IMAGES
of America

SOUTH KNOXVILLE

ON THE COVER: The Vestal baseball team is pictured in the 1910s. (Courtesy of Thompson Photograph Collection, McClung Historical Collection.)

IMAGES
of America

SOUTH KNOXVILLE

Tasha Mahurin and Shannon Mahurin
Introduction by Ray Hill

ARCADIA
PUBLISHING

ISBN 978-0-7385-9421-7

Published by Arcadia Publishing
Charleston, South Carolina

Printed in the United States of America

Library of Congress Control Number: 2012934993

For all general information, please contact Arcadia Publishing:
Telephone 843-853-2070
Fax 843-853-0044
E-mail sales@arcadiapublishing.com
For customer service and orders:
Toll-Free 1-888-313-2665

Visit us on the Internet at www.arcadiapublishing.com

This book is dedicated to our parents and in memory of Fred Berry.

CONTENTS

ACKNOWLEDGMENTS

This book would not have been possible without the support of the South Knoxville community. The community at large is a terrific example of the efforts of those who are dedicated to the preservation of the area they call home.

A special word of thanks to Jeff Berry and the entire Berry family for allowing us access to their personal collection of photographs and for their support throughout the process, Mary Jean Vestal for her willingness to share photographs from her personal scrapbook and family history, Trudy Monaco and Charles Wilson of Candoro Arts and Heritage for being generous with both time and knowledge, Tina Prochaska from Tennessee School for the Deaf for her patience and assistance, Paul James of Ijams Nature Center for pioneering the effort to preserve the history of South Knoxville through Arcadia Publishing, and Ray Hill for sharing his wisdom, insight, and historical knowledge. Thanks also to Anna Chappell of Marble Springs and Amanda Webb of Johnson University, and Mike Brown, Nick Pavlis, and Steve Hunley.

Finally, we would like to thank our family and friends for their support while we completed this project, especially Abigail and Olivia who generously gave their time and patience.

Introduction

South Knoxville has long been considered a special and unique place, especially by those of us who reside in this distinctive community. Tasha Mahurin, with the assistance of Shannon Mahurin, has done a remarkable job of putting together a volume combining historic photographs and commentary for a look at South Knoxville's past.

Their book will not only rekindle our memories of the past and times gone by, but will also serve the important purpose of forever preserving a history that is slowly being eroded with the passage of time. In this wonderful edition, those interested in glimpsing just how things used to be need only open the pages and look inside.

There have been many South Knoxvilians who have made their mark, not only locally, but also nationally. Mildred E. Doyle was the child of a family that traces its lineage back to Tennessee's birth as a state. Mildred's father, Charter, was a long-time member of the county court and his daughter inherited his affinity for politics. Mildred became Knox County's superintendent of schools and served for 30 years. Mildred was also an athlete in her youth and is immortalized in the Women's Basketball Hall of Fame. Charter Doyle Park in South Knoxville was created through a gift of property from the Doyle family and was recently improved as a dog-friendly park through the generosity of Randy Boyd, one of Knoxville's most successful businessmen. Randy Boyd himself is a native South Knoxvilian.

Many folks are familiar with I.C. King Park in South Knoxville, just off Alcoa Highway. I.C. King himself was quite a colorful figure and was the patriarch of a politically potent family active in Republican politics. King served as US marshal during the presidential administrations of Warren G. Harding, Calvin Coolidge, and Herbert Hoover. The King family remained well respected and highly influential in South Knoxville and Knox County for decades. Knox County's Juvenile Court judge Tim Irwin is a descendant of I.C. King.

Sue King married Ben Atchley, who served in the Tennessee General Assembly for 32 years. Few legislators acquired the reputation for honesty, integrity, and ability that Ben Atchley did, yet for those who know Ben and Sue, most would agree Ben's greatest accomplishment was as a picker and chooser. Fewer still would argue that Sue is one iota less accomplished than her formidable husband.

The King family owned and operated one of South Knoxville's most notable institutions, the Ye Olde Steak House, which is still in family hands to this very day. There are few old-time patrons who cannot recall Helen King standing behind the counter of the restaurant, graciously visiting with customers with a smile on her face and a cigarette firmly grasped in one hand.

Tennessee's first governor was a South Knoxvilian. Gov. John Sevier's home still stands in South Knoxville and one of the finest elementary schools in our community is named for the governor's lady, Bonny Kate.

Ben Atchley's predecessor in the Tennessee State Senate, the late Fred O. Berry, built and founded Berry's Funeral Home, which remains yet another South Knoxville monument and continues to prosper under the leadership of the third generation of the Berry family.

The site of Pinkston Motors still exists on Chapman Highway, which was long operated by brothers Howard "Nookie" and Paul Pinkston. For almost two decades, one of the brothers served as South Knoxville's county commissioner. Such was the Pinkston influence at its peak that Gov. Don Sundquist, Sen. Bill Frist, and Sen. Fred Thompson kicked off their 1994 fall campaigns at Pinkston Motors. Entertainers Johnny Knoxville and David Keith are South Knoxvilians, as is Knoxville's new mayor.

For the last 40 years, Knoxvilians have elected residents of West Knoxville as their mayor until 2011, when Madeline Rogero became the first woman to be elected as Knoxville's mayor, as well as the first South Knoxvilian to serve as chief executive since 1971. To compound the delight of South Knoxvilians, their city councilman Nick Pavlis was selected to serve as vice mayor.

Knox County mayor Tim Burchett recently said, "South Knoxvilians have long felt they have been treated like the stepchild at the family reunion, but it looks like South Knoxville's time has come."

From Mayor Burchett's lips to God's ear.

South Knoxville has been my home for practically my entire life. I hope you will open the pages of this book and share the special feeling that can only come from reliving memories that still lurk inside one's head and continue to fill the heart.

—Ray Hill, 2012

One

Community

Traditionally, South Knoxville refers to the section of Knoxville, Tennessee, that lies south of the Tennessee River. The area is currently comprised of various neighborhoods, including Lindbergh Forest, Island Home Park, Old Sevier, Vestal, Lake Forest, and Colonial Village. For most of the 19th century, however, South Knoxville was sparsely populated, most likely due to the lack of a bridge across the Tennessee River, which separates South Knoxville from downtown and other areas of the city.

The Gay Street Bridge, along with the Henley Street Bridge, presently connects South Knoxville to downtown and was completed and opened to traffic on July 9, 1898. The original bridge included a trolley line, which helped to spur residential development in the Island Home Park area, although the Tennessee River would continue to serve as a great divide between South Knoxville and the rest of the city. This segregation of sorts led to the development of a unique community. Even with the connection of the Gay Street Bridge, the area was the last of the four major quadrants (north, south, east, and west) of the city to be acquired and was not annexed by Knoxville until 1917.

The completion of the Henley Street Bridge in 1932, as well as the establishment of the Great Smoky Mountains National Park in 1934, led to extensive commercial development along Chapman Highway, which at the time was the primary route connecting Knoxville with the park. Yet, despite through traffic and the ebb and flow of commercial development, the South Knoxville community, from its origins to the present day, boasts a distinctive culture intrinsic to the area.

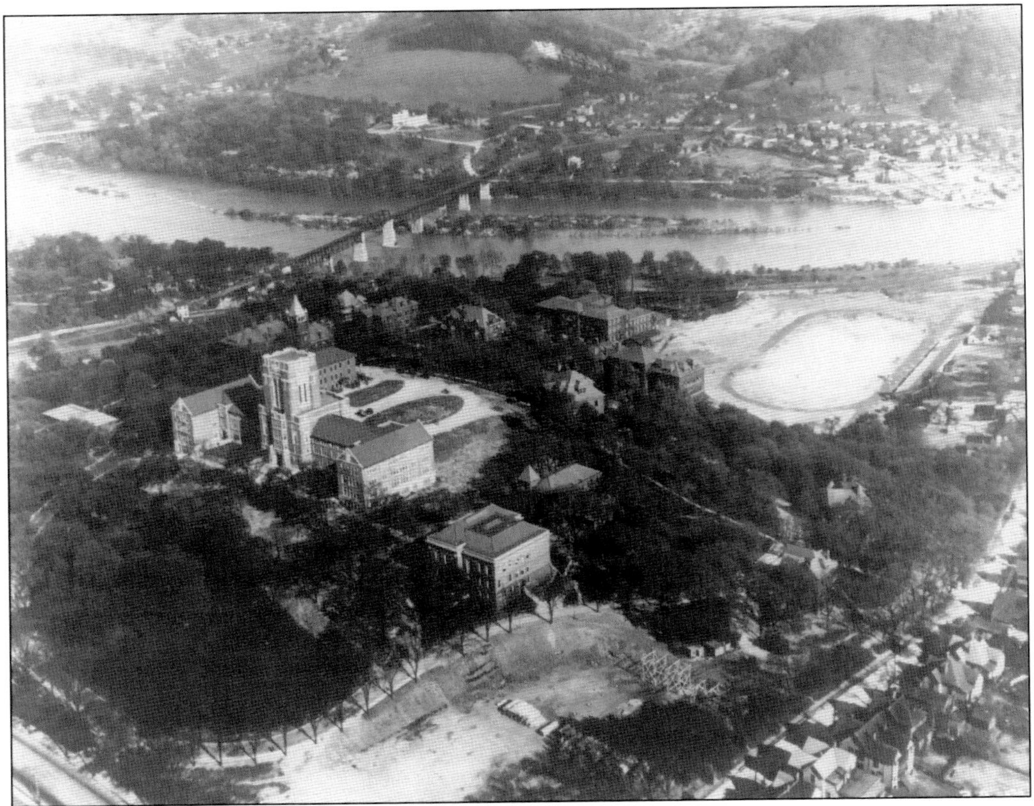

This photograph shows an aerial view of the University of Tennessee and South Knoxville during the 1940s. (Courtesy of the Berry family.)

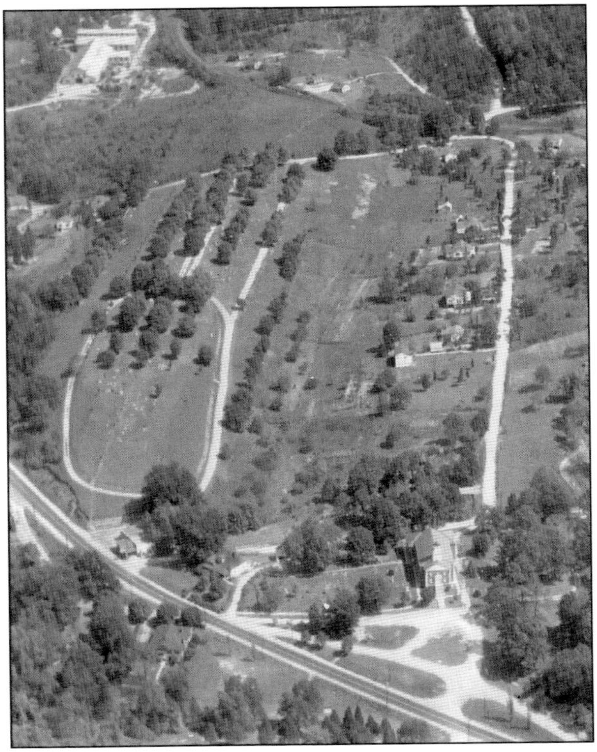

The Mount Olive Community, shown here in an aerial view, was one of the early communities in South Knoxville. Mount Olive Baptist Church is at lower right and the cemetery is to the left. The date is unknown. (Courtesy of the Berry family.)

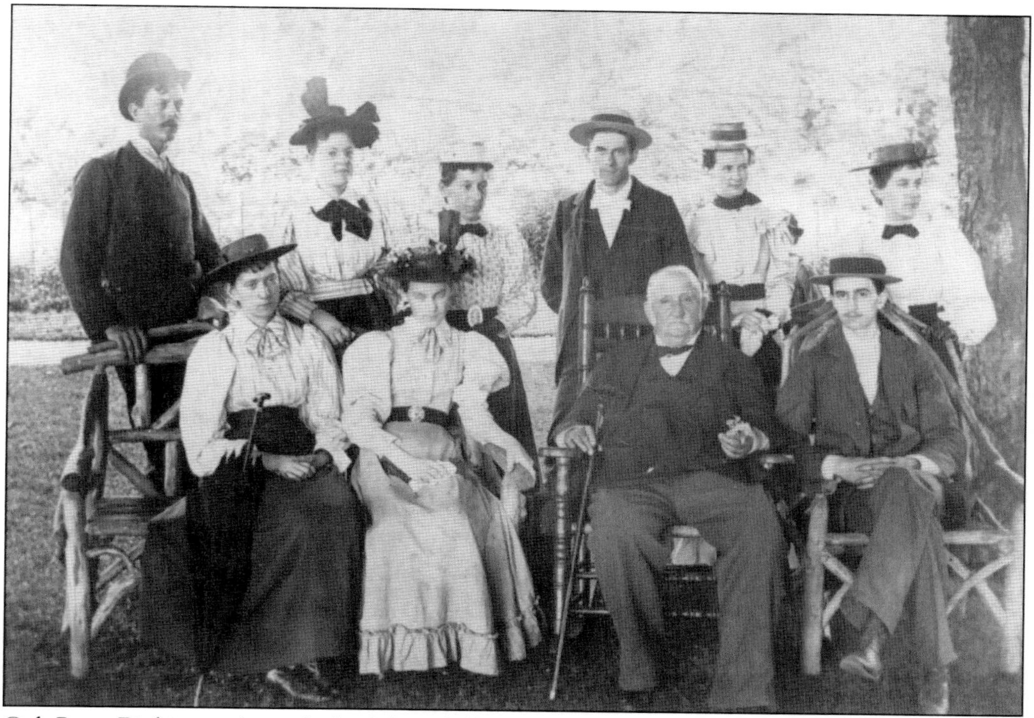

Col. Perez Dickinson (seated, third from left) was one of Knoxville's most beloved early citizens and the cousin of poet Emily Dickinson. He is pictured here with George Broome (seated at right), at Island Home in the 1890s. Others in the photograph include Gertie, Florence, and Edith Broome. (Courtesy of Knox County Two Centuries Photograph Project, McClung Historical Collection.)

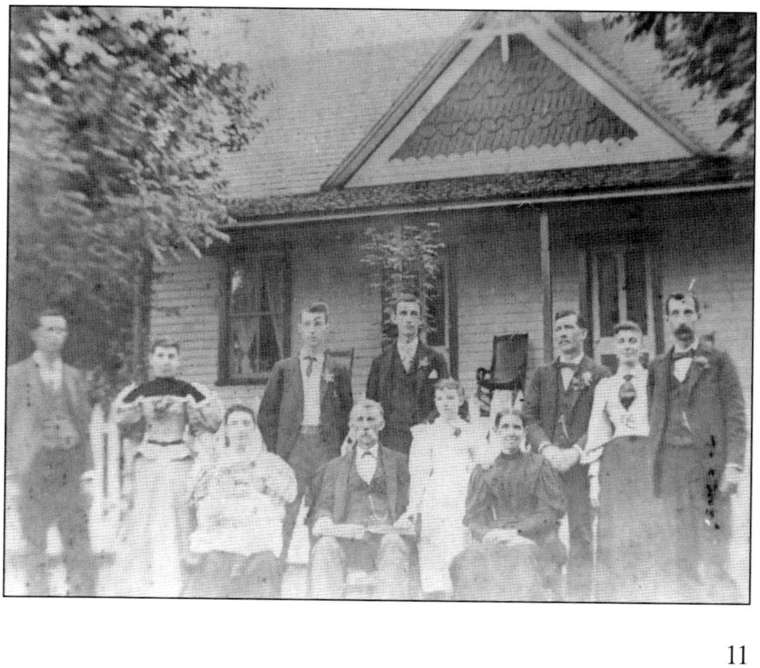

This photograph was taken at the A.M. Gilbert home on Island Home Pike in 1895. Alfred Gilbert is seated holding a Bible while his wife, Jane Henderson Gilbert, is seated wearing a dark dress. (Courtesy of Knox County Two Centuries Photograph Project, McClung Historical Collection.)

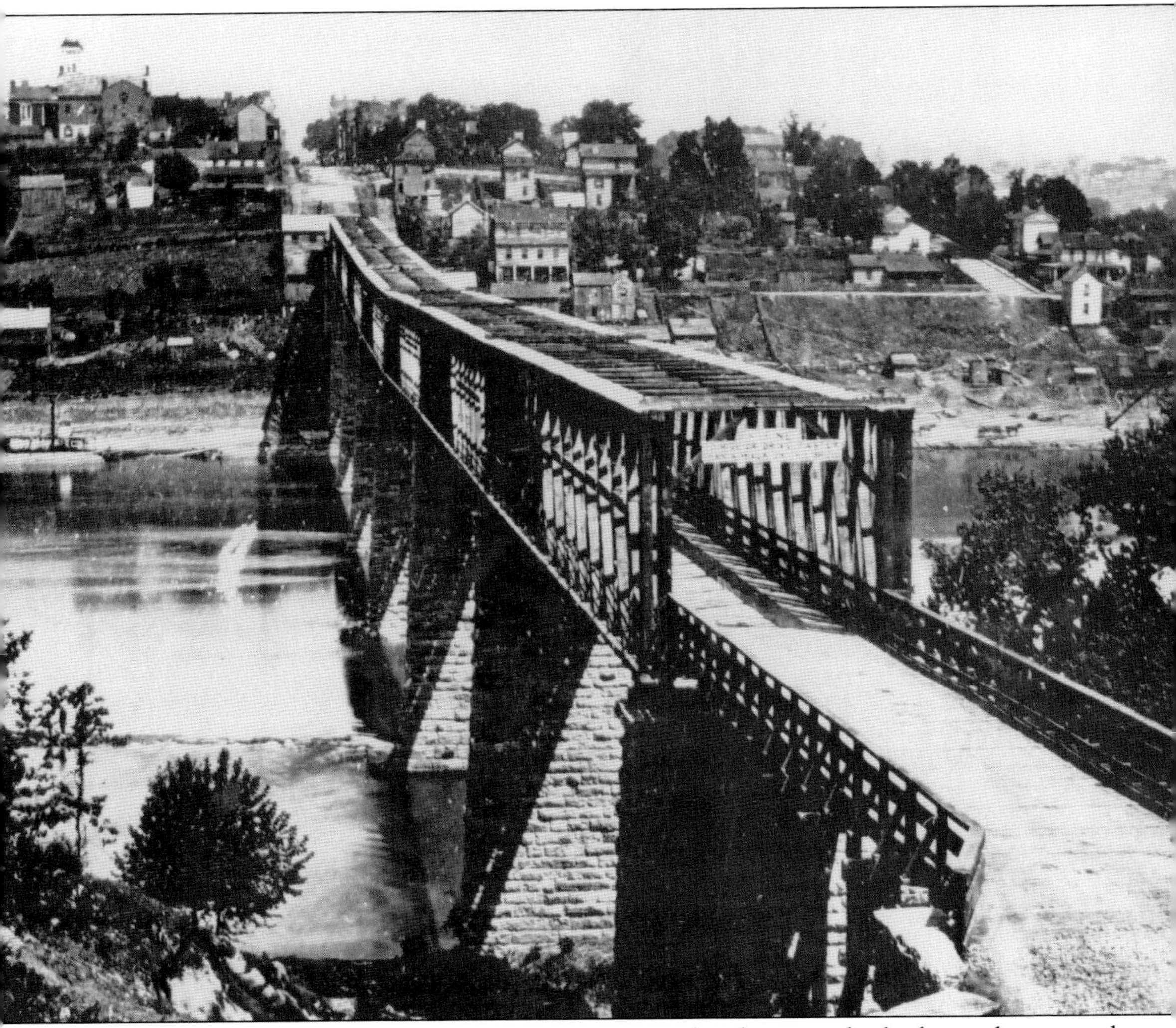

The Gay Street Bridge, which was completed in 1898, replaced two wooden bridges and connected South Knoxville with downtown Knoxville. The first of the two bridges was blown off its stone piers by a sudden gust of wind. The second wooden bridge, shown here, stood on the same stone piers and sagged in the middle. The sign on the bridge promises a fine to those who "ride or drive faster than a walk." (Courtesy of the Berry family.)

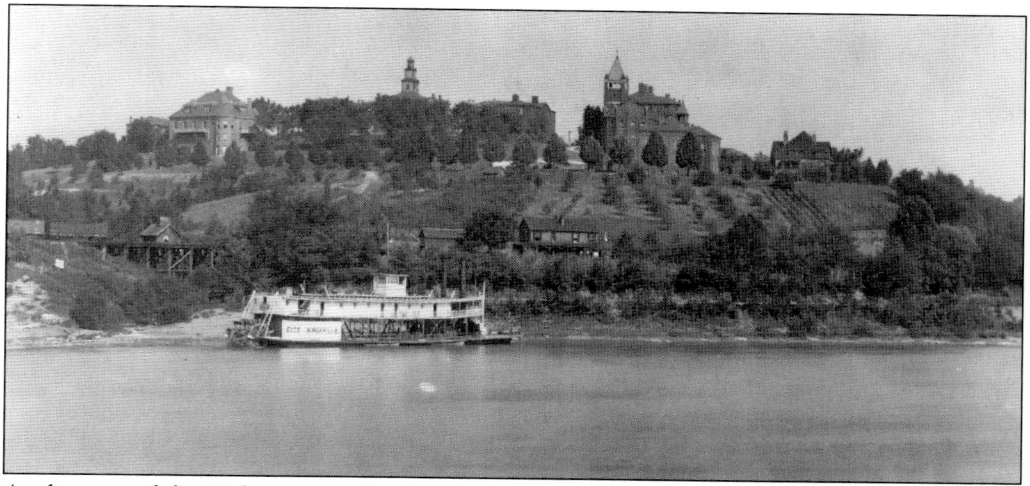

At the turn of the 20th century, the Gay Street Bridge began to bridge the gap between South Knoxville and downtown Knoxville both literally and figuratively. Meanwhile, steamboat traffic, which originally began with the commissioning of the first steamboat in Knoxville (appropriately named the *Knoxville*), remained consistent along the Tennessee River, serving both recreational and industrial purposes. (Courtesy of the Berry family.)

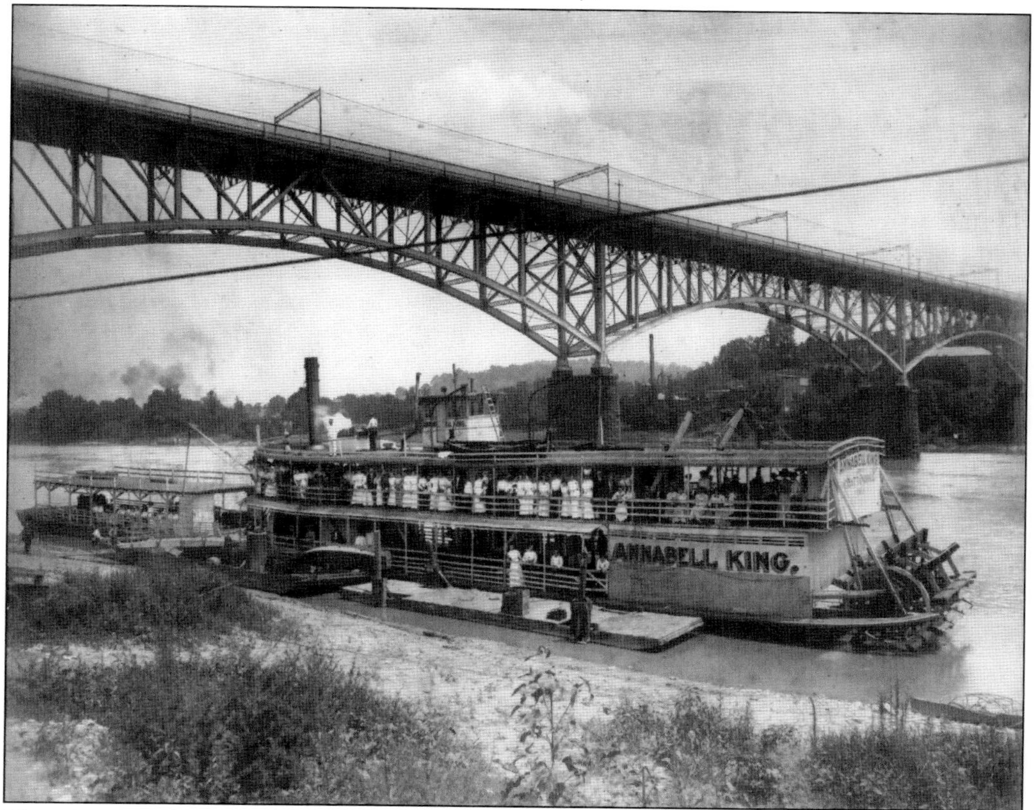

This photograph is of *Annabell King* in port in Knoxville. South Knoxville can be seen in the distance just behind the Gay Street Bridge. The famed Knoxville steamboat sank early one morning in 1911 in the Tennessee River, although the exact location of the incident draws conflicting reports from historical scholars. (Courtesy of the Berry family.)

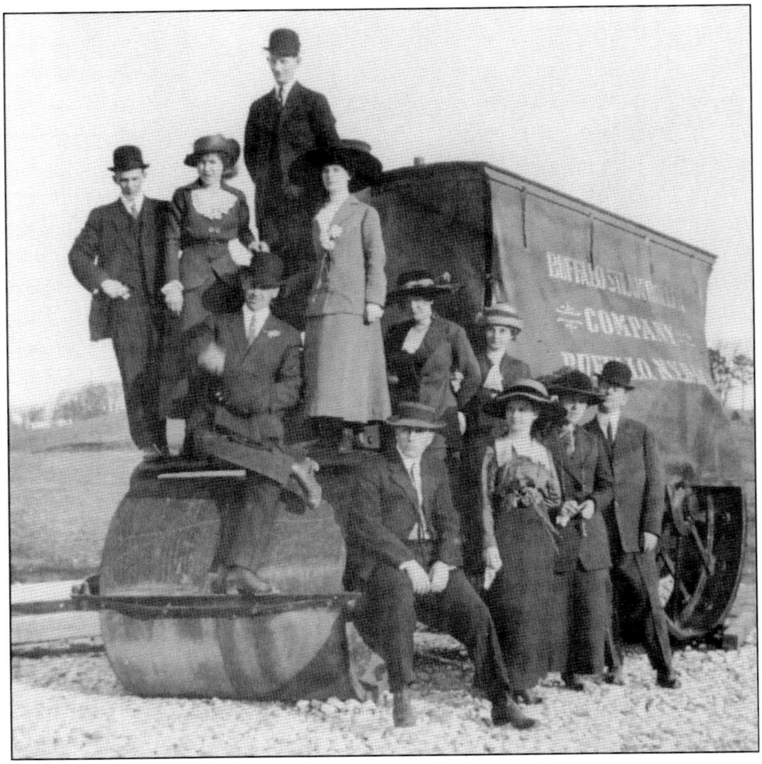

The Cole family poses near Island Home in 1914 in front of a steamroller from the Buffalo Steamroller Company. Standing from left to right on the steamroller are W.D. Pettigrew, Katherine Ellis Cole, Vernon Edward Cole (highest), Helen Cole, Mae Ellis, and Katherine Cole. The rest are unidentified. (Courtesy of Knox County Two Centuries Photograph Project, McClung Historical Collection.)

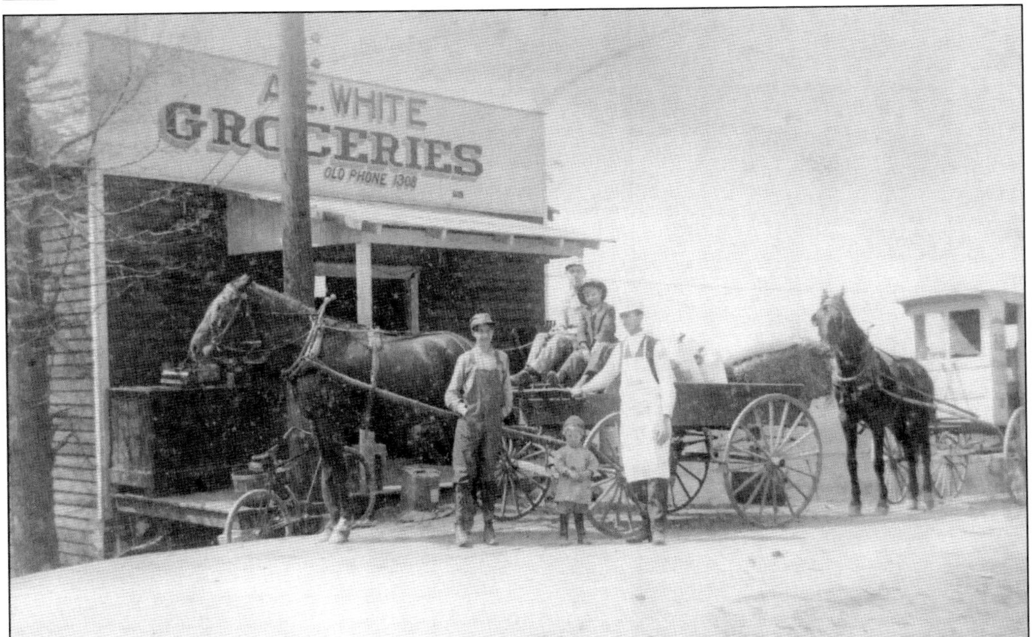

This photograph of A.E. White Groceries, located on Island Home Pike, was taken in 1915. It shows an Island Home Dairy truck with Chester Thomas, driver (left) and A.E. White in the white apron. The smallest boy in the photograph is James White. (Courtesy of Knox County Two Centuries Photograph Project, McClung Historical Collection.)

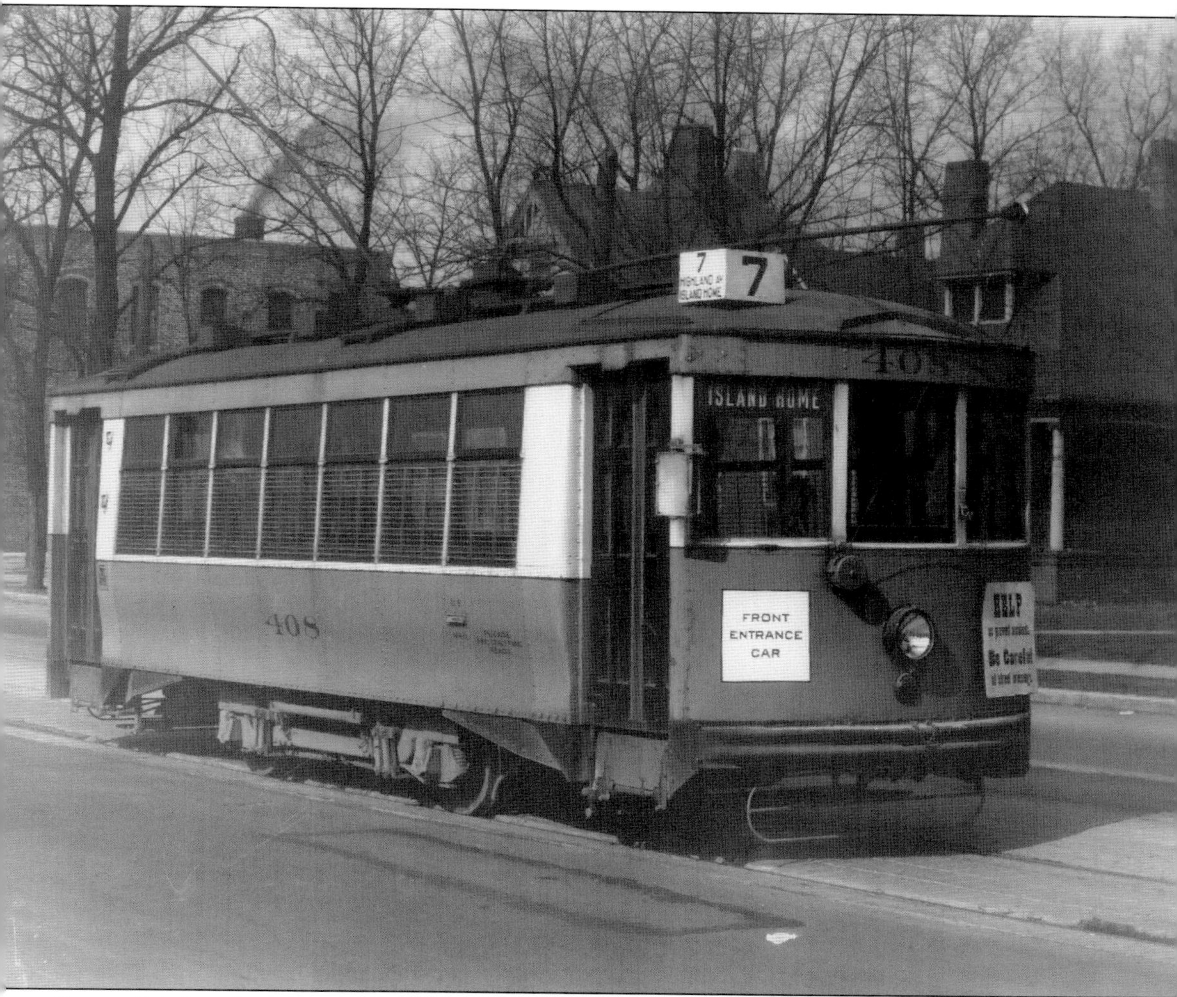

Knoxville's first electric streetcar line opened in 1890. This photograph is of Island Home streetcar 408 in the 1920s. The sign at front says, "Help us prevent accidents. Be careful at street crossings," while the small lettering on the side near the US mail slot says, "Please have exact fare ready." (Courtesy of Thompson Photograph Collection, McClung Historical Collection.)

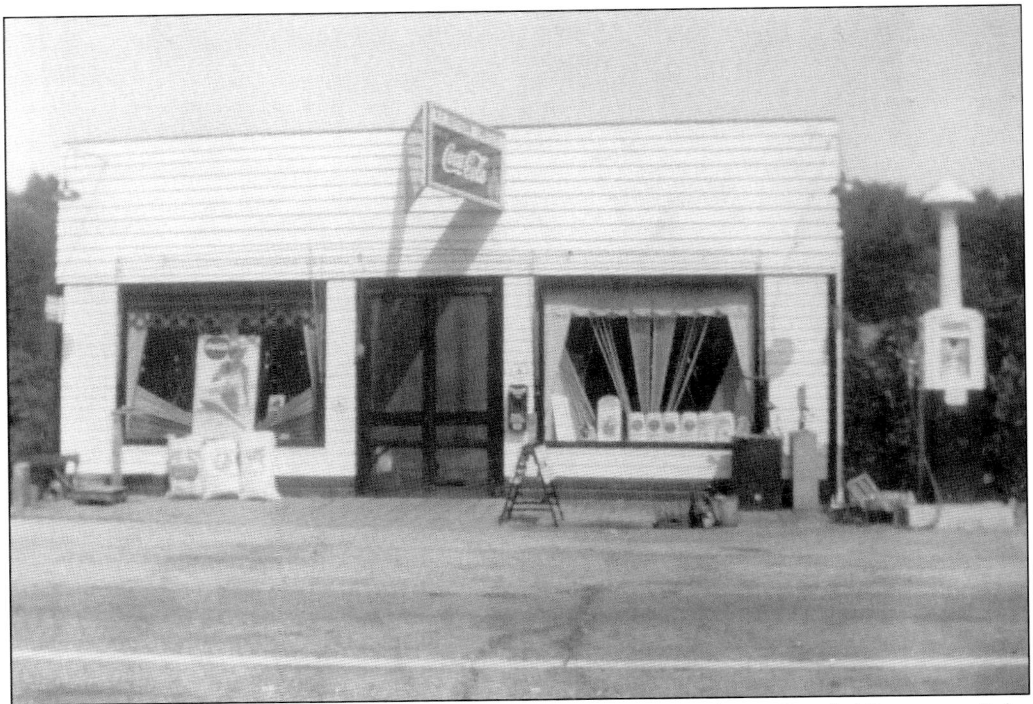

This 1930s image shows Burleson Store on Maryville Pike at Maloney Road. (Courtesy of the Berry family.)

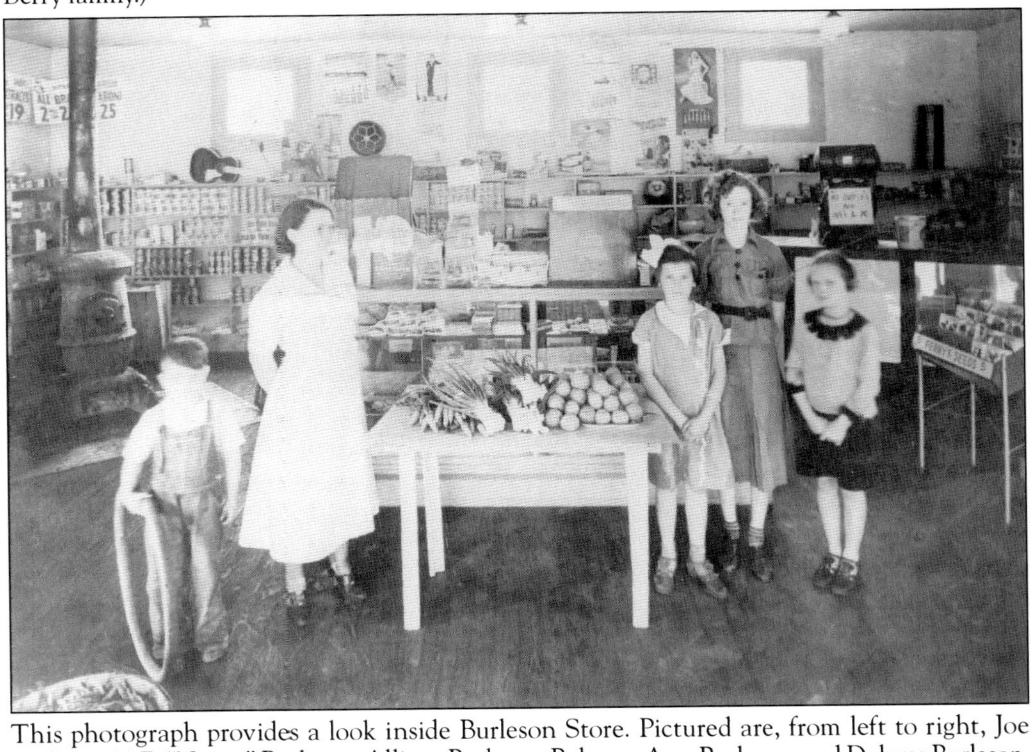

This photograph provides a look inside Burleson Store. Pictured are, from left to right, Joe Burleson, N.E. "Nancy" Burleson, Alliene Burleson, Rebecca Ann Burleson, and Dolores Burleson. (Courtesy of the Berry family.)

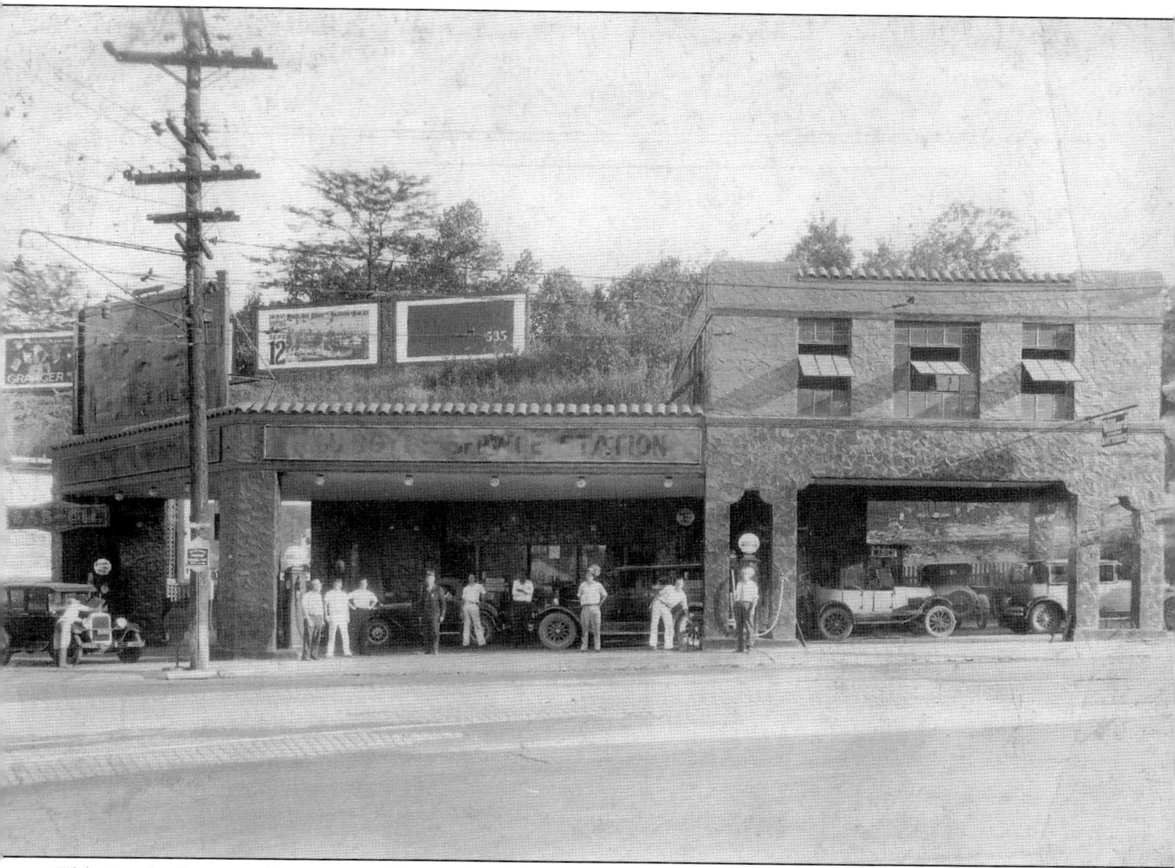

Ebb Doyle Service Station was located at the end of Gay Street in South Knoxville. The police officer pictured is Roy Nelson; the fourth person to the right leaning on the car is Fred Berry. (Courtesy of the Berry family.)

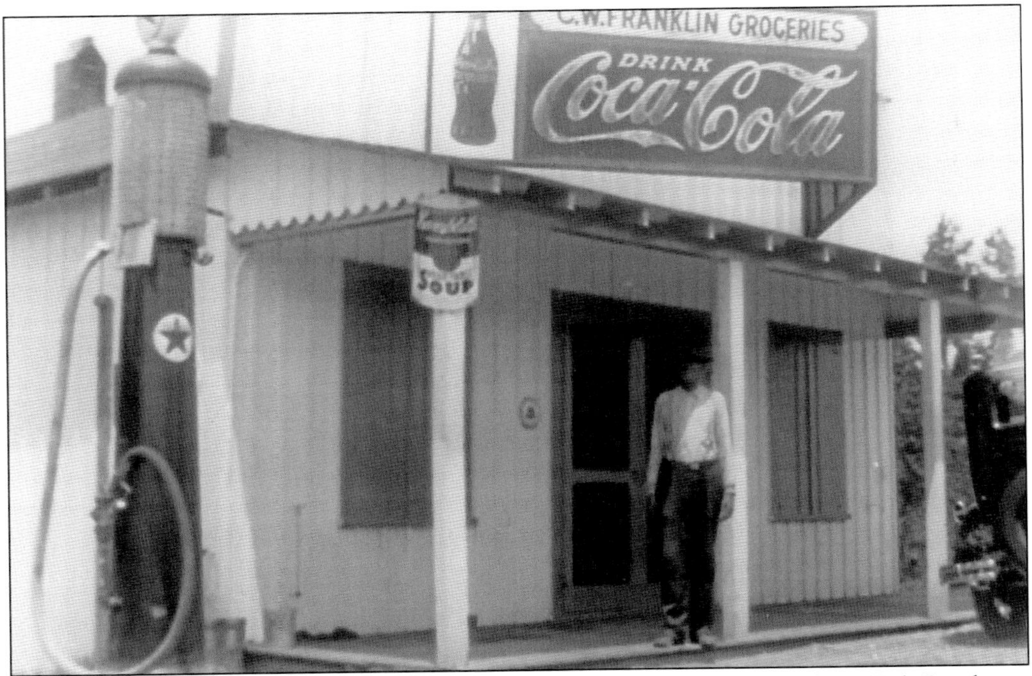

C.W. Franklin Store was built in the 1920s and was located on Maryville Pike at Belt Road, just one mile from Burleson Store. (Courtesy of the Berry family.)

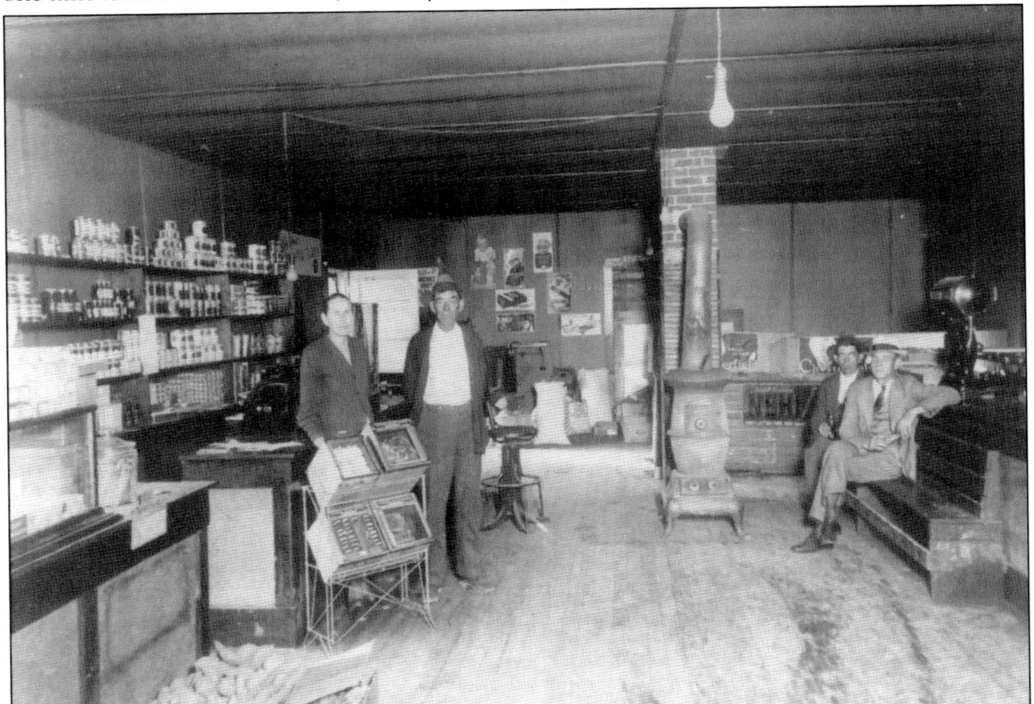

This photograph shows the inside of Franklin Store where men from the community frequently gathered to discuss weather and politics. Pictured are, from left to right, Nannie Rollins Franklin, Charles Wesley Franklin, Willie Jones, and Wilbur Hutson. (Courtesy of the Berry family.)

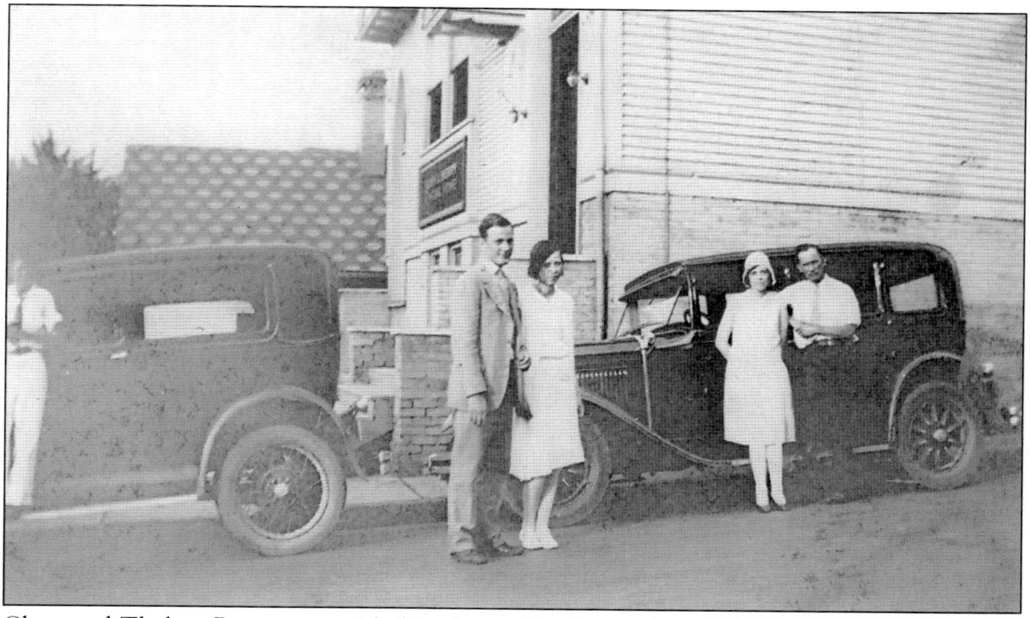

Clara and Thelma Berry pose with friends on Gay Street during the 1930s. (Courtesy of the Berry family.)

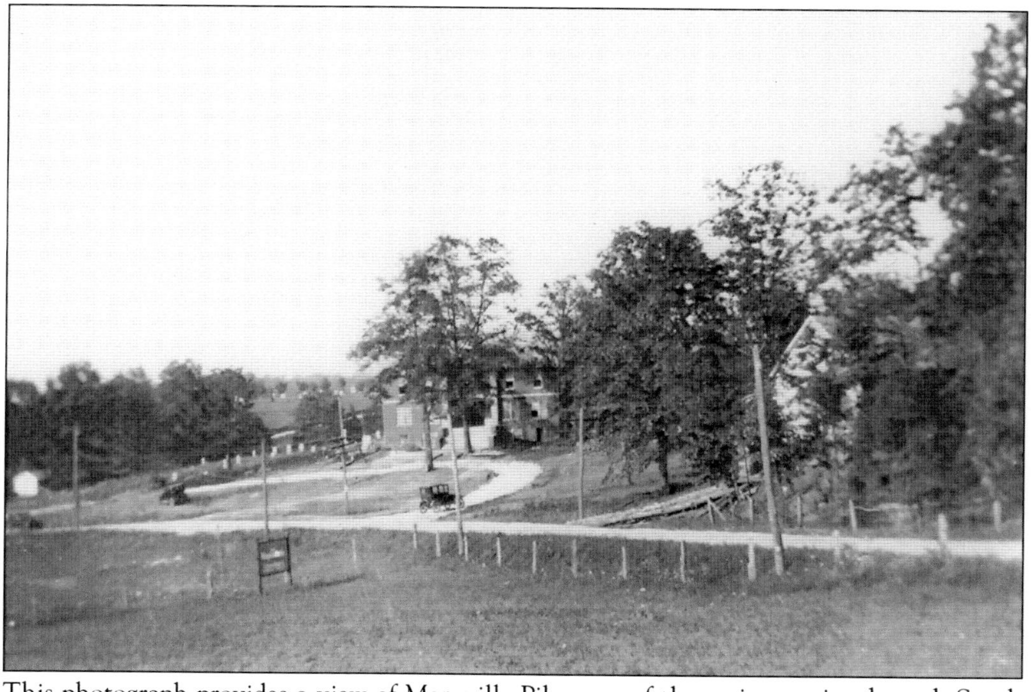

This photograph provides a view of Maryville Pike, one of the main arteries through South Knoxville before 1925. Note the Grand Army Hall to the right. (Courtesy of the Berry family.)

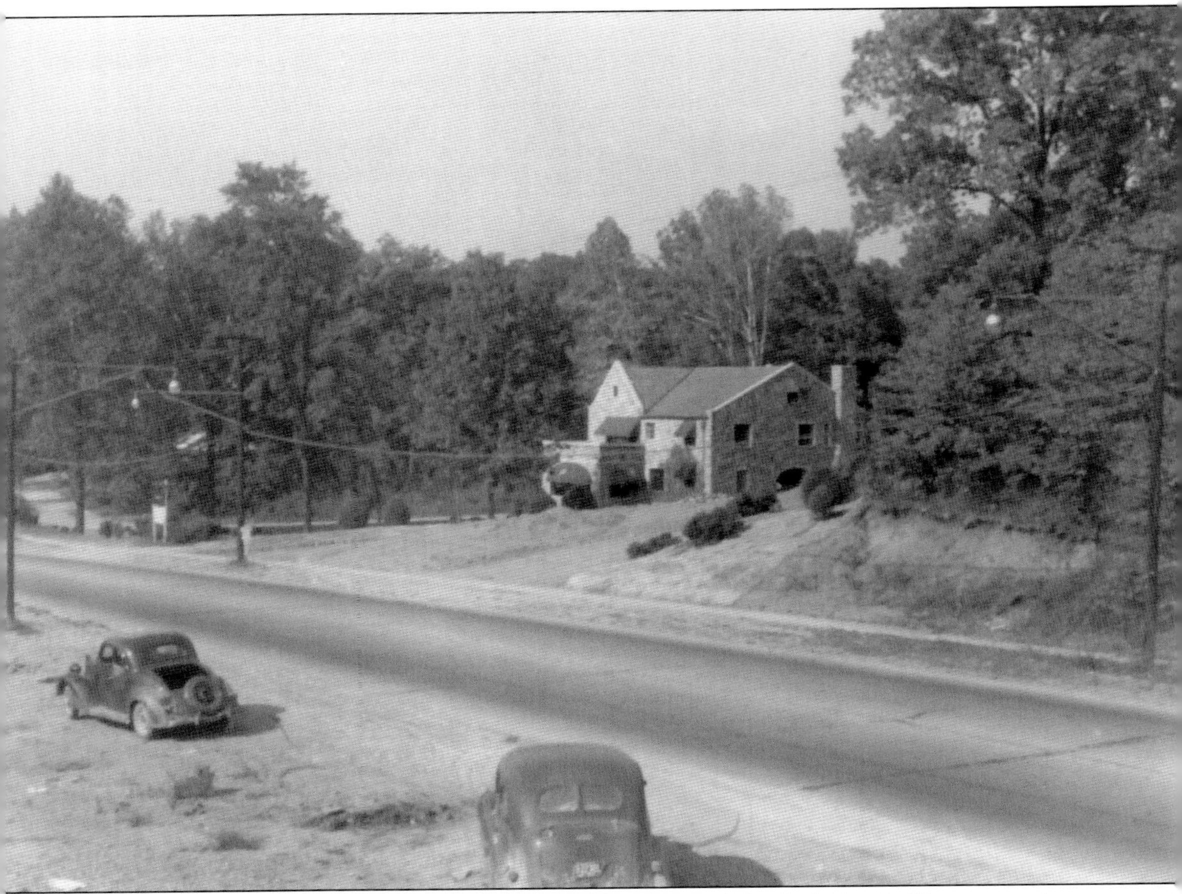

Chapman Highway, seen here during the 1940s, is named for Col. David Chapman, who was instrumental in the designation of Great Smoky Mountains National Park. A government commission met in 1924 to consider locations for a new national park. Colonel Chapman led what is known as the "Knoxville Raid" on the meeting. Chapman, a wholesale druggist, used his sales abilities to move the Smoky Mountains to the top of the list of areas considered. (Courtesy of the Berry family.)

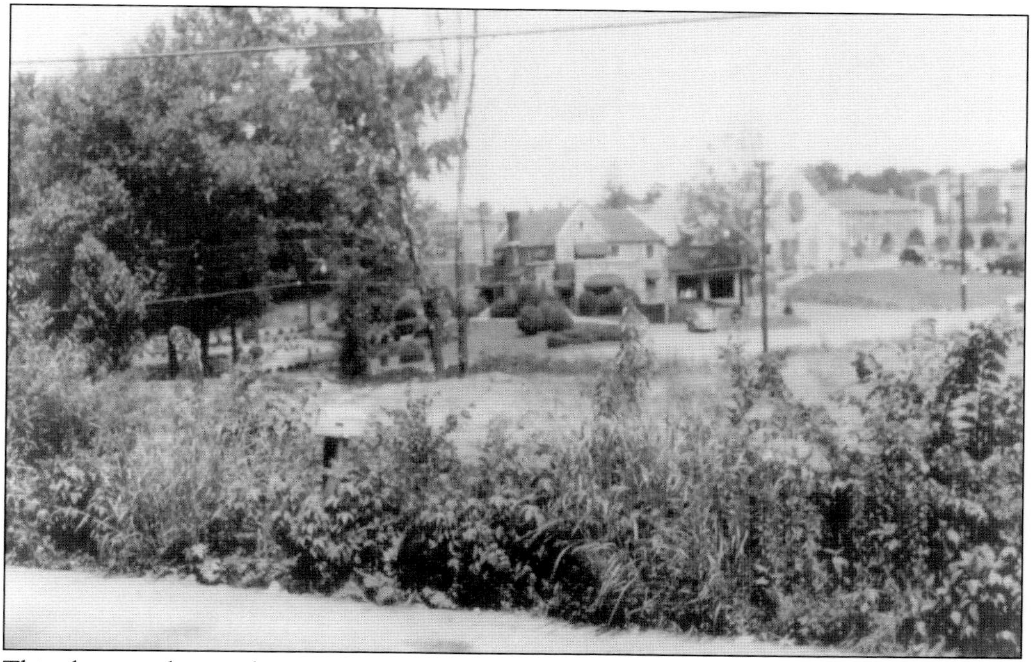

This photograph provides another view of Chapman Highway during the 1940s. (Courtesy of the Berry family.)

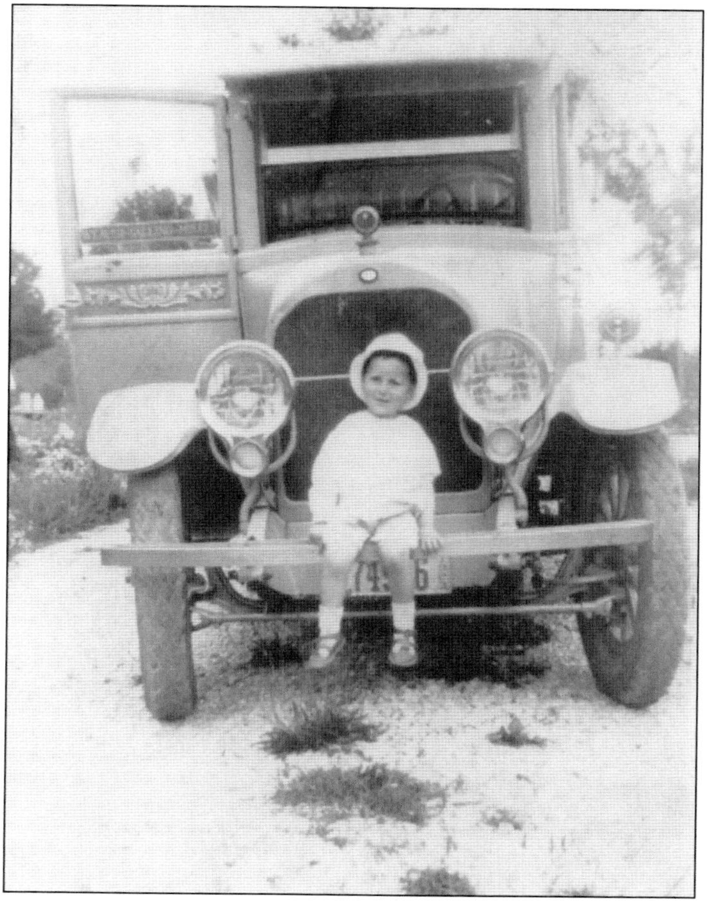

A young Ralph Lawson Berry Jr. sits on the bumper of a Weaver-Sallings-Mikels funeral coach in Mount Olive Cemetery in 1923. (Courtesy of the Berry family.)

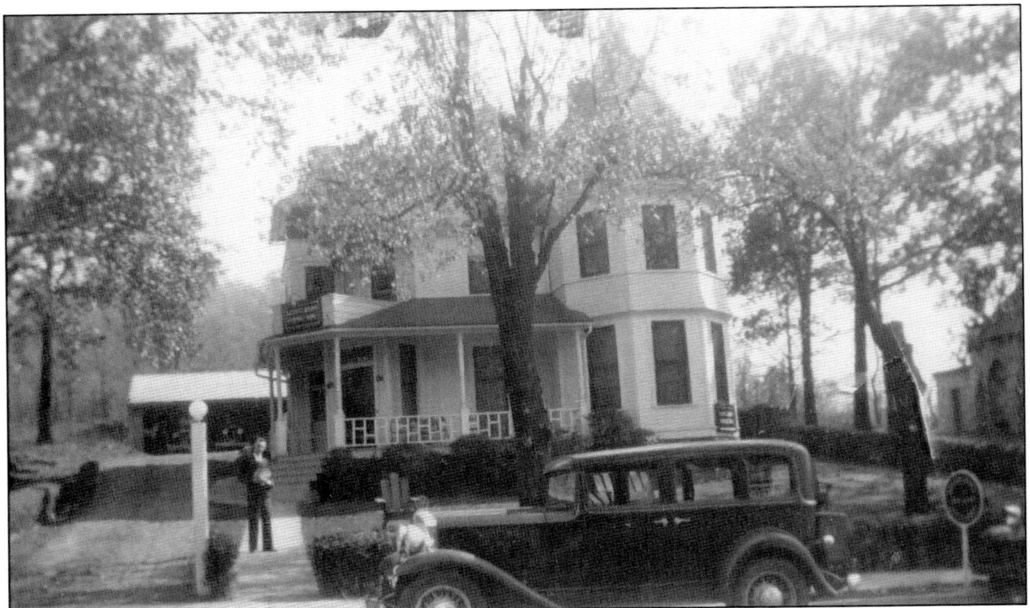

Berry Funeral Home moved from its location at 400 Island Home Boulevard to another location on Blount Avenue in 1935. (Courtesy of the Berry family.)

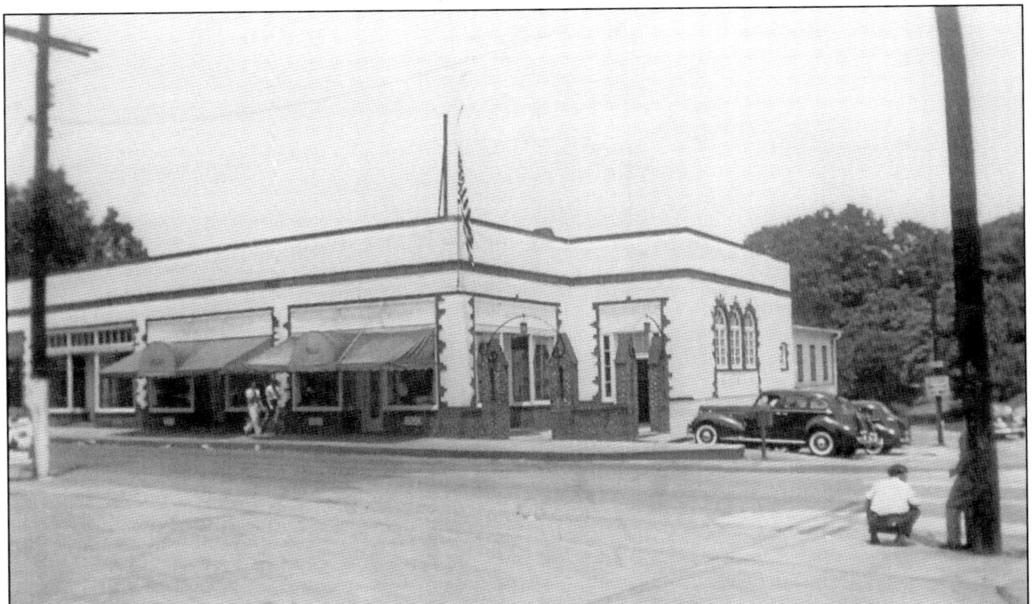

Berry Funeral Home was located at the end of Gay Street during the late 1930s. (Courtesy of the Berry family.)

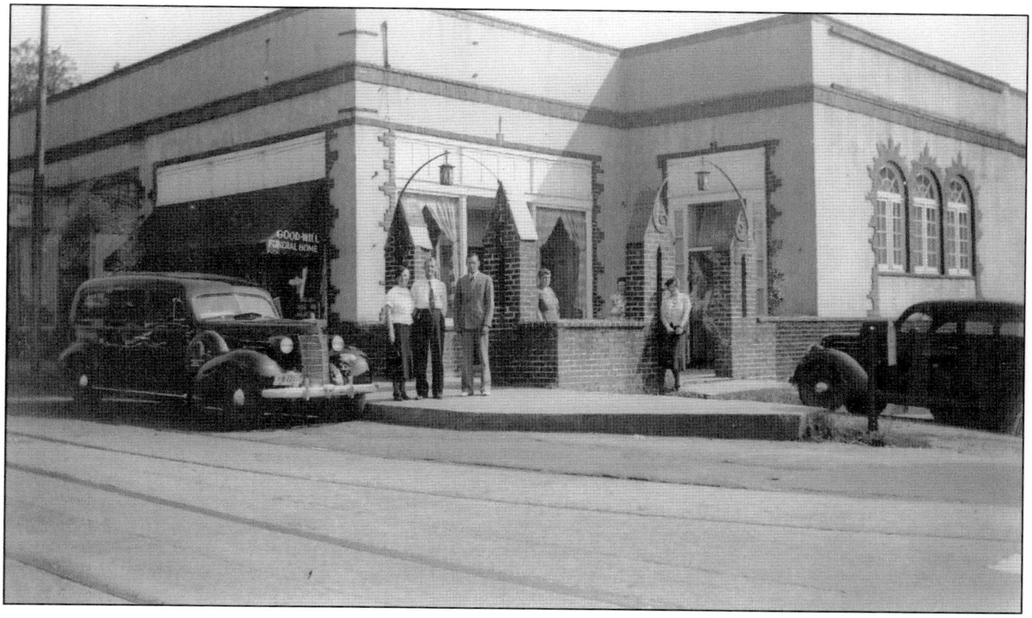

These images are additional photographs of Berry Funeral Home when it was located at the end of Gay Street in South Knoxville during the 1930s. (Both, courtesy of the Berry family.)

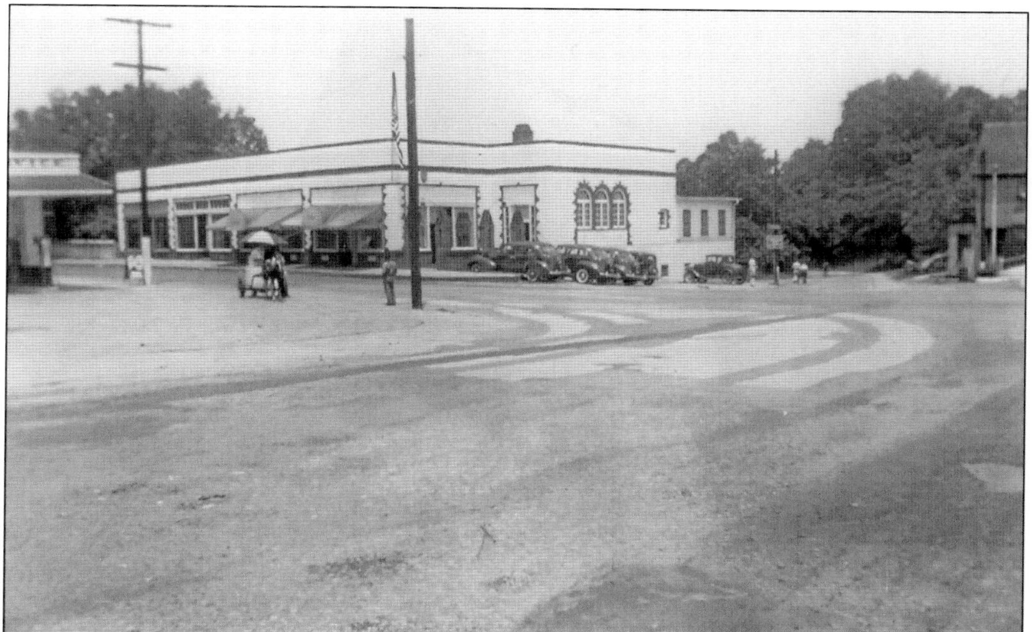

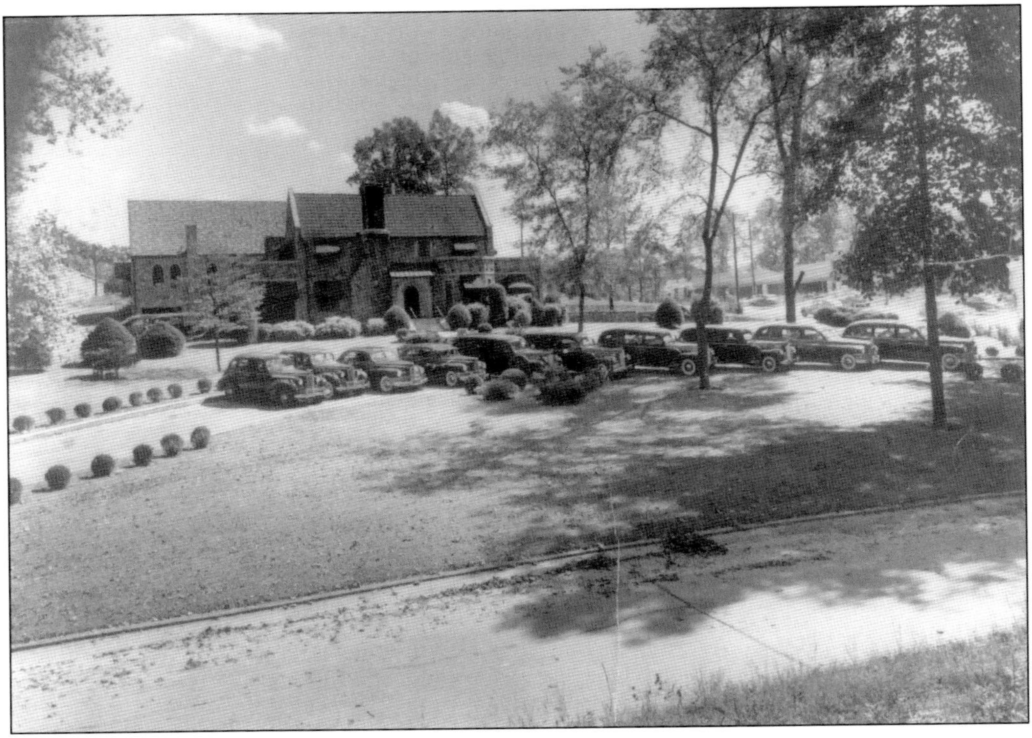

In 1949, Berry Funeral Home opened a new location, seen here in the 1950s, at 3704 Chapman Highway. In 1951, founder Ralph L. Berry Sr. passed away. By 1957, Fred Jr. and G. Edward had joined the business, representing the third generation of the Berry family to enter the funeral business. The Gloria Dei Lutheran Church began in Berry Funeral Home Chapel in the late 1940s. (Courtesy of the Berry family.)

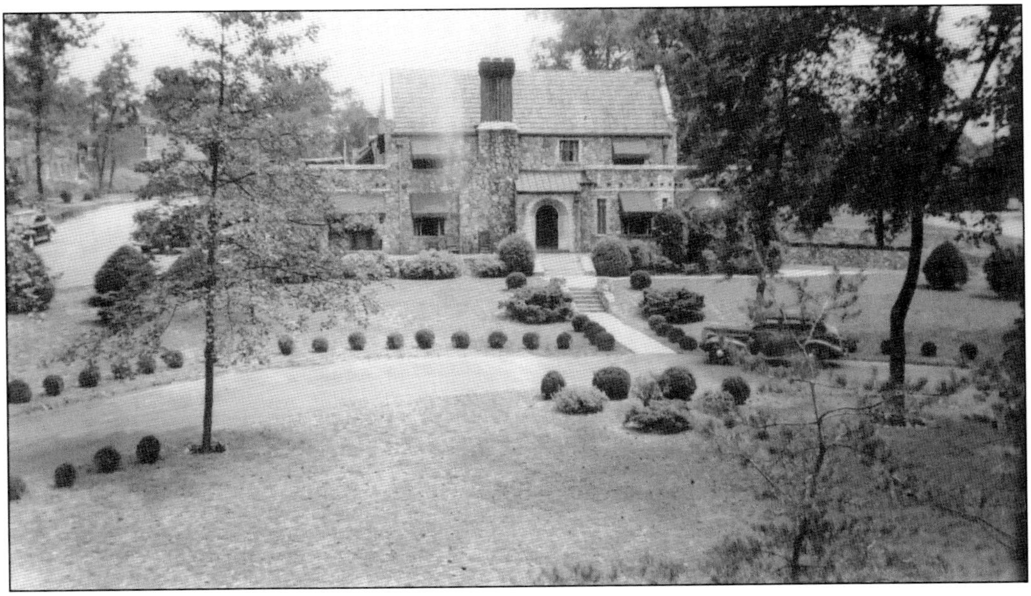

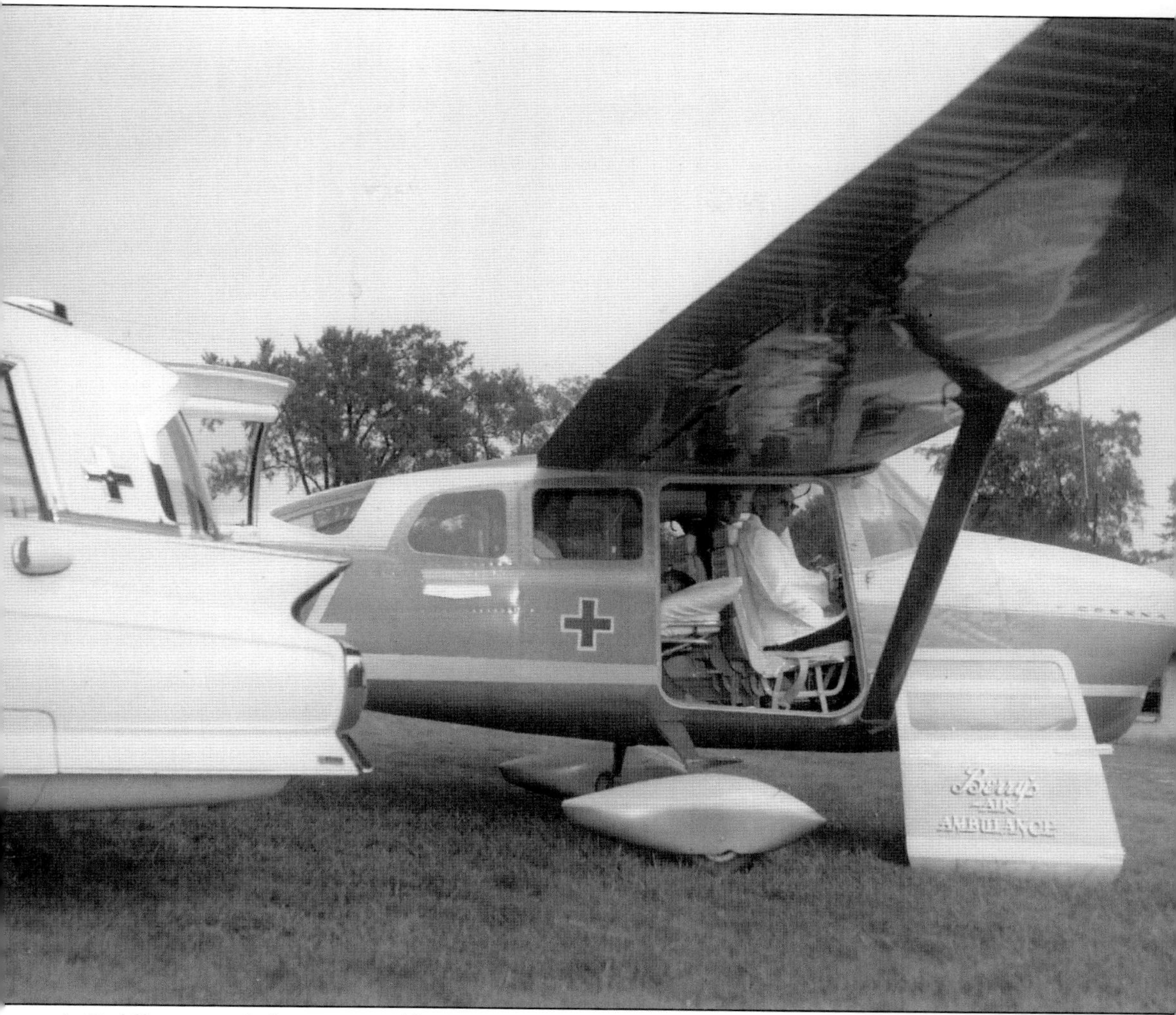

A Cadillac air ambulance owned by Berry Funeral Home is pictured here in 1962. Fred O. Berry Sr. served as an aviator technician in the US Air Force. Through his experiences and observations, he realized the benefits that air transport afforded the sick and injured. When he returned home, he was determined to pioneer an air ambulance service. He obtained one of the first three custom-made air ambulances delivered in the United States by the Beechcraft company. Berry's air ambulances flew over all 50 states, Canada, and Mexico, until the air ambulance service was discontinued in 1967. (Courtesy of the Berry family.)

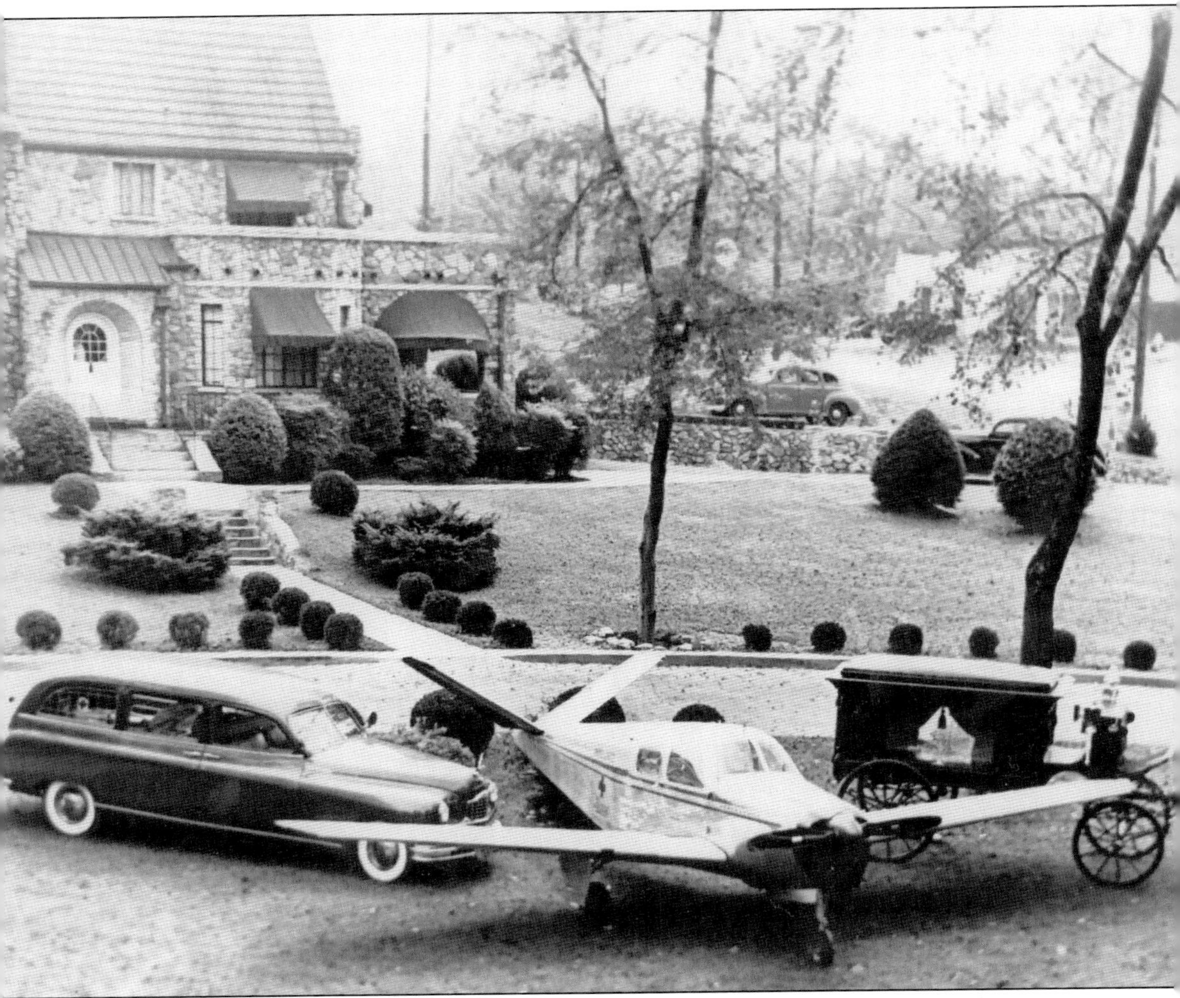

This photograph shows the various modes of transportation used by Berry Funeral Home since its founding by Ralph Lawson Berry in 1928. (Courtesy of the Berry family.)

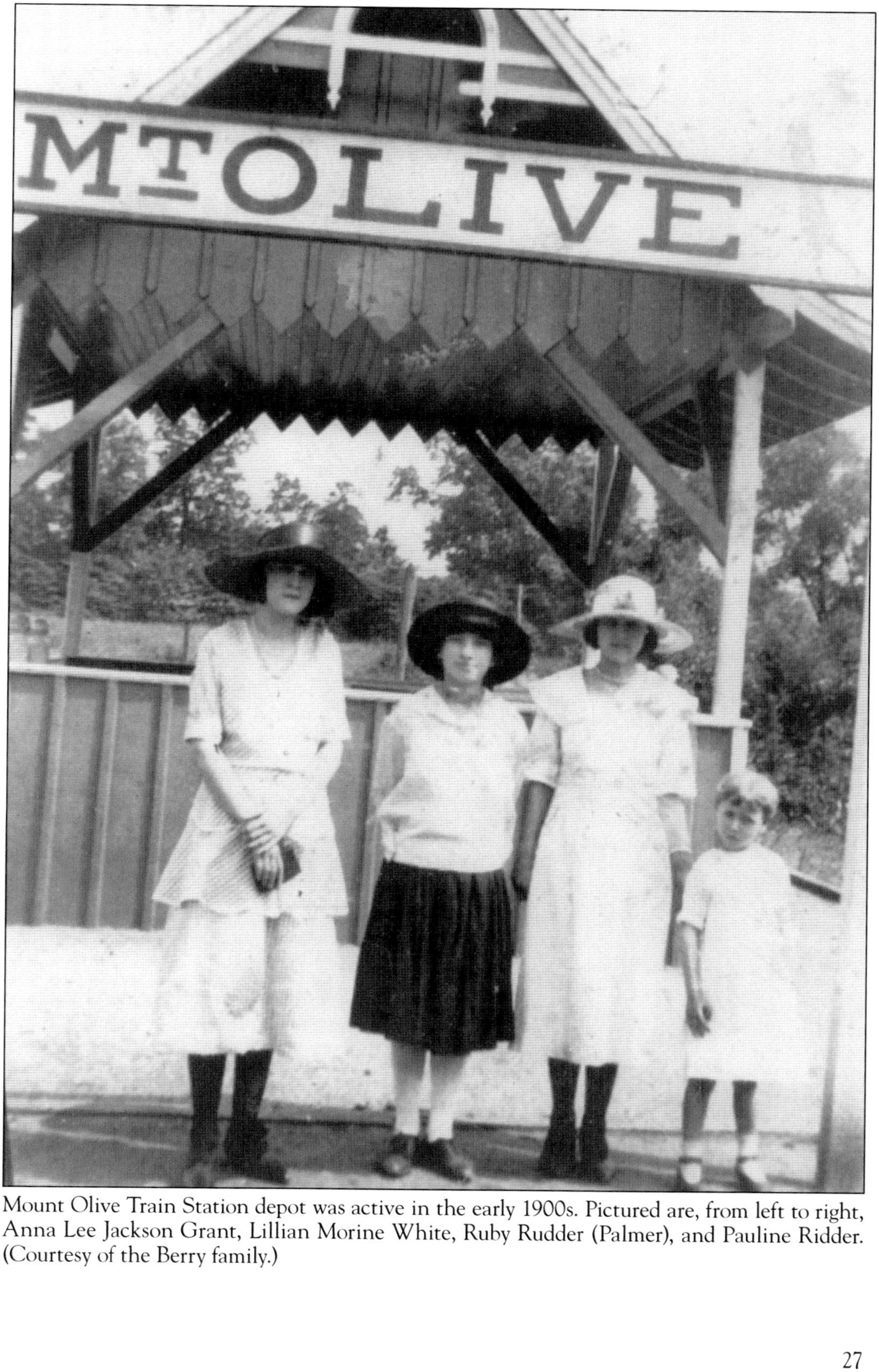

Mount Olive Train Station depot was active in the early 1900s. Pictured are, from left to right, Anna Lee Jackson Grant, Lillian Morine White, Ruby Rudder (Palmer), and Pauline Ridder. (Courtesy of the Berry family.)

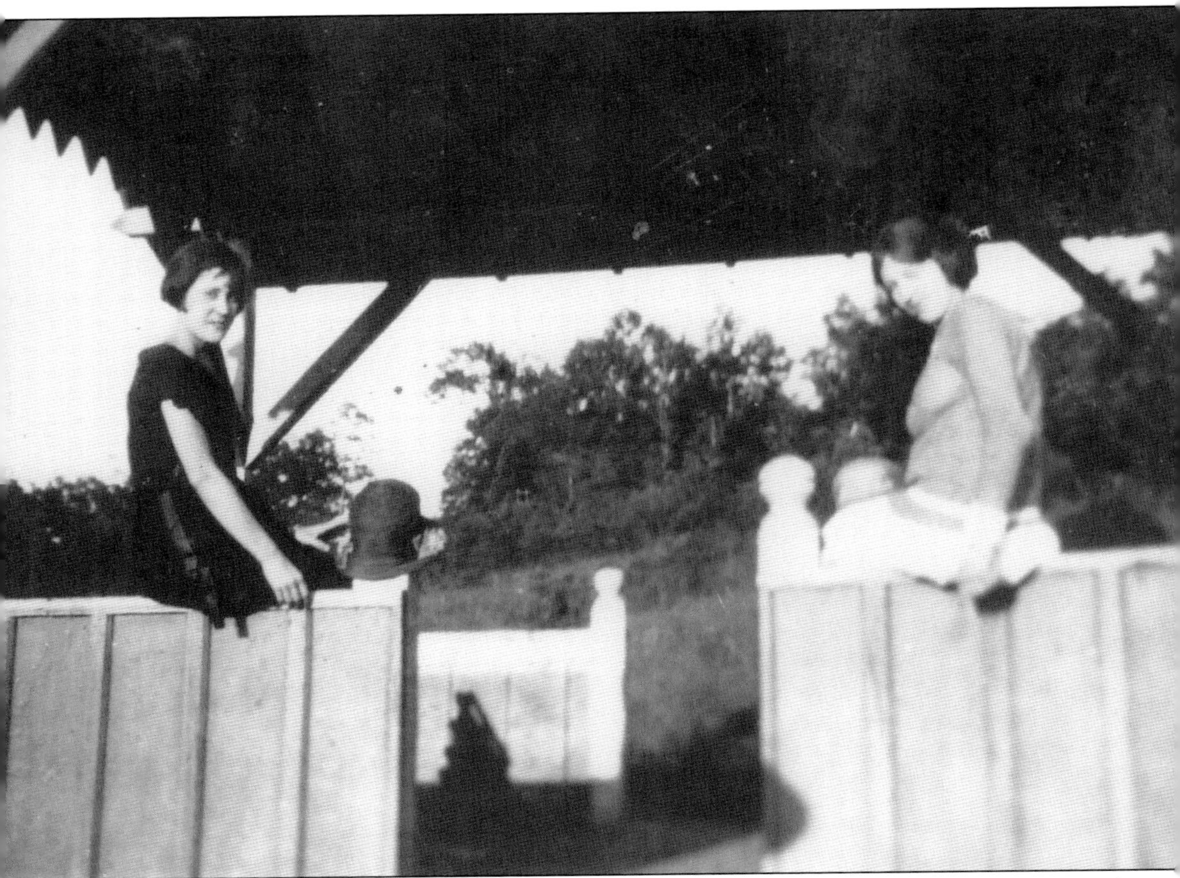

Mount Olive Train Station was on the Knoxville and Augusta track, which later became part of the Southern Railway. The station was located on the corner of Mount Olive and Berry Roads. Rail transportation played a critical role in the early growth of the city of Knoxville. (Courtesy of the Berry family.)

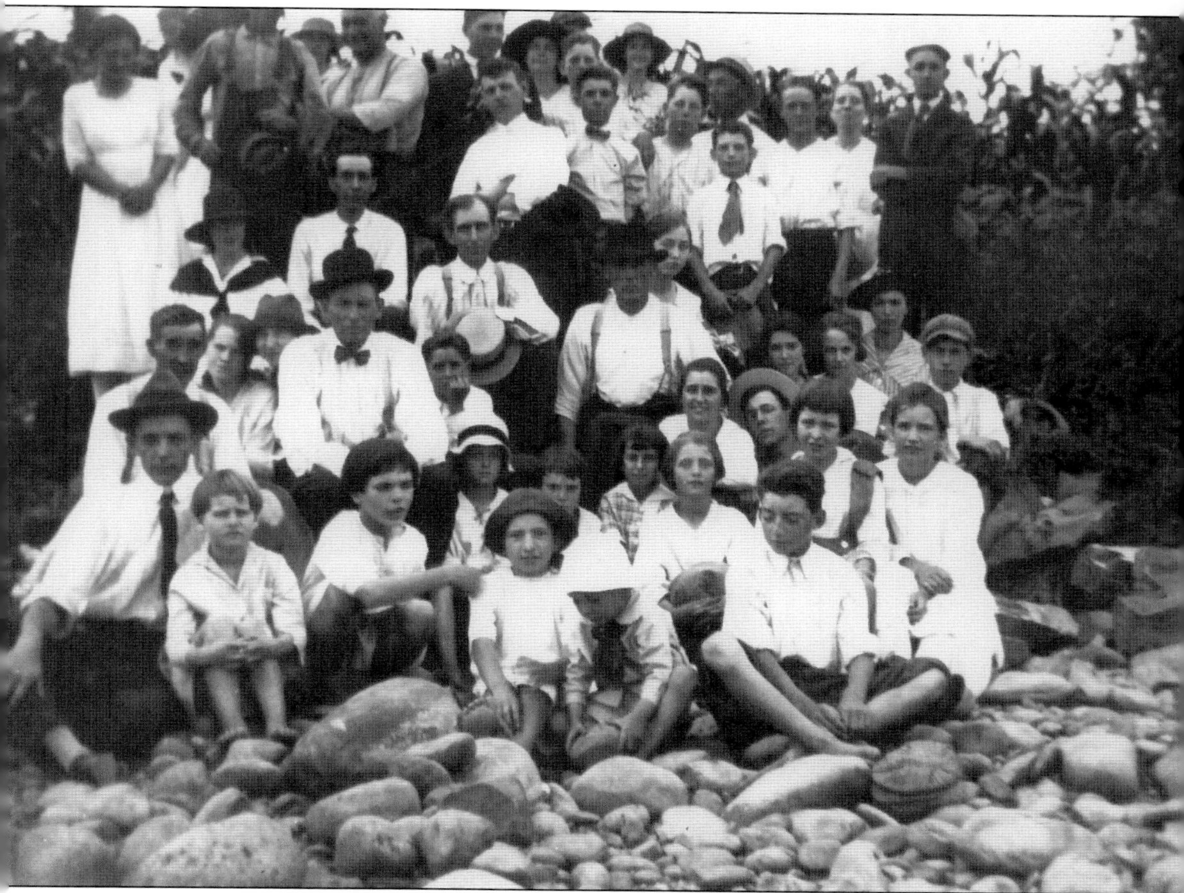

This photograph of citizens of the Mount Olive community was taken around 1910. (Courtesy of the Berry family.)

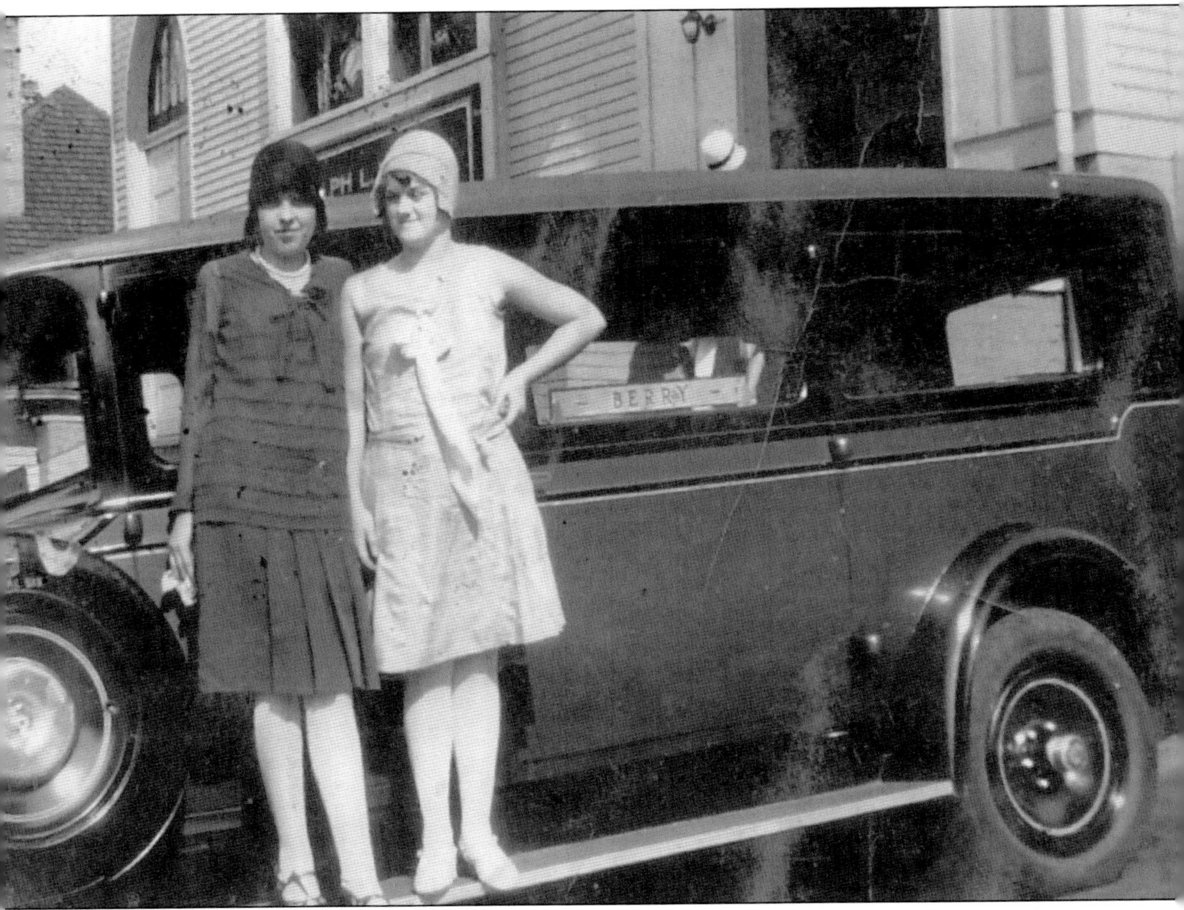

Thelma Ford (left) poses with a friend on the step rails of a car in front of Berry Funeral Home. (Courtesy of the Berry family.)

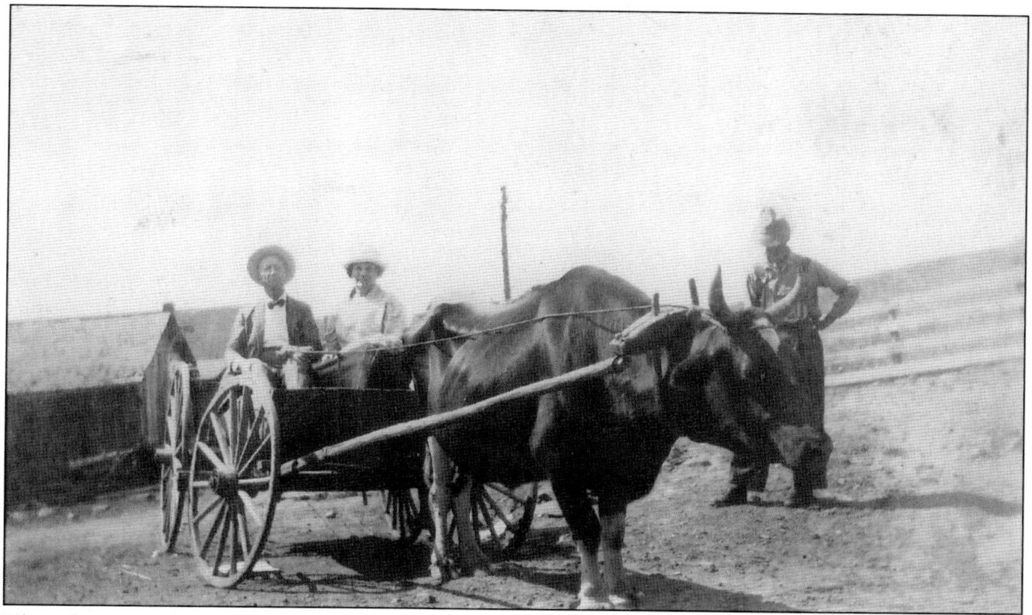

This photograph of Stanley Farm was taken in the late 1800s. A portion of the land was deeded to the family by Tennessee governor William Blount's half-brother Willie Blount in the early 1800s. Agriculture was the main focus from the beginning and the Davenport Farm became one of the largest wheat producers in Knox County. One hundred years later, produce and cut flowers took center stage. Most of these products were sold downtown on Market Square. (Courtesy of Monte Stanley.)

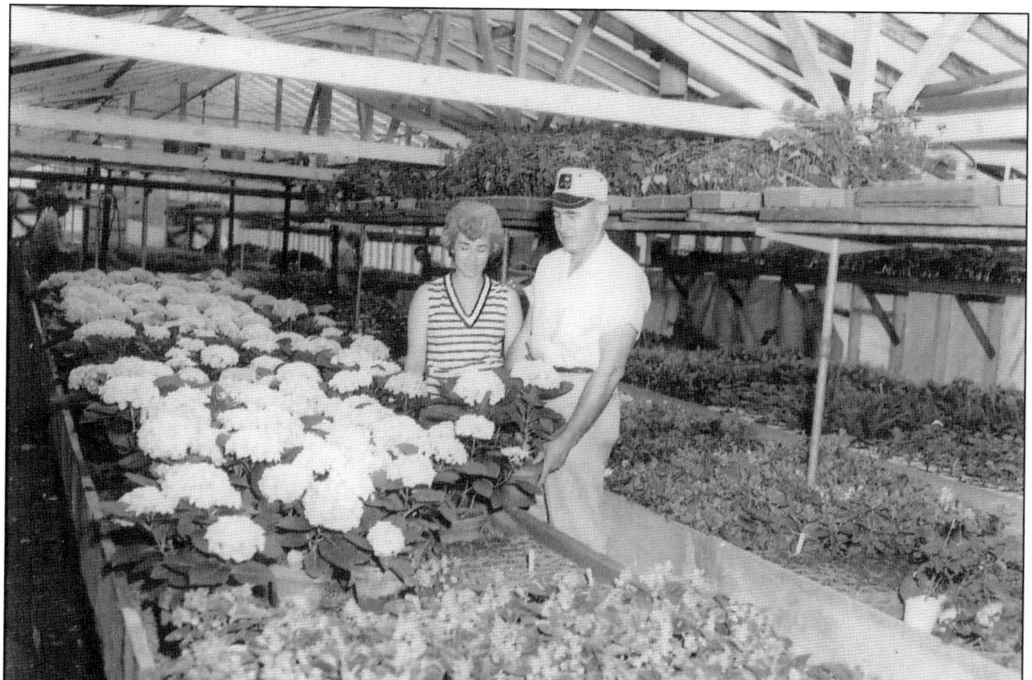

Charles Stanley Sr. and Mary Kathryn Stanley pose for a photograph in the 1960s. (Courtesy of Monte Stanley.)

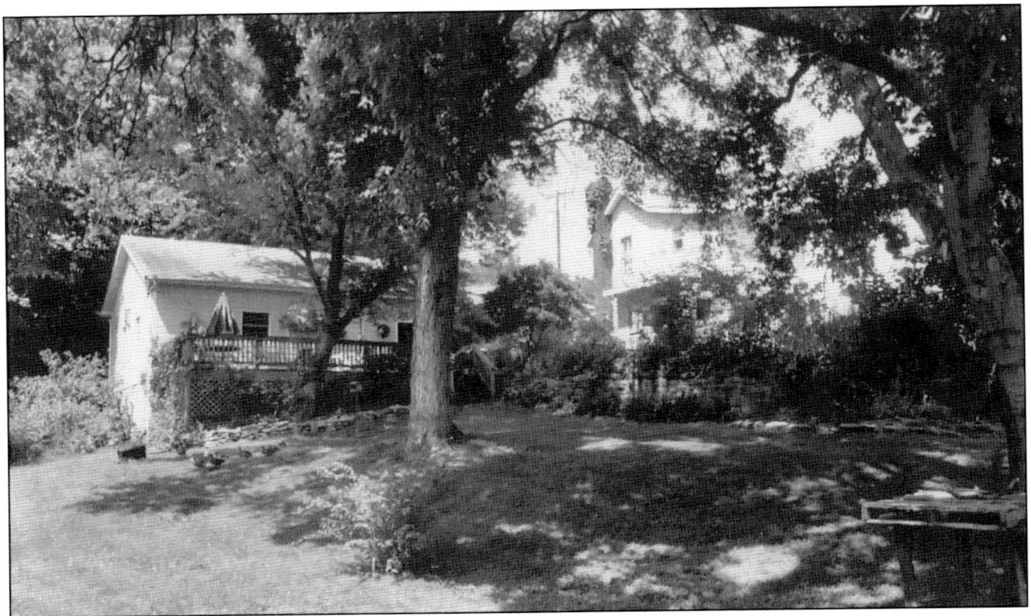

The Stanley home, seen in the distance, was built in the late 1790s. The original structure is log, now covered with siding. (Courtesy of Monte Stanley.)

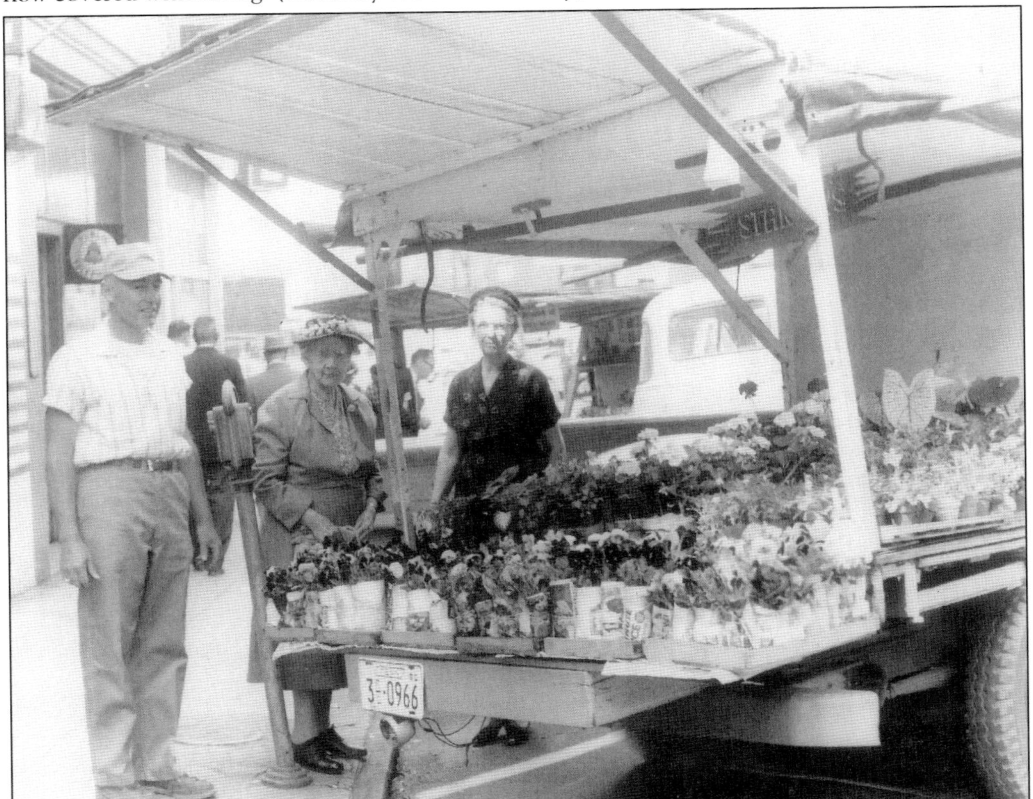

Charles Stanley and Mrs. Lonas traveled to Market Street in downtown Knoxville in the 1950s to sell flowers from Stanley's Greenhouse. (Courtesy of Monte Stanley.)

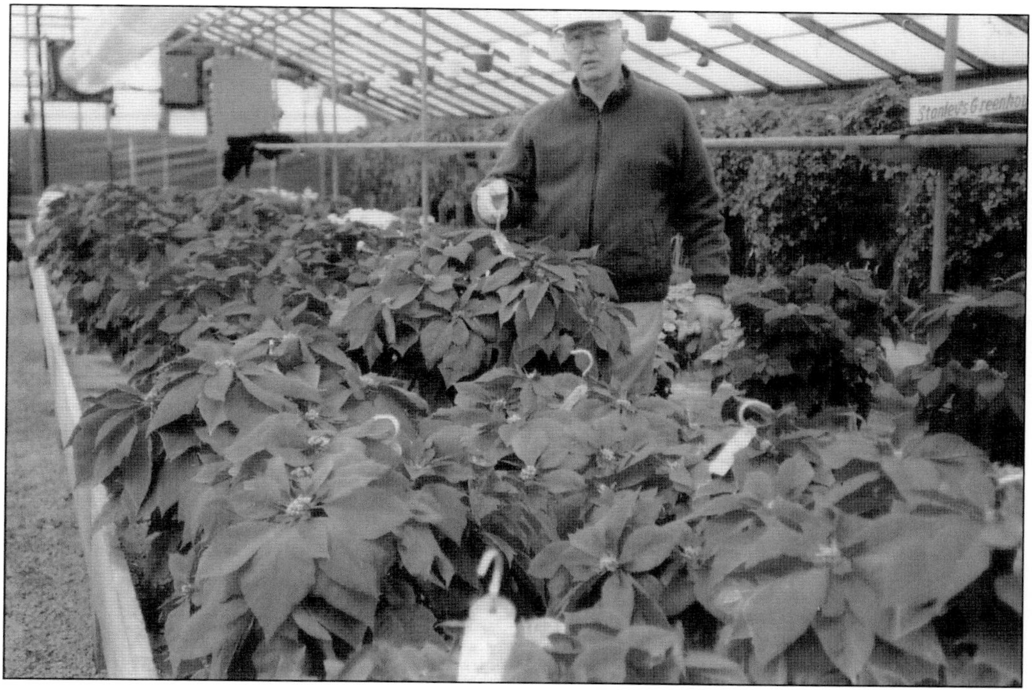

These two photographs show the inside of Stanley's Greenhouse. (Courtesy of Monte Stanley.)

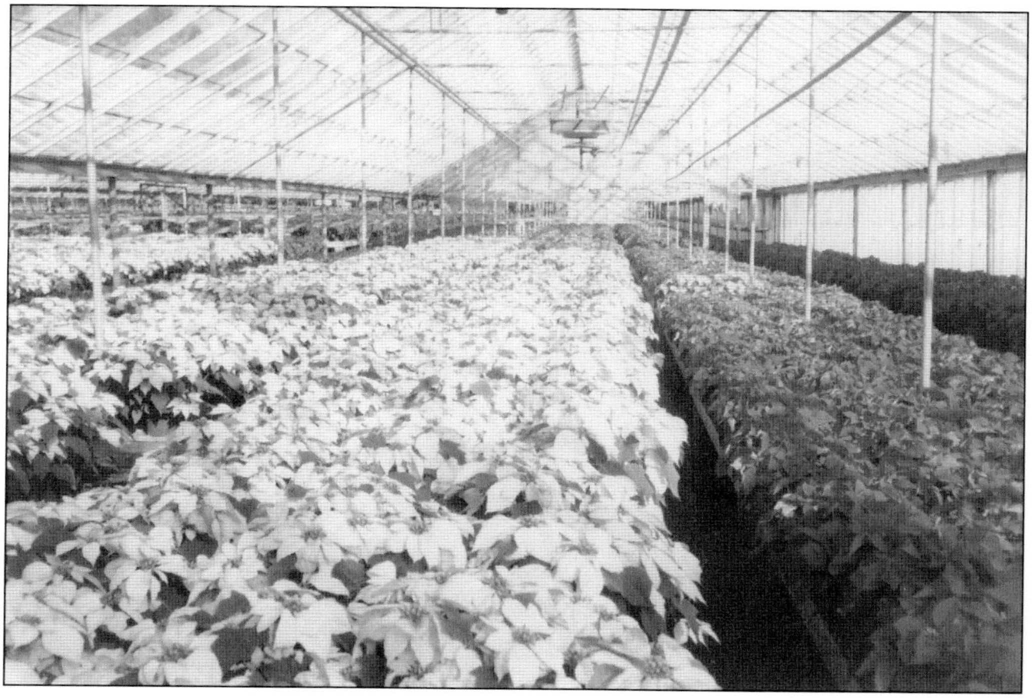

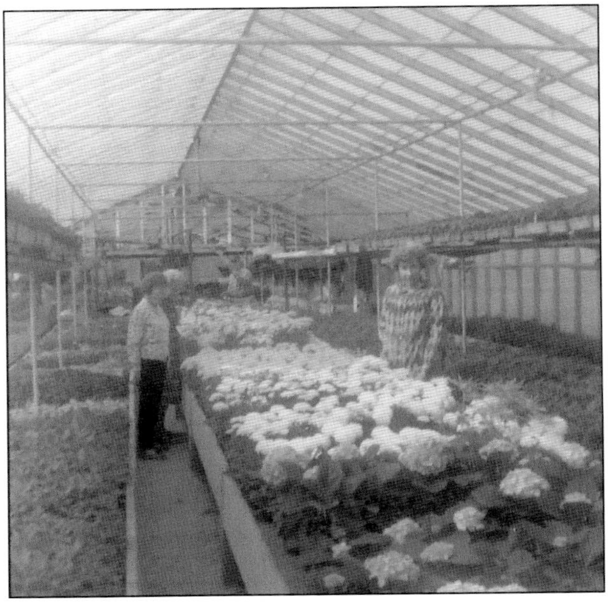

Charles Stanley, Charlie Davenport's grandson, built the first greenhouse in 1955, changing the focus more toward horticulture. (Courtesy of Monte Stanley.)

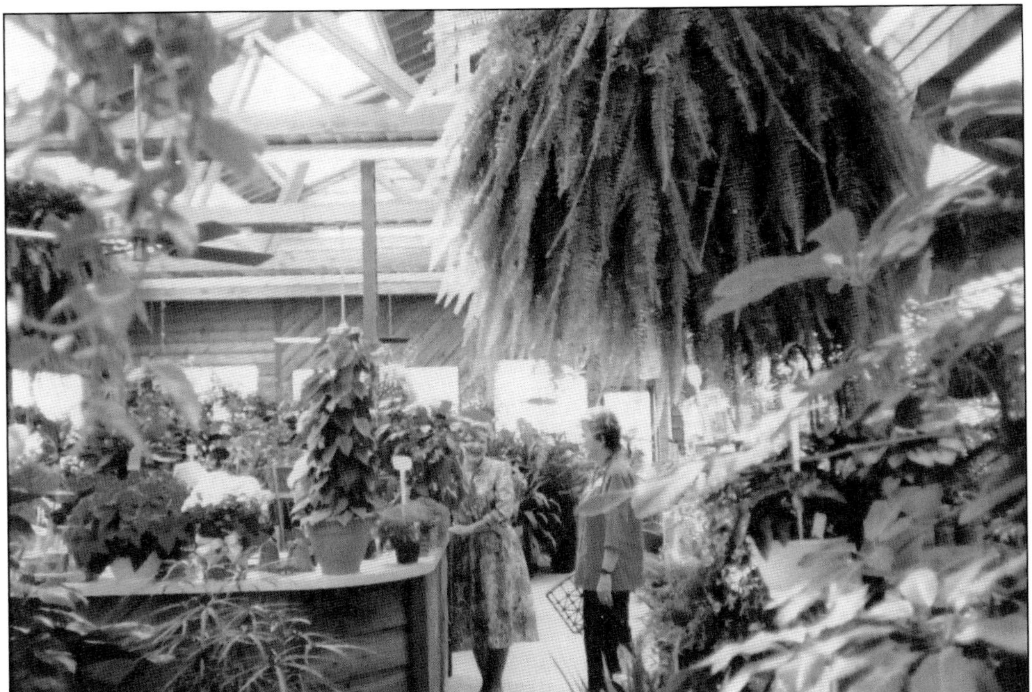

Stanley's Greenhouses & Plant Farm now totals over 190,000 square feet with the addition of the 36,000-square-foot retail center that opened in 2001. (Courtesy of Monte Stanley.)

Two

EARLY HISTORY

Although technically located in South Knox County and not within the city limits of South Knoxville, Marble Springs reflects the earliest notable history of the South Knoxville area. Marble Springs is the historic site of the home of Tennessee resident Gov. John Sevier. Sevier settled in the East Tennessee area after leaving his home state of Virginia in the early 1770s. He fought in the Battle of King's Mountain and was instrumental in defeating the Cherokee at the Battle of Boyd's Creek. Sevier was also the only governor of the state of Franklin and served as the governor of Tennessee for six terms. Later in life, he served as a state senator and a US congressman. Sevier officially obtained the property that he named Marble Springs in 1796.

The South Knox area remained fairly quiet and sparsely populated until the 1860s. South Knoxville played a significant role during the Civil War. Fort Higley, Fort Dickerson, Fort Stanley, and Sevierville Hill were erected by Union forces on the south side of the Tennessee River in 1863. Famed entrepreneur and Knoxville resident Perez Dickinson, cousin of poet Emily Dickinson, purchased William's Island in 1869. He later built a mansion known as "Island Home" on what is now the campus of Tennessee School for the Deaf.

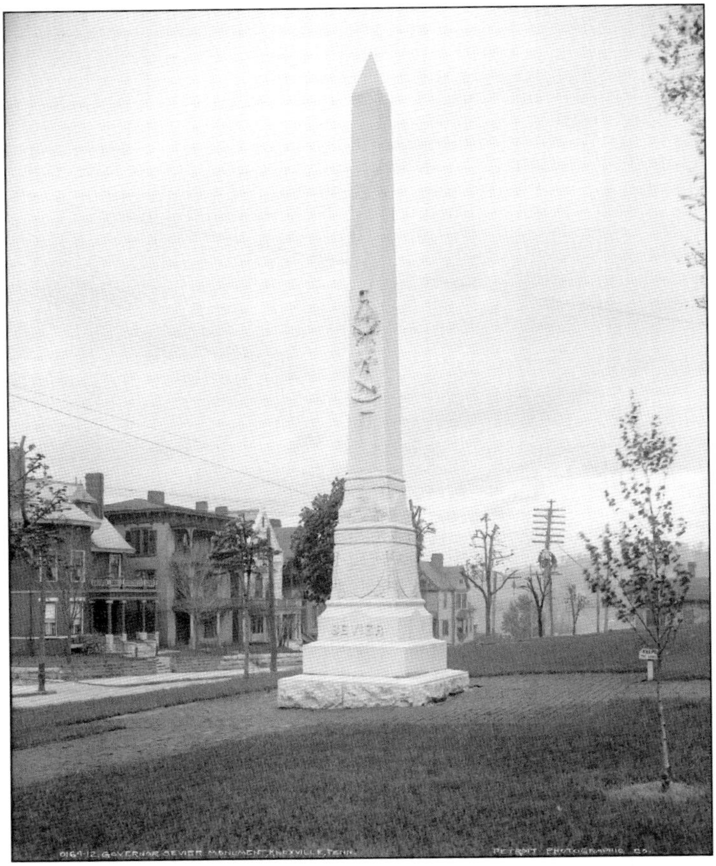

This is a photograph of the Gov. John Sevier monument located in Knoxville around 1900. The famed governor and his wife, Bonny Kate, lived in South Knox County from the 1790s until his death in 1815. The monument sits on the east lawn of the Knox County Courthouse. (Courtesy of the Library of Congress.)

John Sevier received a grant for a parcel of land in South Knox County at the foot of Bays Mountain. He named the place Marble Springs because of the numerous springs and ample deposits of marble located on the property. Because he loved farm life, he built a home on this land and moved his family rather than living in the city. (Courtesy of Marble Springs.)

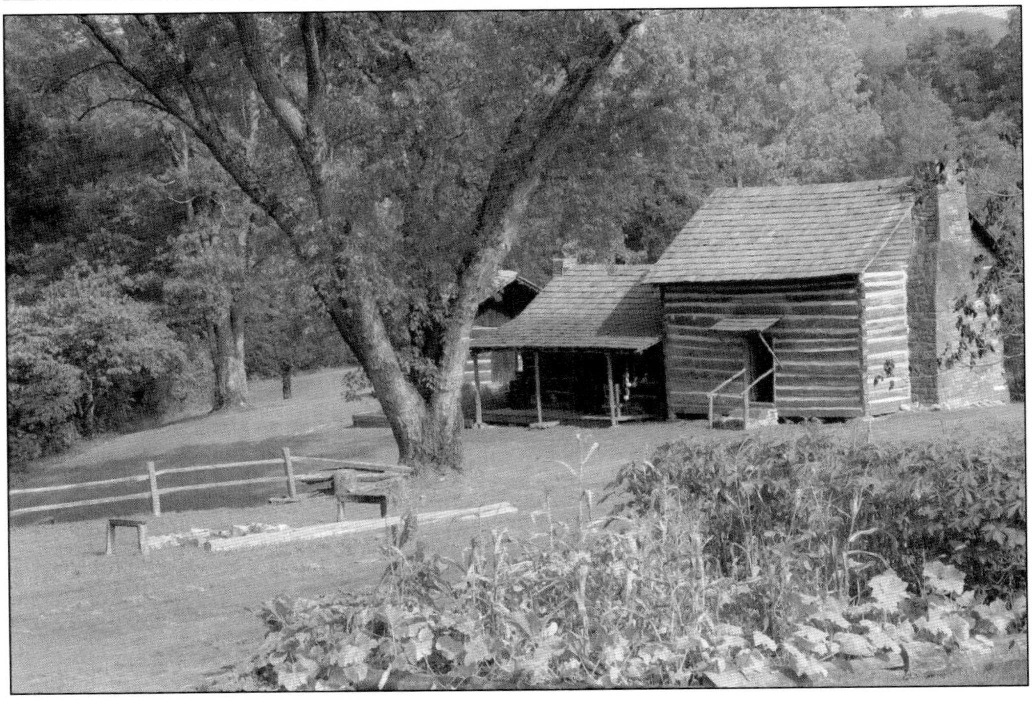

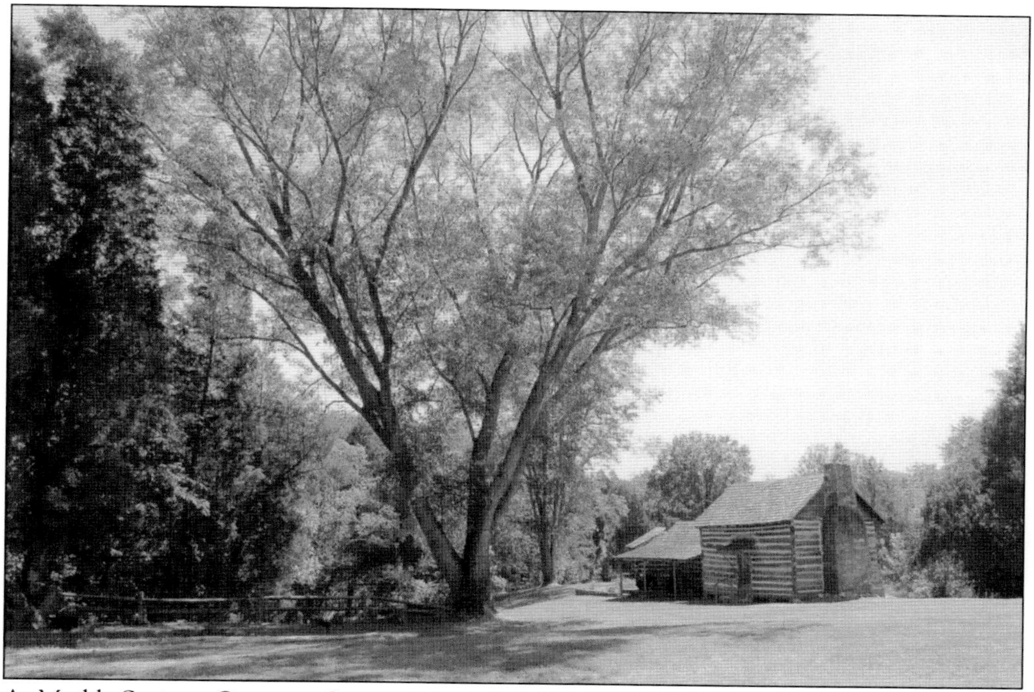

At Marble Springs, Governor Sevier built a log home similar to his home at Plume Grove near Bristol, where he lived when he first moved to East Tennessee. The main house consisted of one main room and an overhead sleeping loft. The kitchen was separate in order to protect the main house in the event of a fire. (Courtesy of Marble Springs.)

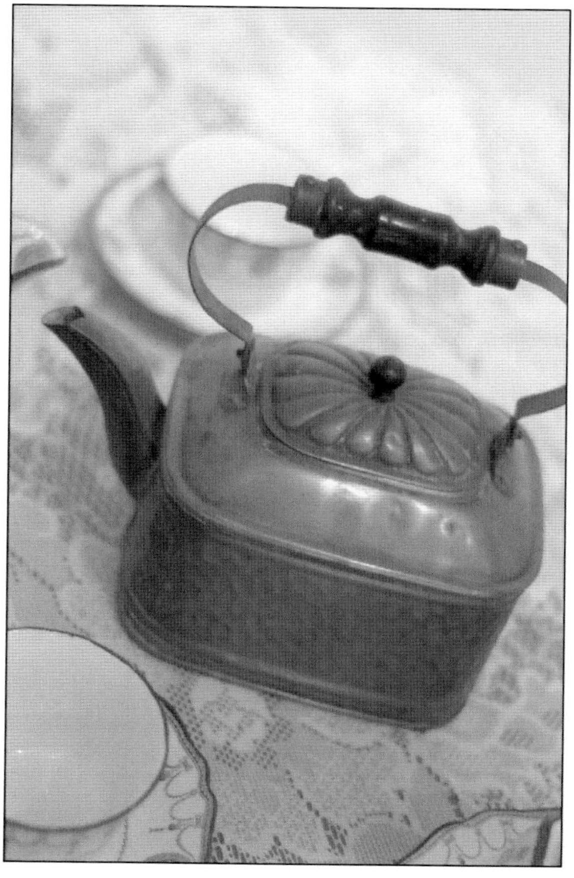

This is a photograph of a teakettle owned by Bonny Kate, the second wife of John Sevier. As Tennessee's first lady, Bonny Kate hosted many visitors and was known for her hospitality. No visitor, friend, or petitioner left Marble Springs without enjoying some refreshments. She frequently entertained high-society visitors with formal tea. (Courtesy of Marble Springs.)

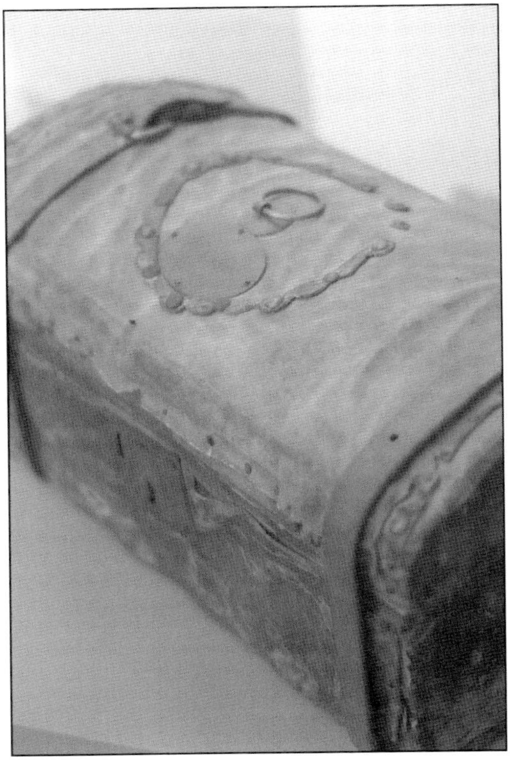

This is a trunk owned by Gov. John Sevier, the first governor of Tennessee. During his travels throughout the region, he used this trunk to transport personal items and important documents. (Courtesy of Marble Springs.)

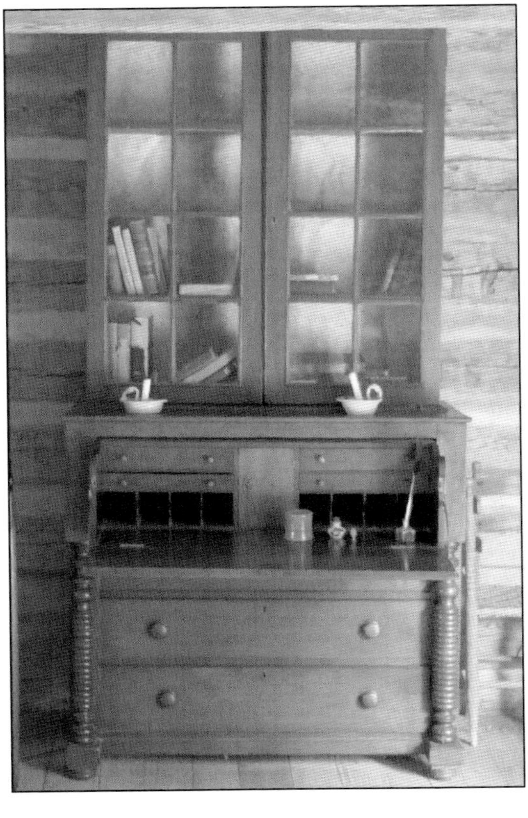

As an early political leader and eventual governor, John Sevier would have engaged in a significant amount of correspondence, which would have been written on a writing desk such as this one. (Courtesy of Marble Springs.)

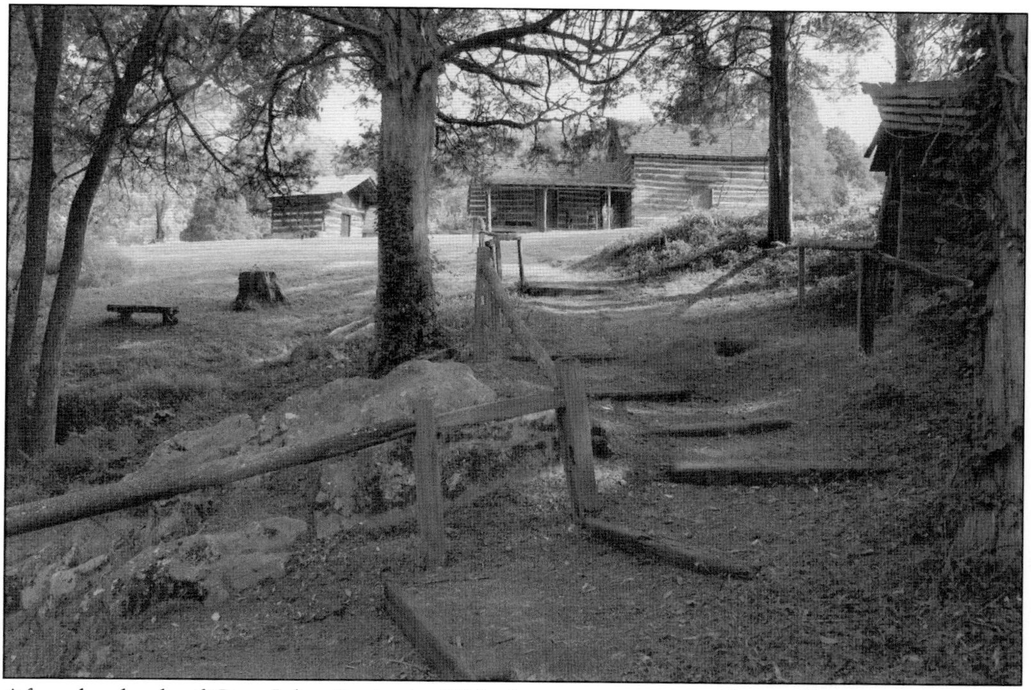

After the death of Gov. John Sevier in 1815, the property was sold at public auction in 1818. It remained in private hands until 1941, when the General Assembly of Tennessee purchased 40 acres of land at Marble Springs; at that time, only the original cabin remained. (Courtesy of Marble Springs.)

The historic Franklin Home was located on Maryville Pike across from Hardin Appliance Store and Mary Knox. The Flenniken family, who were early settlers of the Mount Olive community, built the home in 1772. (Courtesy of the Berry family.)

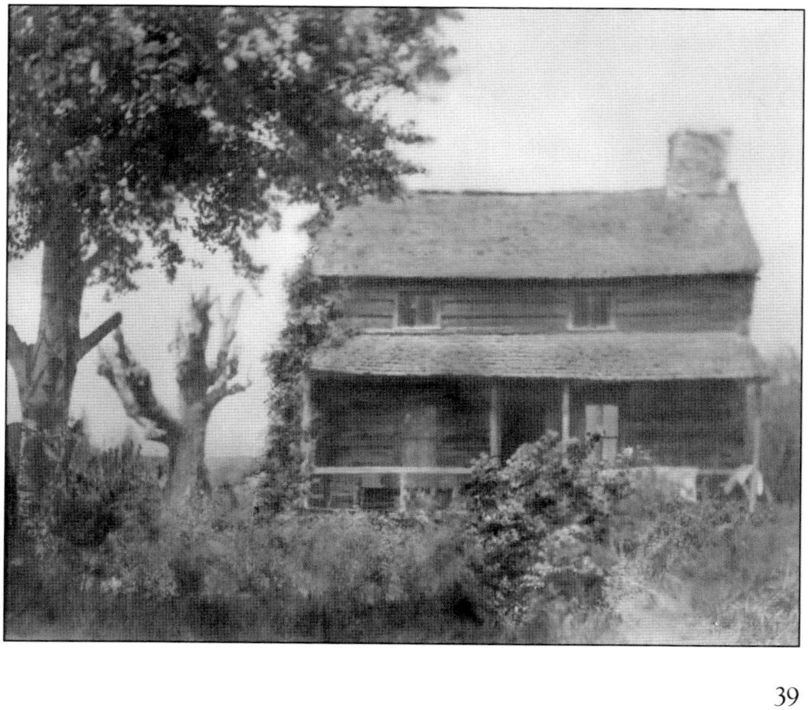

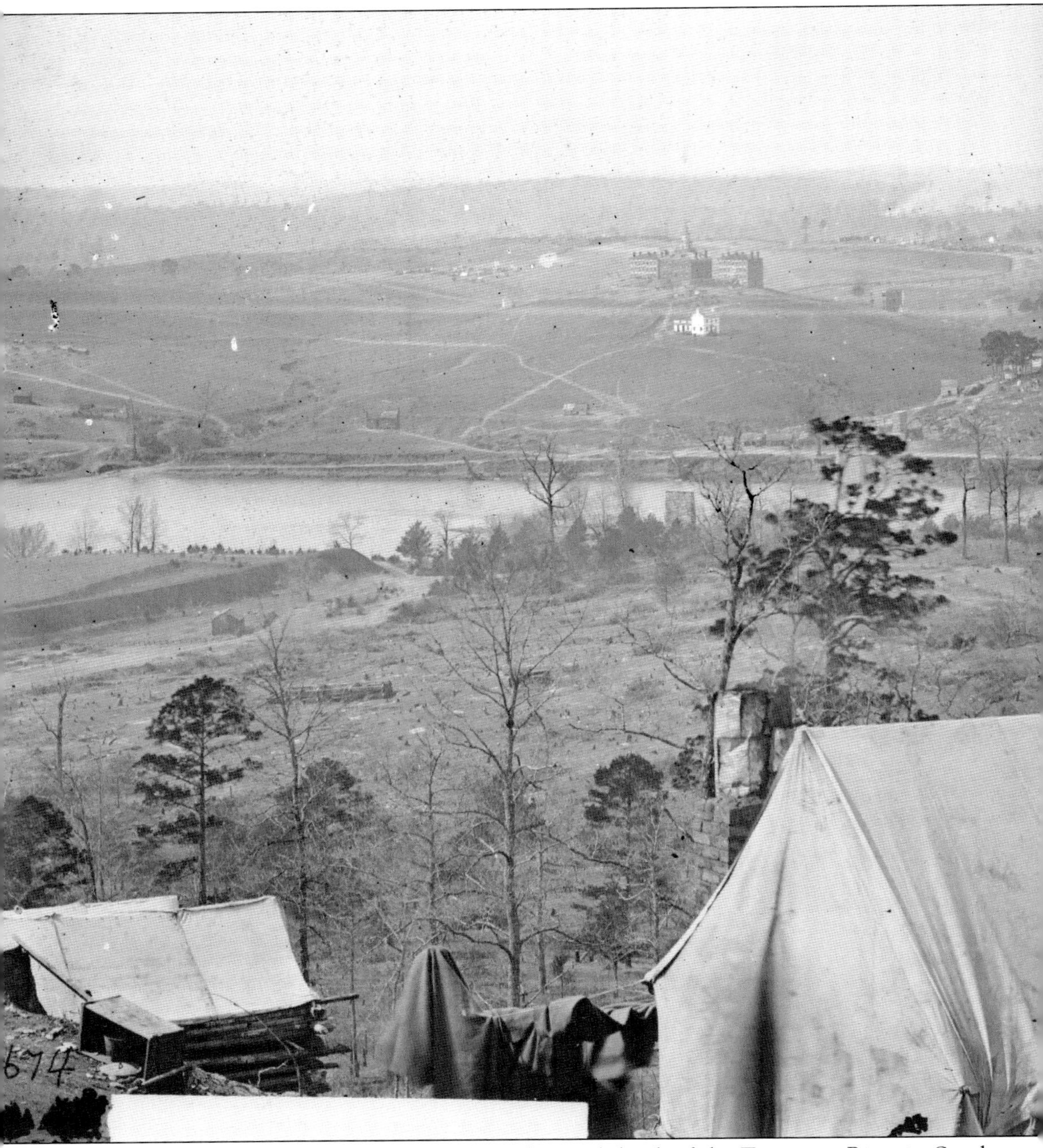

The environs of Knoxville are shown from the south bank of the Tennessee River in South Knoxville. This photograph is from the Siege of Knoxville in late 1863. The difficult strategic situation of the federal armies after Chickamauga enabled Bragg to detach a force under Longstreet, which aimed to drive Burnside out of East Tennessee and did shut him up in Knoxville, which he defended successfully. This view, taken after Longstreet's withdrawal on December 3, shows Strawberry Plains, which was on his line of retreat. George N. Barnard was photographer of the chief engineer's office, military division of the Mississippi, and his views were transmitted with the report of the chief engineer of Burnside's army on April 11, 1864. (Courtesy of the Library of Congress.)

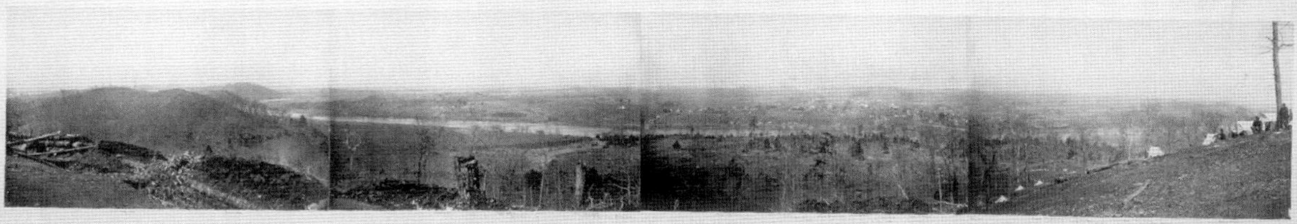

This photograph depicts Knoxville as seen from Fort Stanley in 1864. Fort Dickerson lies to the west and Fort Stanley to the east of what is now Chapman Highway. The forts were the center two of four fortified heights held by Union forces south of the river during the siege of Knoxville from November 17 to December 4, 1863. The outlying heights were Fort Higley and Sevierville Hill. Maj. Gen. Jos. Wheeler, CSA, made a vain effort to seize these hills with cavalry on November 15–16, 1863. He came via Sweetwater and Maryville. (Courtesy of the Library of Congress.)

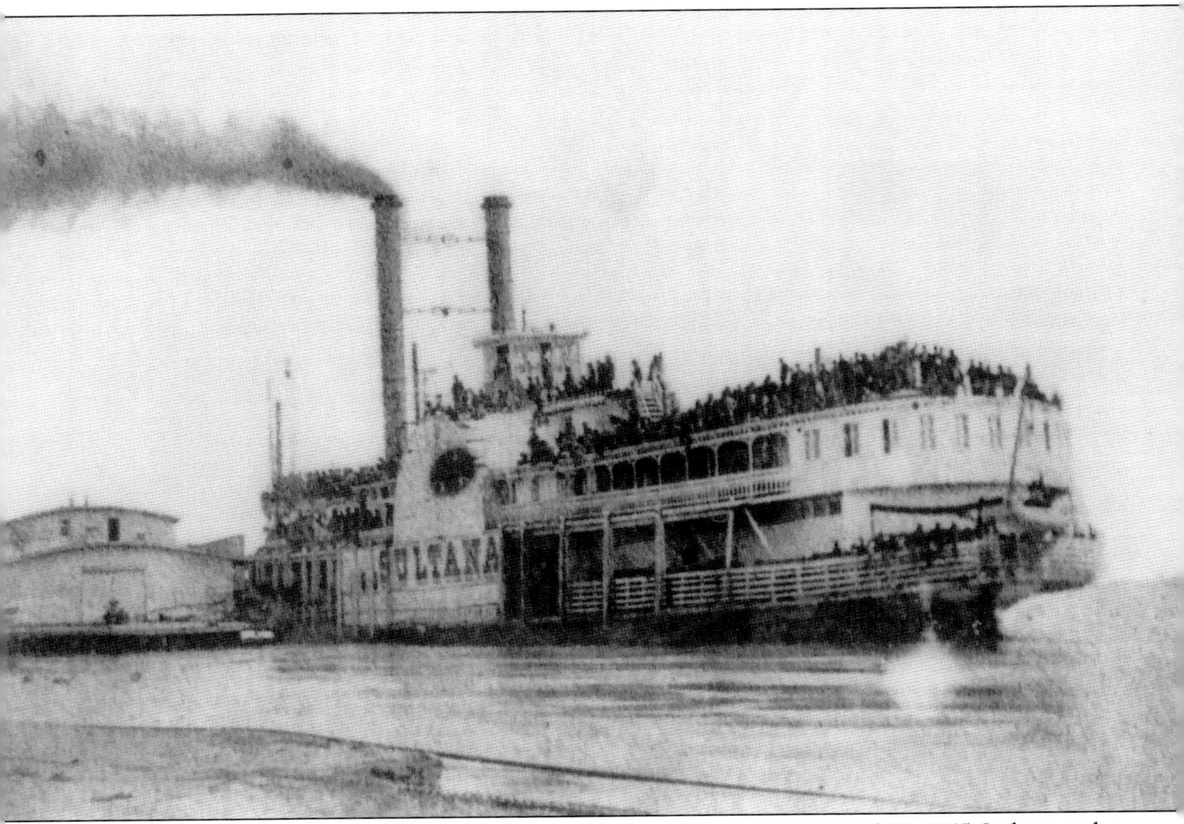

This photograph shows the ill-fated *Sultana* in Helena, Arkansas, on April 27, 1865. It depicts the overloaded steamboat on the Mississippi River the day before her boilers exploded and she sank on April 27. Many of her passengers were Union soldiers from Tennessee, Kentucky, Michigan, Ohio, Indiana, and Virginia, who were on their way home following their release from the Confederate prisons at Andersonville and Cahaba. Built to carry only 376 passengers, *Sultana* had over 2,300 on board at the time of the disaster. (Courtesy of the Library of Congress.)

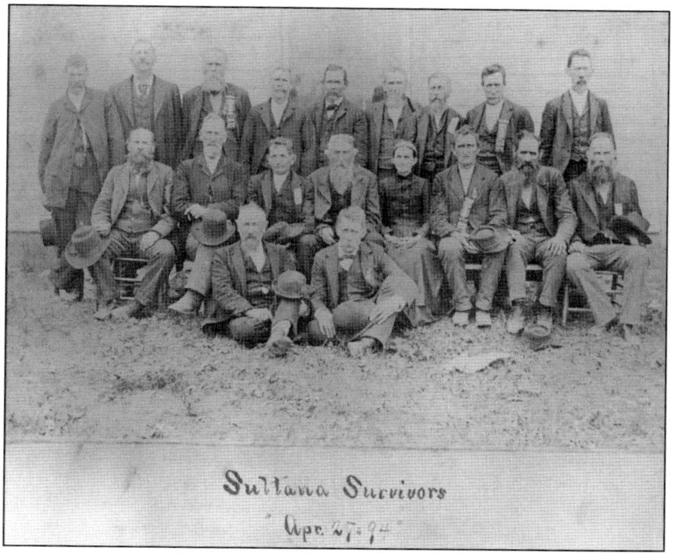

The remaining survivors of the *Sultana* disaster are shown in South Knoxville in 1894. Although reports vary, no less than 1,400 passengers died in the disaster. Many of the survivors and casualties alike were from the South Knoxville area. The East Tennessee Sultana Survivors Association was formed by John Simpson and a group of East Tennessee Civil War veterans in 1880. The group met annually on April 27 for 50 years until there were only four left in 1928. (Courtesy of the Berry family.)

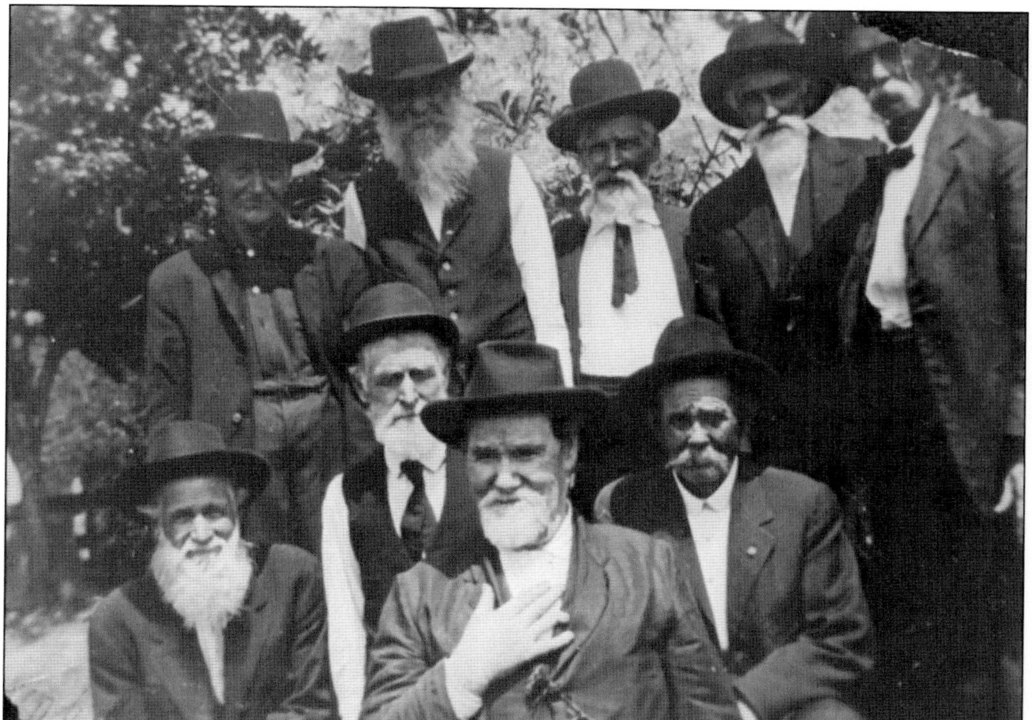

The East Tennessee Sultana Survivors Association is posing for a photograph in 1910. (Courtesy of the Berry family.)

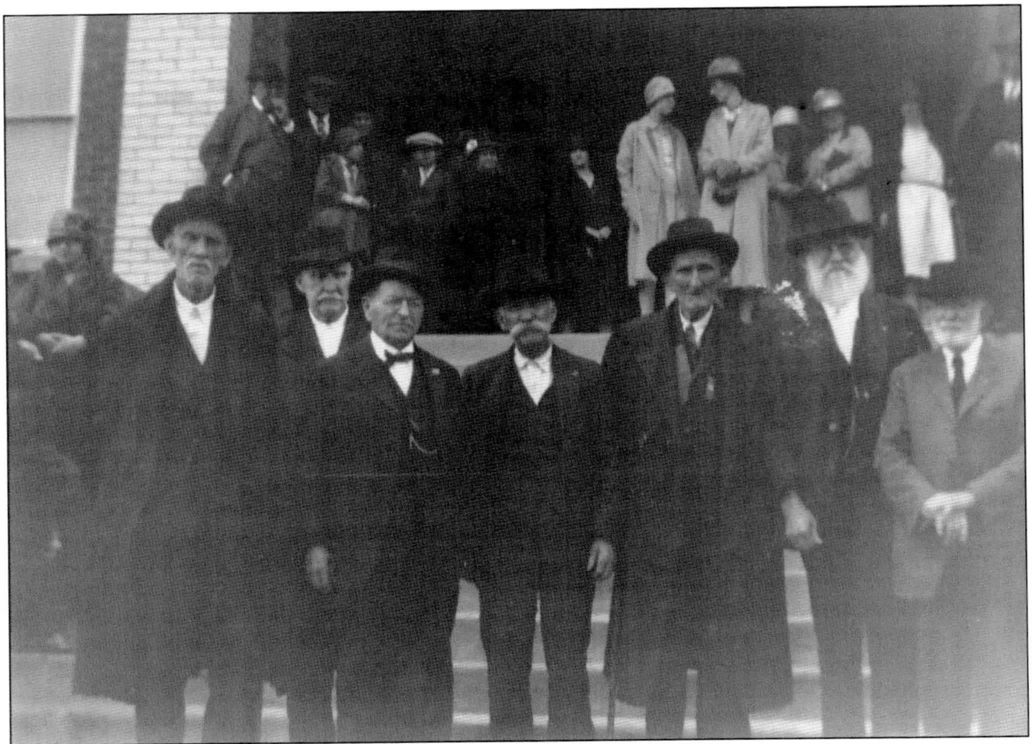

This is a later shot of the East Tennessee Sultana Survivors Association. Pictured are, from left to right, two unidentified, Pleasant M. Keeble, unidentified, Daniel Hendrick, John Simpson, and unidentified. (Courtesy of the Berry family.)

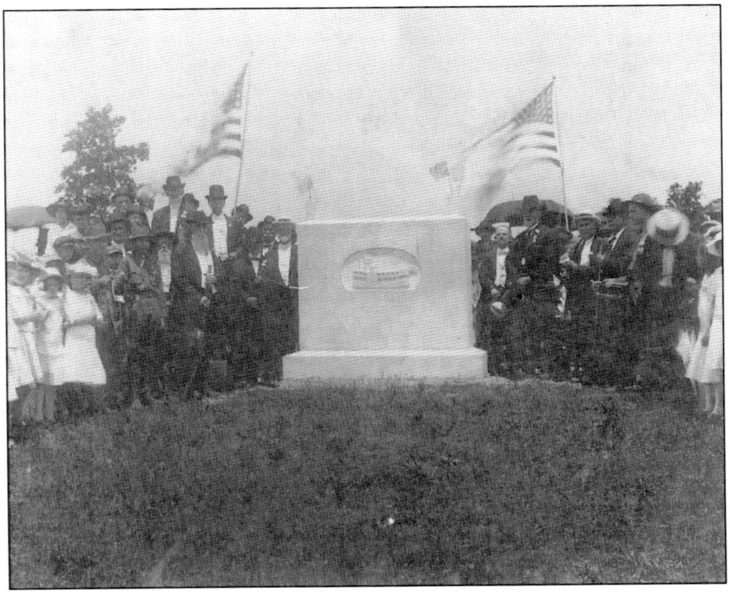

A monument was erected in the Mount Olive Cemetery in 1916 to memorialize those Tennesseans who lost their lives in the disaster. The inscription reads, "In memory of the men who were on the *Sultana* that was destroyed April 27, 1865, by explosion on the Mississippi River near Memphis, Tenn." The stone was donated by Gray Eagle Marble Co. and was carved by Joseph Henry Troutt. (Courtesy of the Berry family.)

Three

Industry

The abundance of natural resources, population growth, and the growth of the railroad in Knoxville led to the rise of a significant manufacturing sector in the late 19th century that remained strong through the early 20th century. Many industries such as iron works, machine shops, textile mills, lumber yards, and marble flourished in the city. In fact, Knoxville was once commonly referred to as the Marble City due to its thriving marble industry. South Knoxville in particular is home to major outcroppings of Tennessee marble. This led to the development of several marble quarries and finishing facilities in the late 19th century. The industry continued to thrive up until World War II. The most notable of the operations in South Knoxville were the Ross-Republic quarries, which are now part of Ijams Nature Center, and the Candoro Marble Works located in Vestal.

Additionally, Vestal Lumber Company began operation at a band mill located at 529 Martin Mill Pike in 1902. The location was particularly convenient because it was between two different railroads just two miles south of what was then the city limits. Vestal Lumber Company was a large employer in the area and also continued to thrive through World War II.

The completion of the Henley Street Bridge and the establishment of the Great Smoky Mountains National Park led to explosive industrial and economic growth in South Knoxville. The economy in South Knoxville continued to thrive until the 1970s.

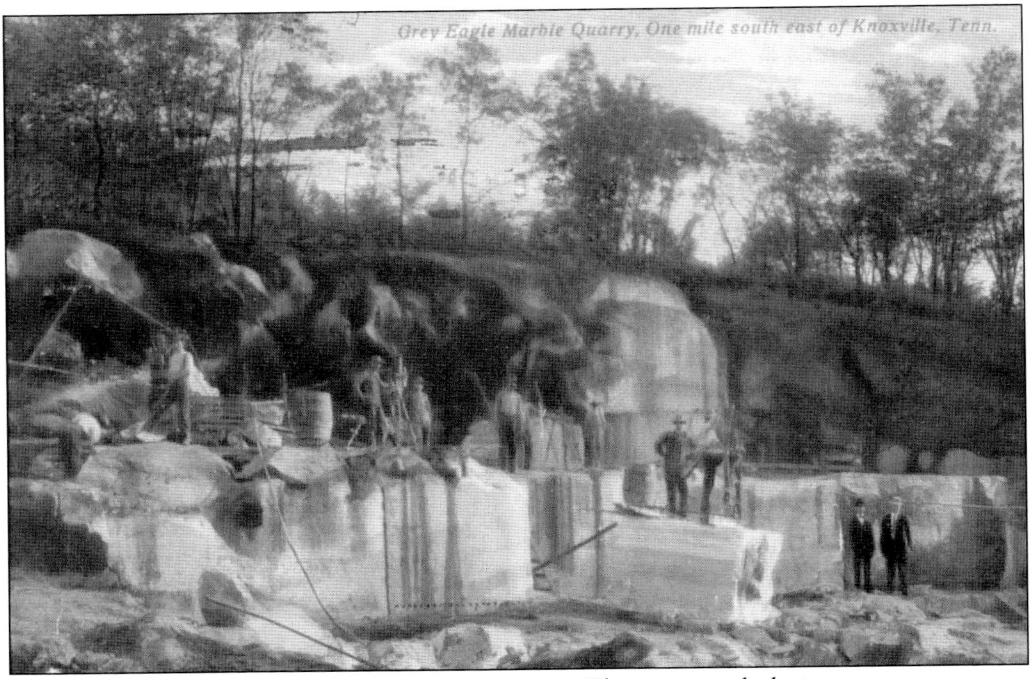

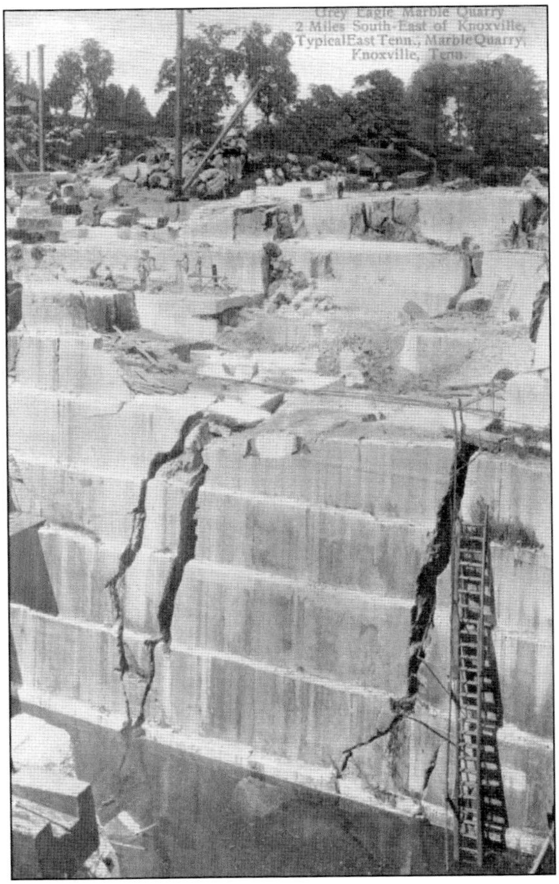

These postcards depict quarry operations in South Knoxville. (Courtesy of Paul James.)

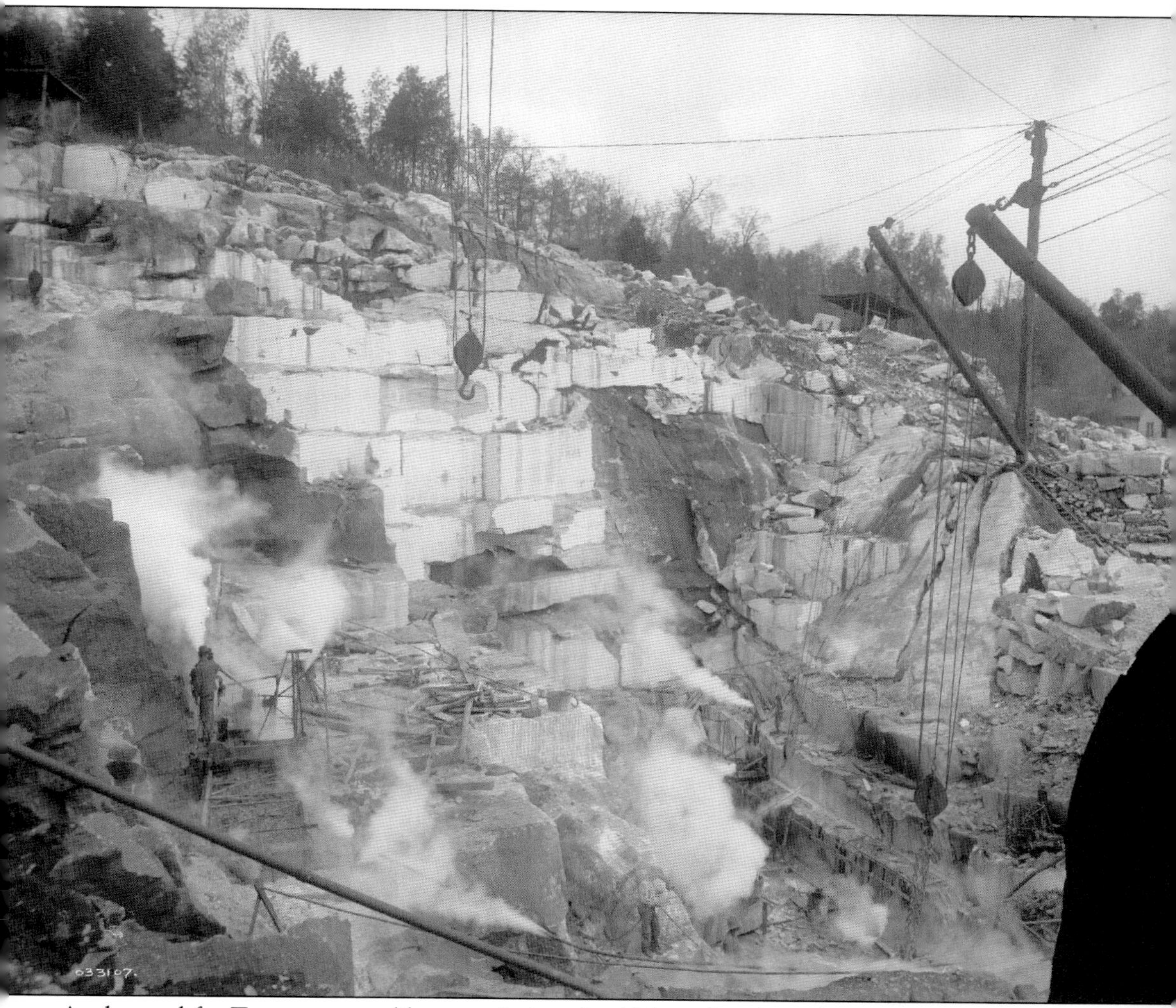

As demand for Tennessee marble grew during the 19th and early 20th century, a number of quarries and mills opened in Knoxville. Steam powered saw blades and steam derricks were used to cut and lift the marble to be shipped to the mills. This photograph shows a quarry managed by the Ross-Republic Marble Company, which was established when the Republic Marble Company merged with the Ross Marble Company in 1892. The Ross Marble Company operated the Island Home Quarry, later named Mead's Quarry, in South Knoxville, which was established in 1881.

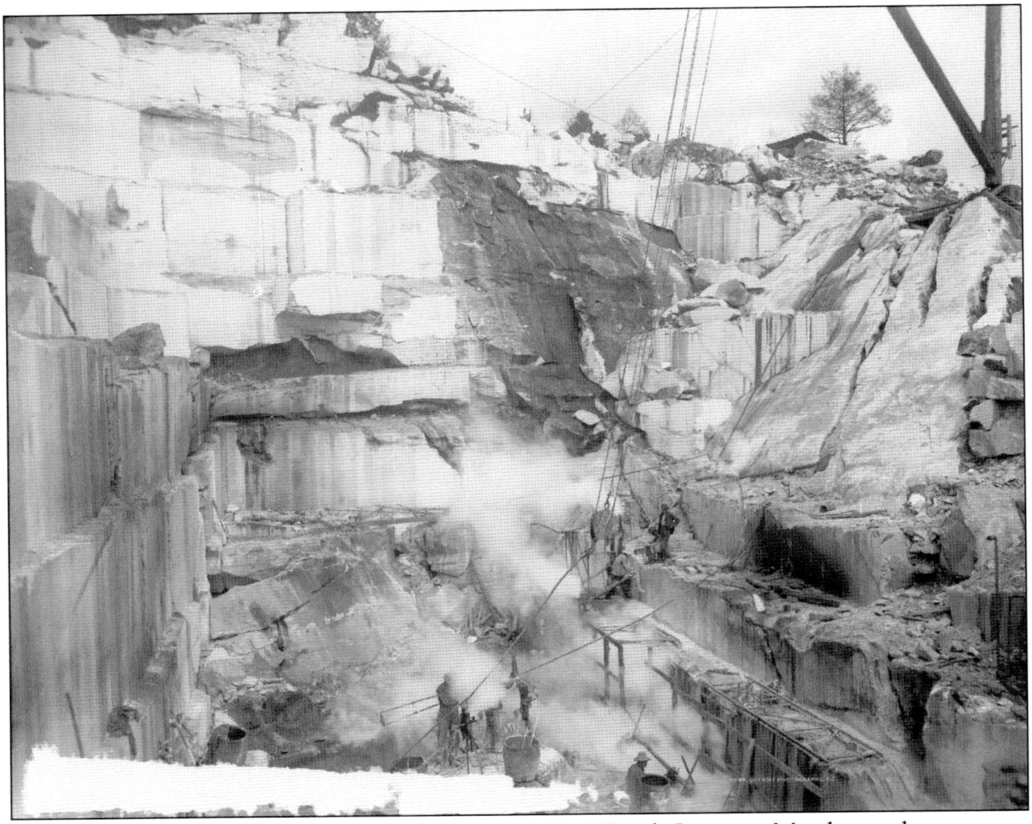

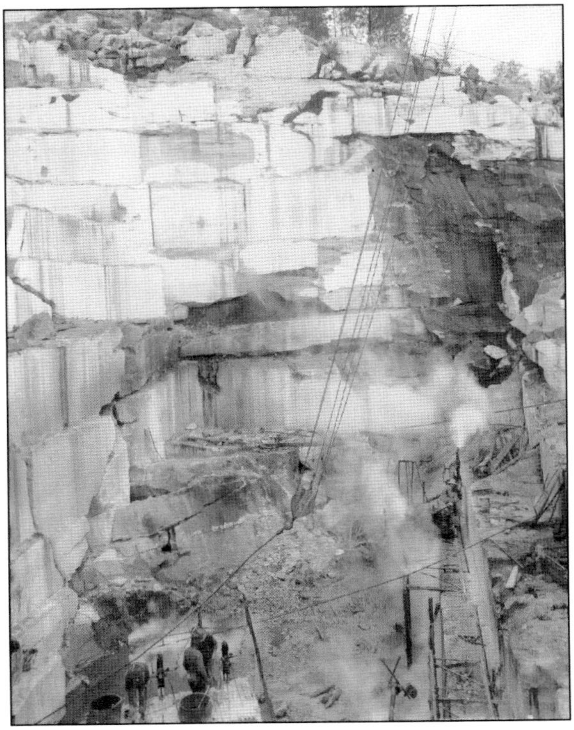

Frank Seymour Mead served as president of the new company after the merger of the Republic Marble Company and the Ross Marble Company. The company operated three quarries in the Island Home area of South Knoxville similar to those shown in these undated photographs. These images illustrate the difficult and often dangerous task of cutting and lifting the marble. Two of the quarries operated by the Ross-Republic Marble Company in Island Home, including Mead's Quarry, have been transformed into recreational areas at Ijams Nature Center. (Both, courtesy of the Library of Congress.)

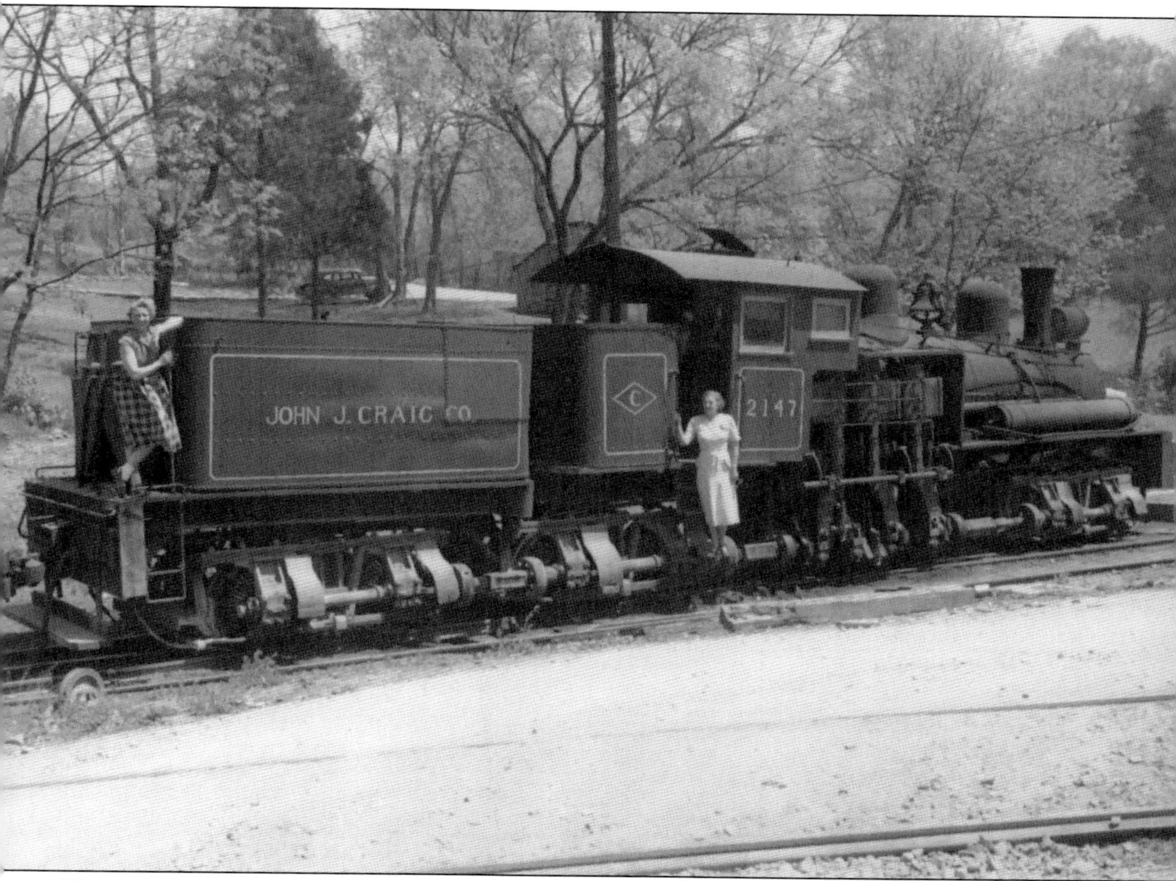

This is a photograph of a steam locomotive engine owned by the John J. Craig Co. in the early 1900s. Candoro Marble was affiliated with the John J. Craig Company, which operated several quarries in the vicinity of Knoxville. Marble from Craig quarries was processed at Candoro and used in many historically significant building projects, including the beloved pair of lion sculptures entitled "Patience" and "Fortitude" at the entrance of the New York Public Library. Marble that was quarried from Craig quarries and processed through Candoro Marble Company adorns the exterior of the National Gallery of Art in Washington, D.C.. At one point, Candoro Marble Company was the largest producer of pink marble in the United States. (Courtesy of Candoro Arts and Heritage.)

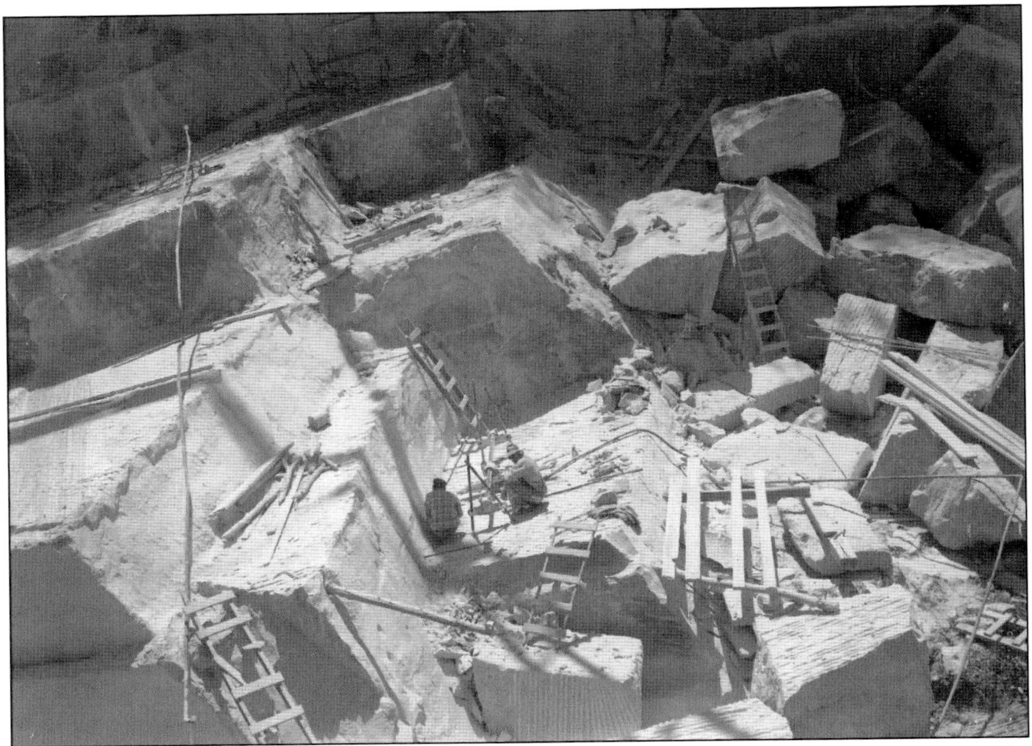

These photographs demonstrate the mining of marble to later be finished at Candoro Marble. They were taken from a sales manual used by representatives of Candoro Marble. (Courtesy of Candoro Arts and Heritage.)

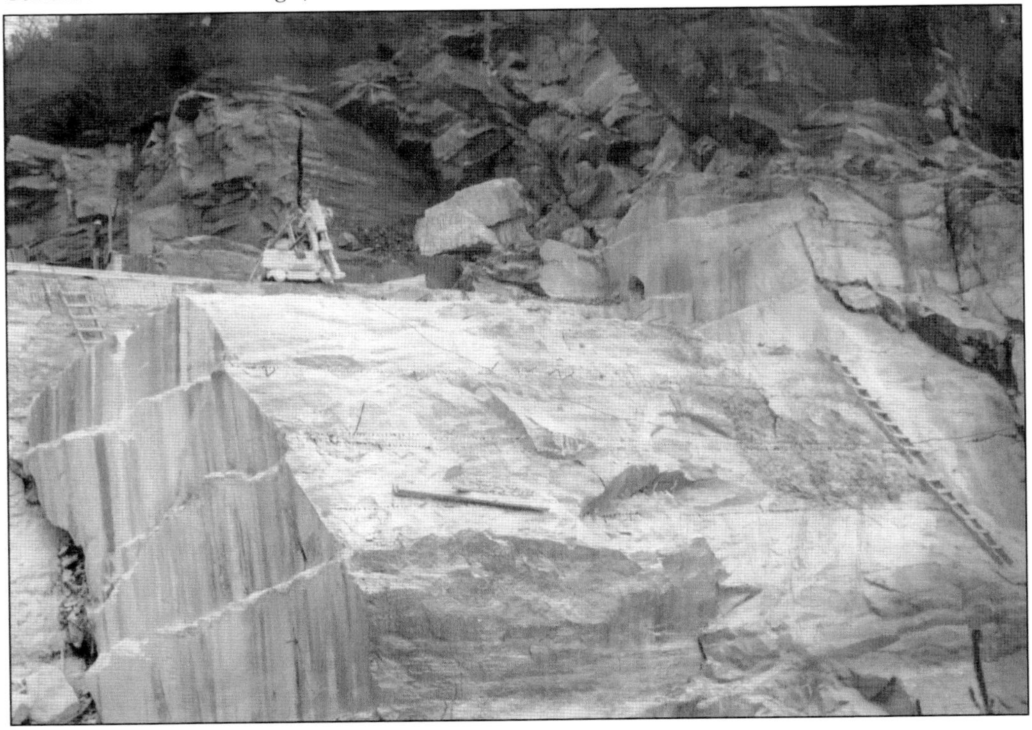

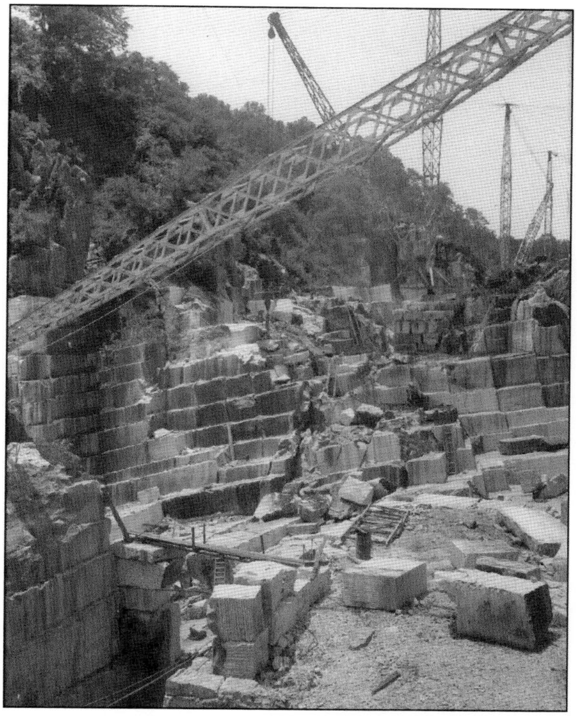

The grounds of Candoro Marble consist of the showroom, garage, and three additional buildings all built in 1914. The cutting facility is a large steel frame warehouse-style building where marble slabs were cut into blocks like the ones seen here. The polishing and shipping/receiving building is a concrete and steel structure with angular roofs covering each individual bay. This building once housed the complex's polishing machinery and shipping bay. The boiler room and office, constructed in 1914, consists of a one-story front section that contained the complex's offices and a two-story back section that contained the complex's boiler. The interior of the office section contains East Tennessee marble floors, wainscoting, and railing. (Courtesy of Candoro Arts and Heritage.)

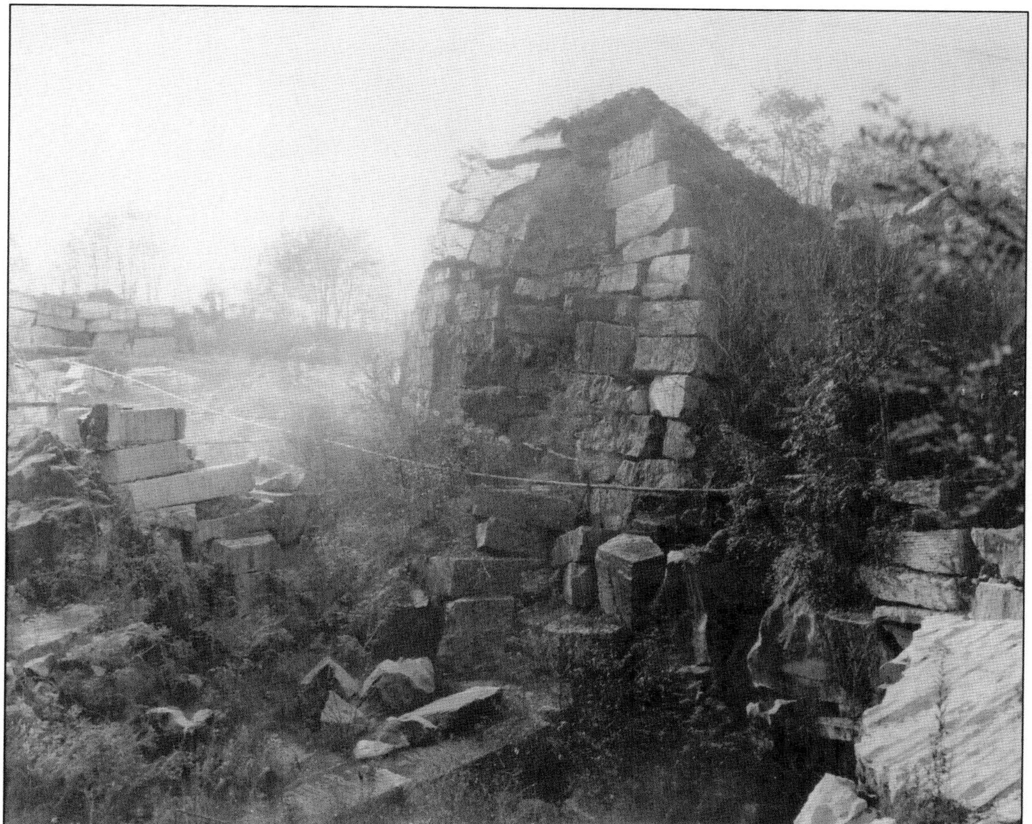

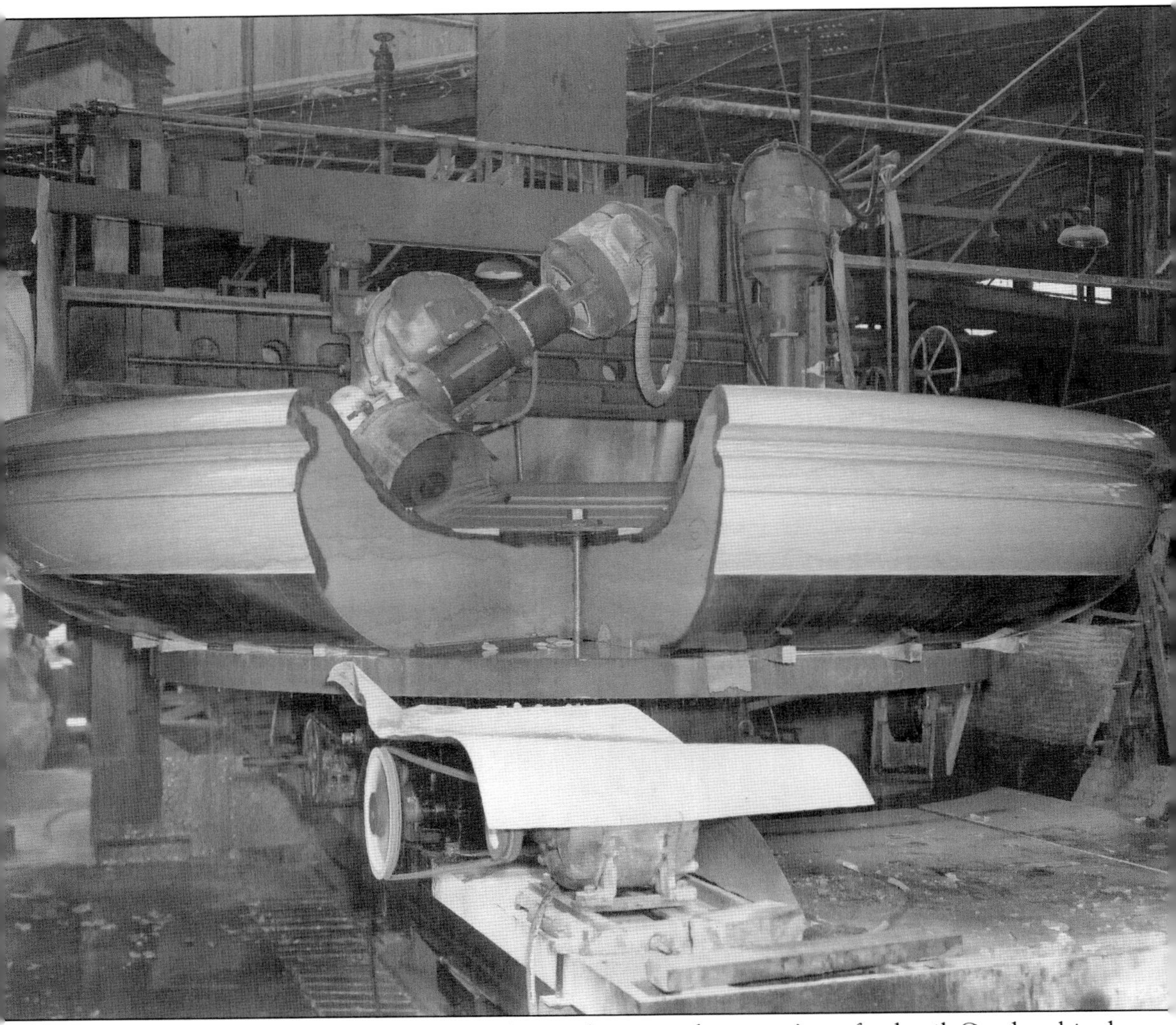

Marble processing required both complex machinery and an artist's eye for detail. Candoro hired famous Italian stone carver Albert Milani in 1927. Milani worked at Candoro for 40 years and during this time Candoro provided marble for the Smithsonian Museum of History and Technology and the National Gallery of Art in Washington, D.C., as well as local buildings such as the Knoxville Post Office building. More intricate hand carvings by Milani include the *History of the World* relief at the Pennsylvania State Capitol and the four eagle sculptures flanking the entrances of the Knoxville Post Office. According to Candoro's records, Milani's carvings were shipped to customers as far away as Pakistan and Japan. (Courtesy of Candoro Arts and Heritage.)

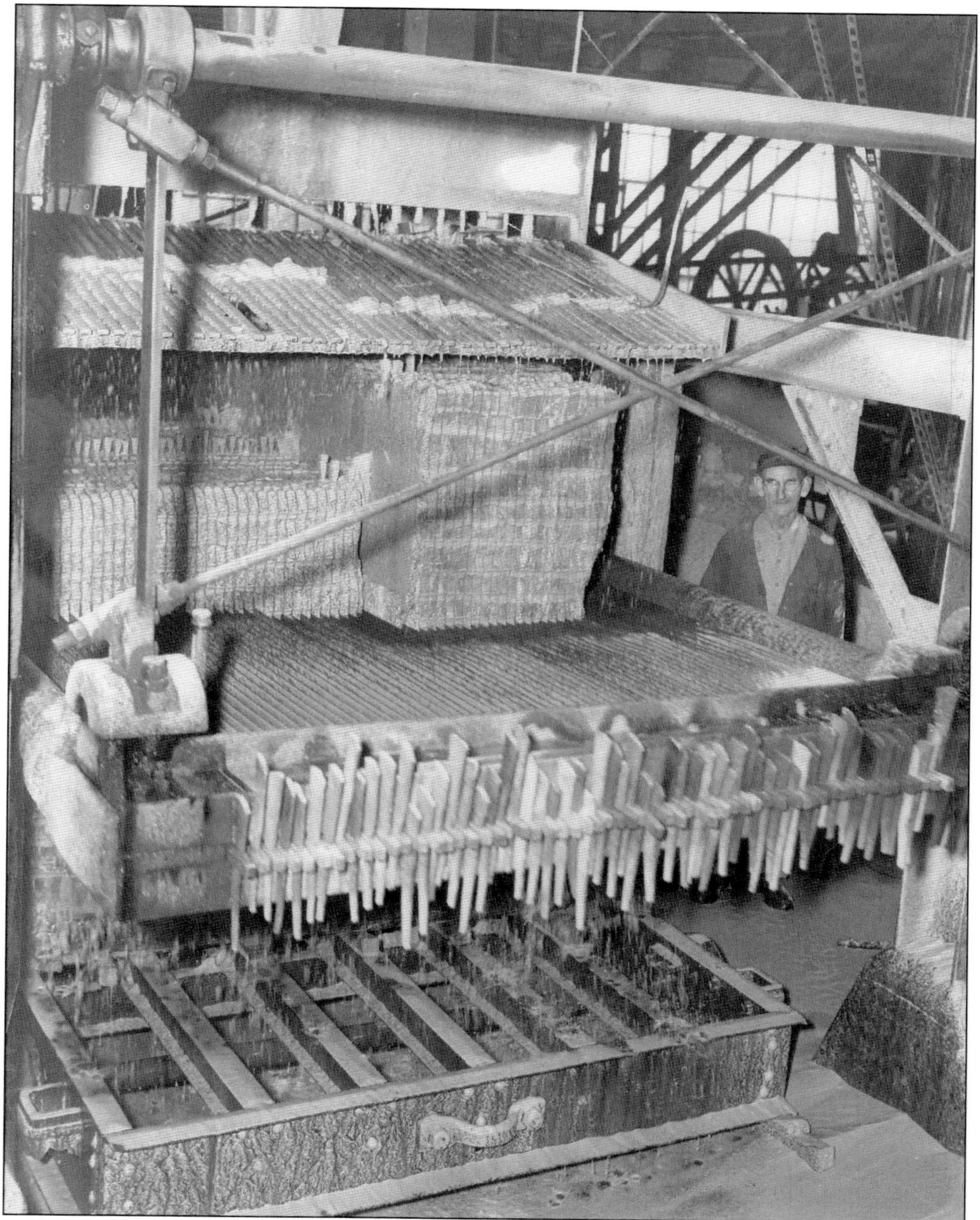

The industrial complex constructed by the Candoro Marble Company included a cutting facility and a polishing facility. This photograph shows some of the machinery used in the processing and finishing of the beautiful marble that came from Candoro Marble. (Courtesy of Candoro Arts and Heritage.)

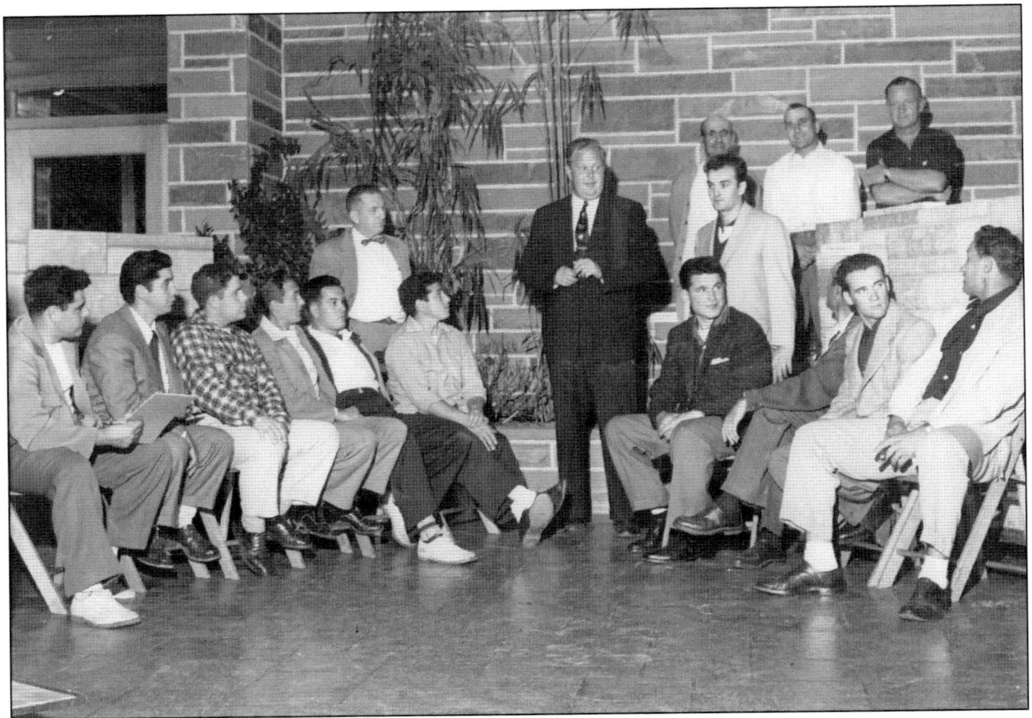

While marble occurs in several colors, the East Tennessee quarries were particularly renowned for pink marble because of the striking color and relative ease of processing and polishing. Above, sales staff and representatives of Candoro Marble meet before going out on the road. Note the tools laying on the block of marble below. (Both, courtesy of Candoro Arts and Heritage.)

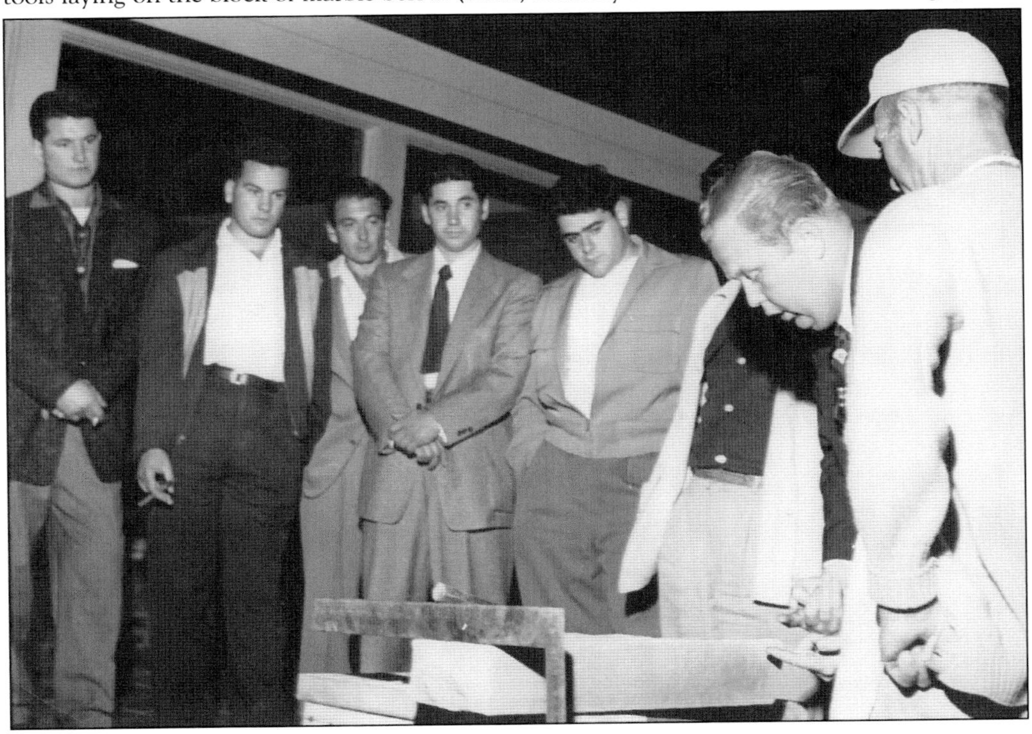

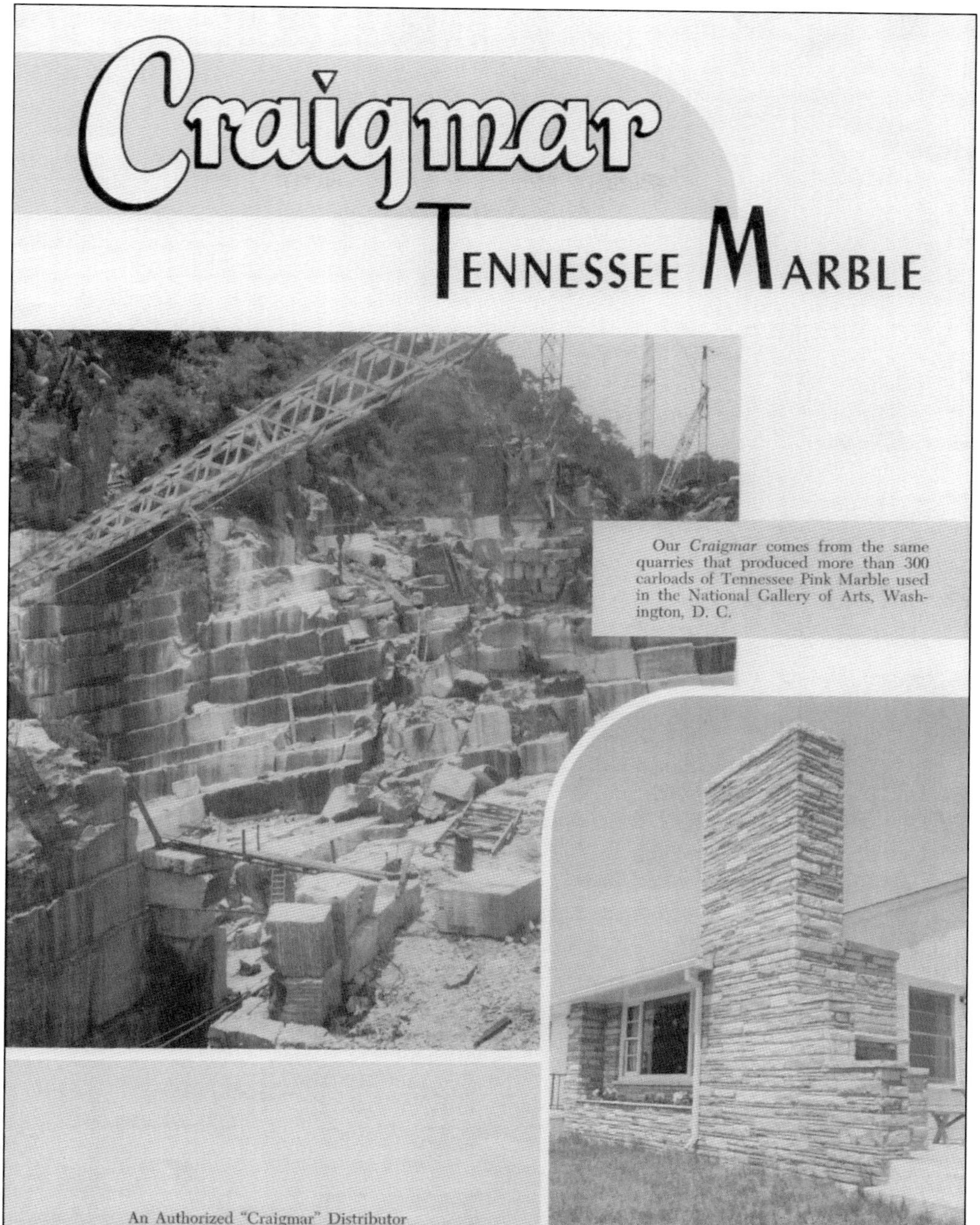

Brochures such as the one shown here showcased the unique qualities of Tennessee marble and were used by salesmen from Candoro Marble. After World War II, alternative building materials became cheaper and more widely available and the use of marble began to decline, leading to the closing of many marble companies, including Candoro, which closed in the 1980s. Even today, however, Tennessee marble remains popular in government buildings, monuments, and museums. (Courtesy of Candoro Arts and Heritage.)

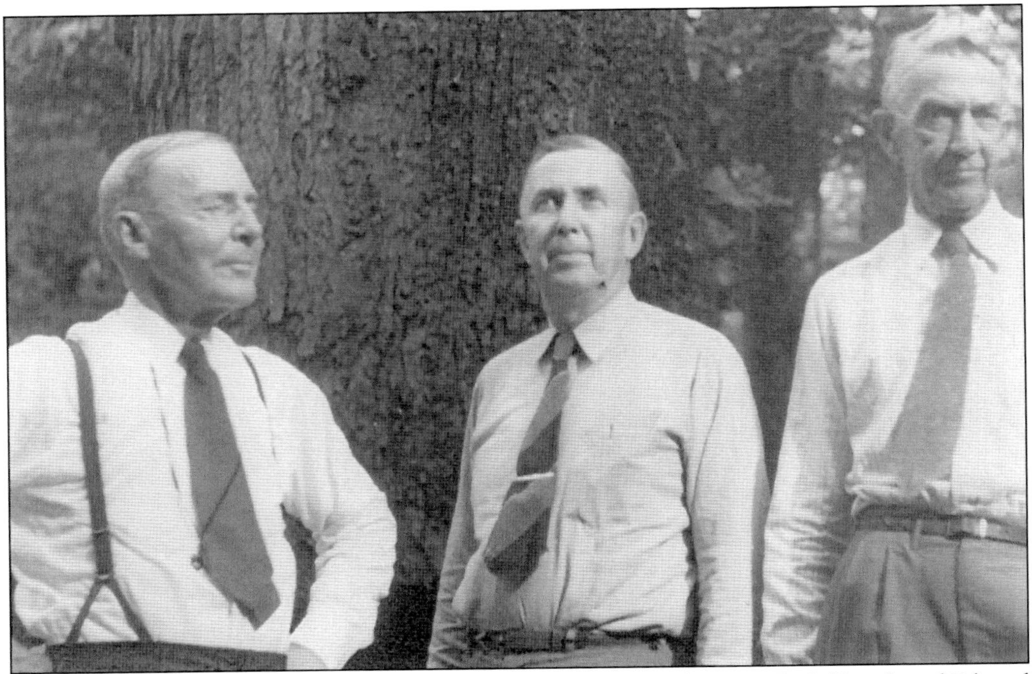

This 1940s photograph shows, from left to right, George E. French, James Park Vestal, and Edward Vestal. Shortly after the Vestal's father, Robert Vestal Sr., died in 1889, Mena Vestal, the older sister, went to work in a lumber office in Knoxville. There she met Mr. French, a visiting lumber broker from Boston. Three years later Mr. French took not only a bride but also her 14-year-old brother, James Park, back to Boston where James Park attended business school and worked in Mr. French's Atlantic Lumber Co. office. Around the turn of the century, Mr. French suggested forming a southern corporation with the Vestal brothers in Knoxville. (Courtesy of the Vestal family.)

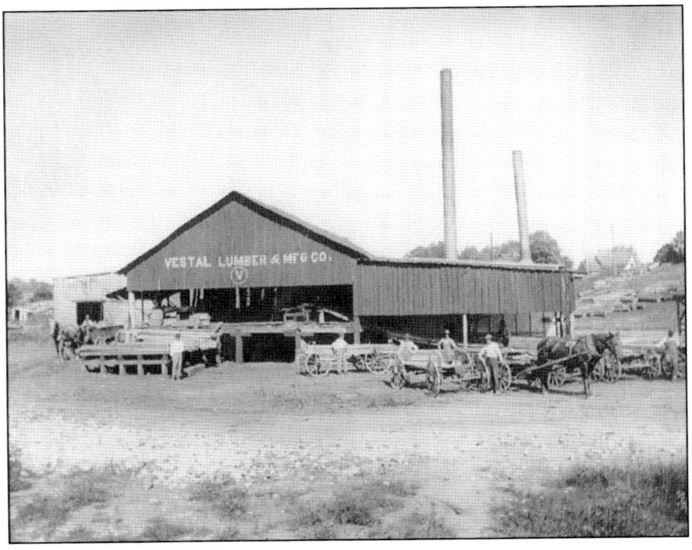

Vestal Lumber & Manufacturing Co. was incorporated in 1901. The band mill was built a year later at 529 Maryville Pike between two railroads, two miles south of the city of Knoxville. The area was known as Vestal, Tennessee, until it was annexed around 1917. This photograph shows an active 1920s lumber mill during the height of Knoxville's manufacturing boom. (Courtesy of the Vestal family.)

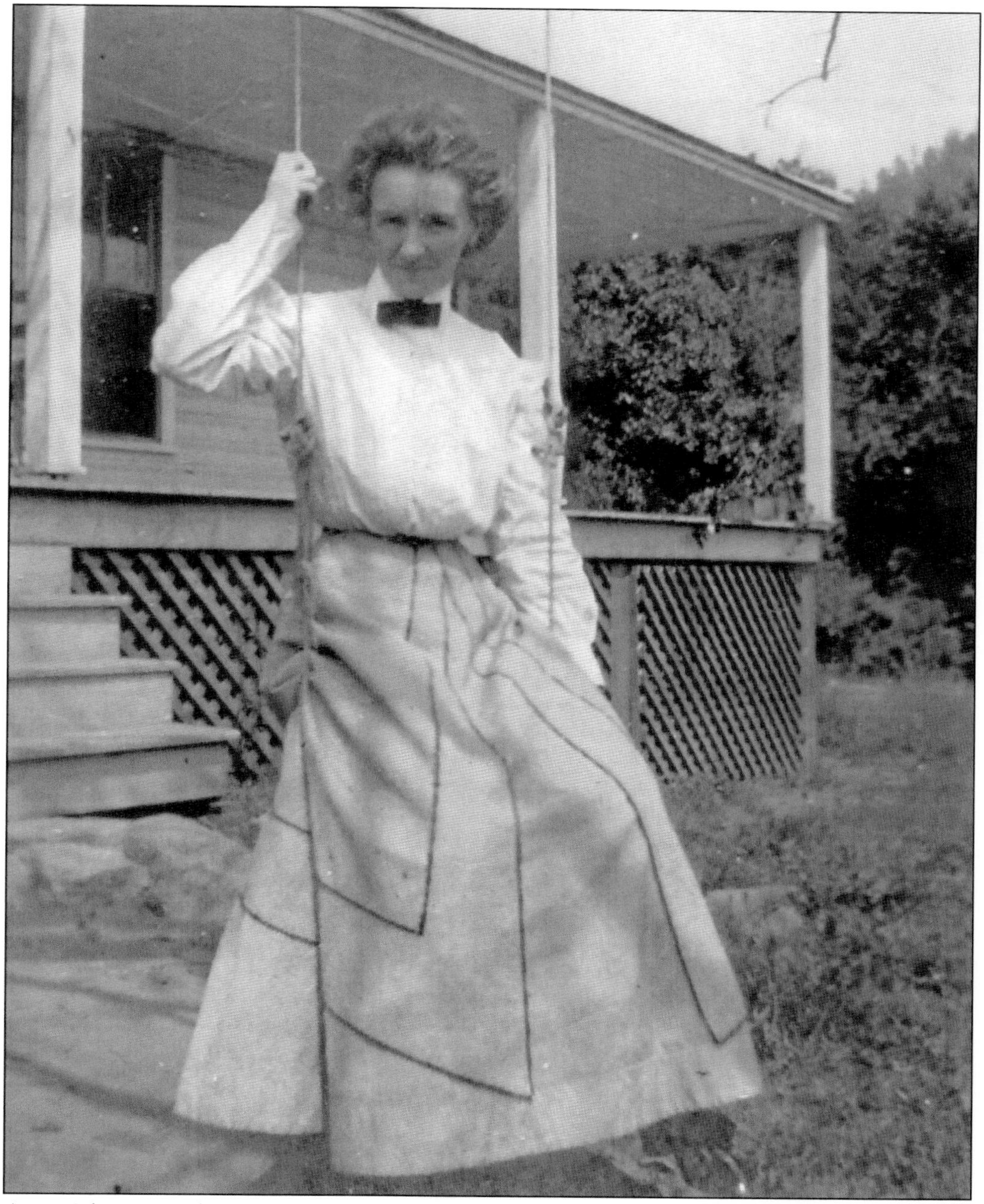

Ann Nelson Vestal was married to Robert Vestal Jr., the oldest of Mary Vestal's sons. Robert Jr. was president of the Lumber & Manufacturing Co. from 1902 to 1913. (Courtesy of the Vestal family.)

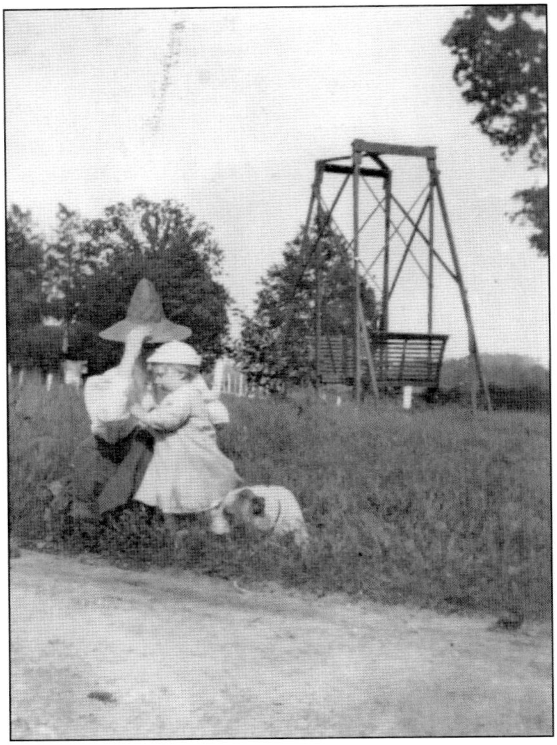

Ella Horne Vestal and her son, Park Gibbs Vestal, are pictured in 1908 at their home which today is still on a hill facing Martin Mill Pike and close to Moody Avenue. (Courtesy of the Vestal family.)

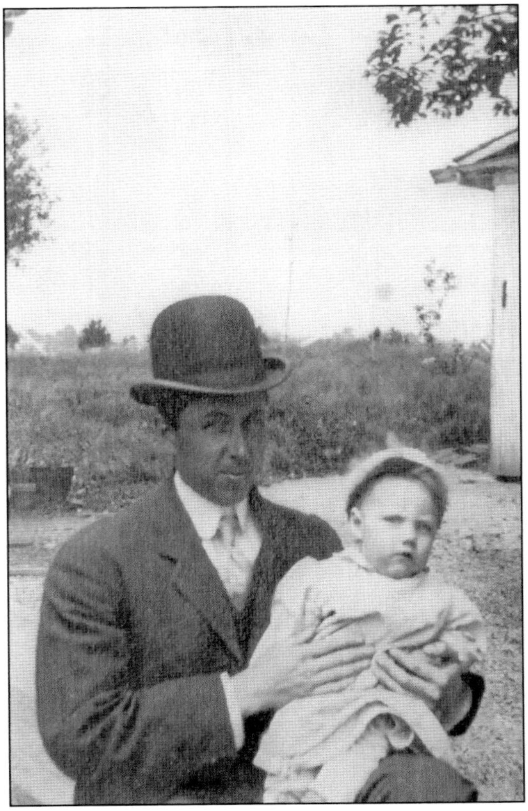

James Park Vestal is pictured in 1908 with his second son, Park Gibbs Vestal, at their home overlooking the family lumber mill. James Park Vestal was the longest serving president and treasurer of Lumber & Manufacturing Co. from 1913 to the time he died in 1951. (Courtesy of the Vestal family.)

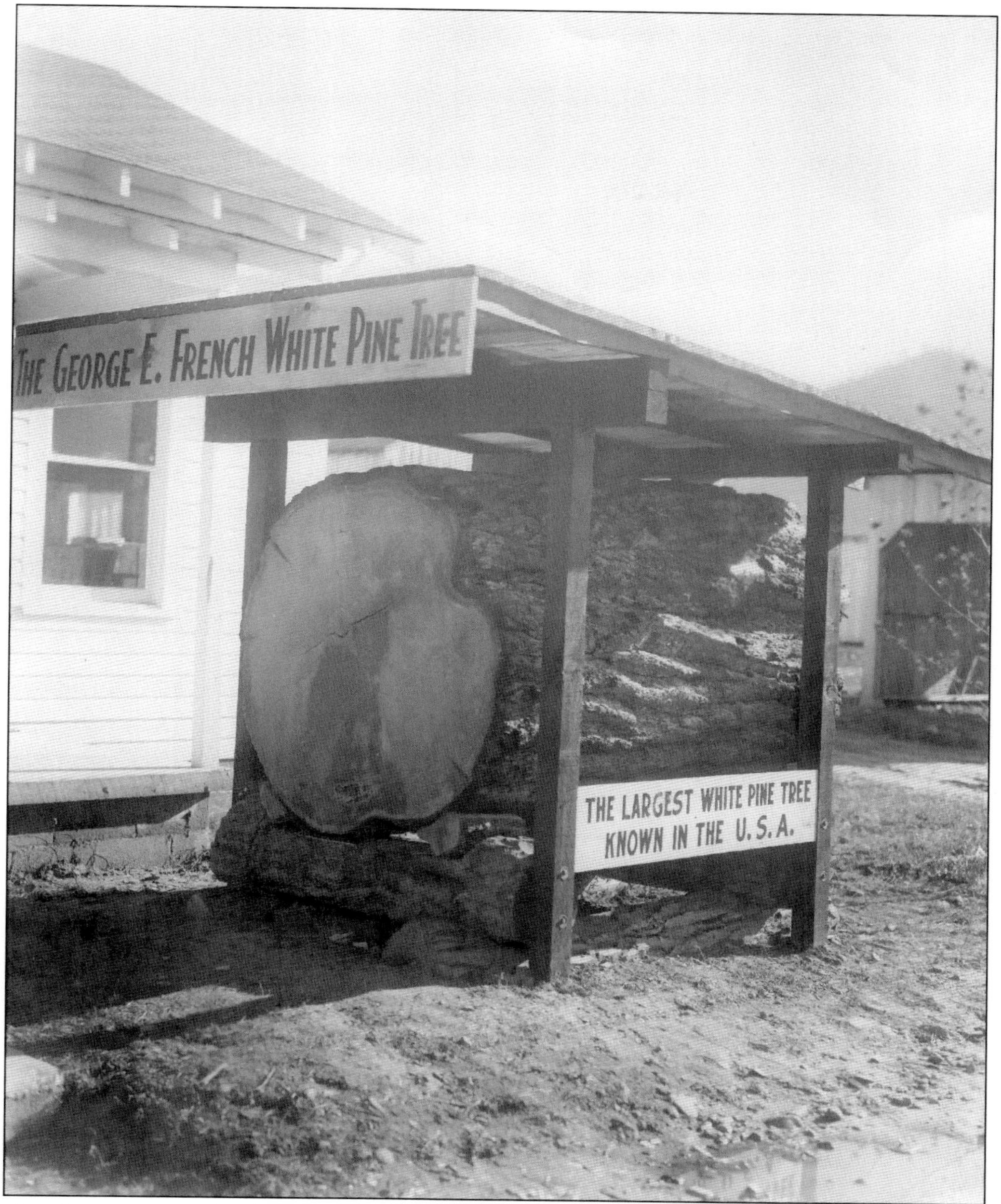

The George E. French white pine tree gained a great deal of press coverage. In 1949, the tree was the largest known white pine in the United States. It was found on Rich Mountain with its top broken off and water damaging the timber. After consulting with state forestry experts, James Park Vestal was advised to fell it. The giant tree measured 6 feet 2 inches across, 19 feet 2 inches around, and 168 feet tall. A section of the tree estimated to be approximately 353 years old was given to the UT forestry department in 1970. This section was later given to Ijams Nature Center for exhibit. (Courtesy of the Vestal family.)

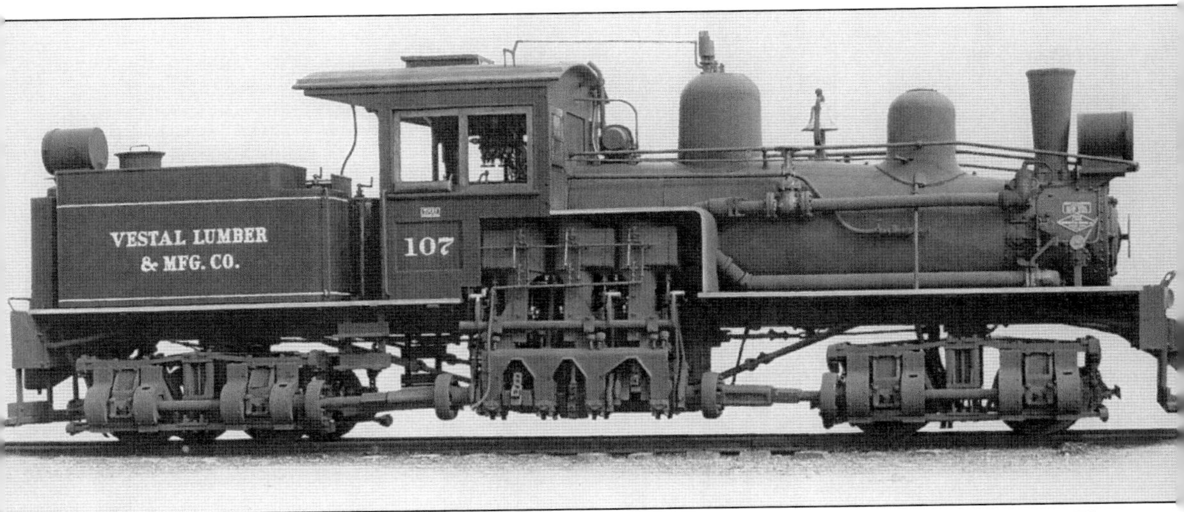

The locomotive shown here carried lumber for the Vestal Lumber & Manufacturing Co. The arrival of the railroad to Knoxville, and South Knoxville in particular, helped shape the area industry and sustain manufacturing in Knoxville. Much of the raw timber that was processed at the lumber company arrived by rail from areas throughout the southeast. (Courtesy of Mary Jean Vestal.)

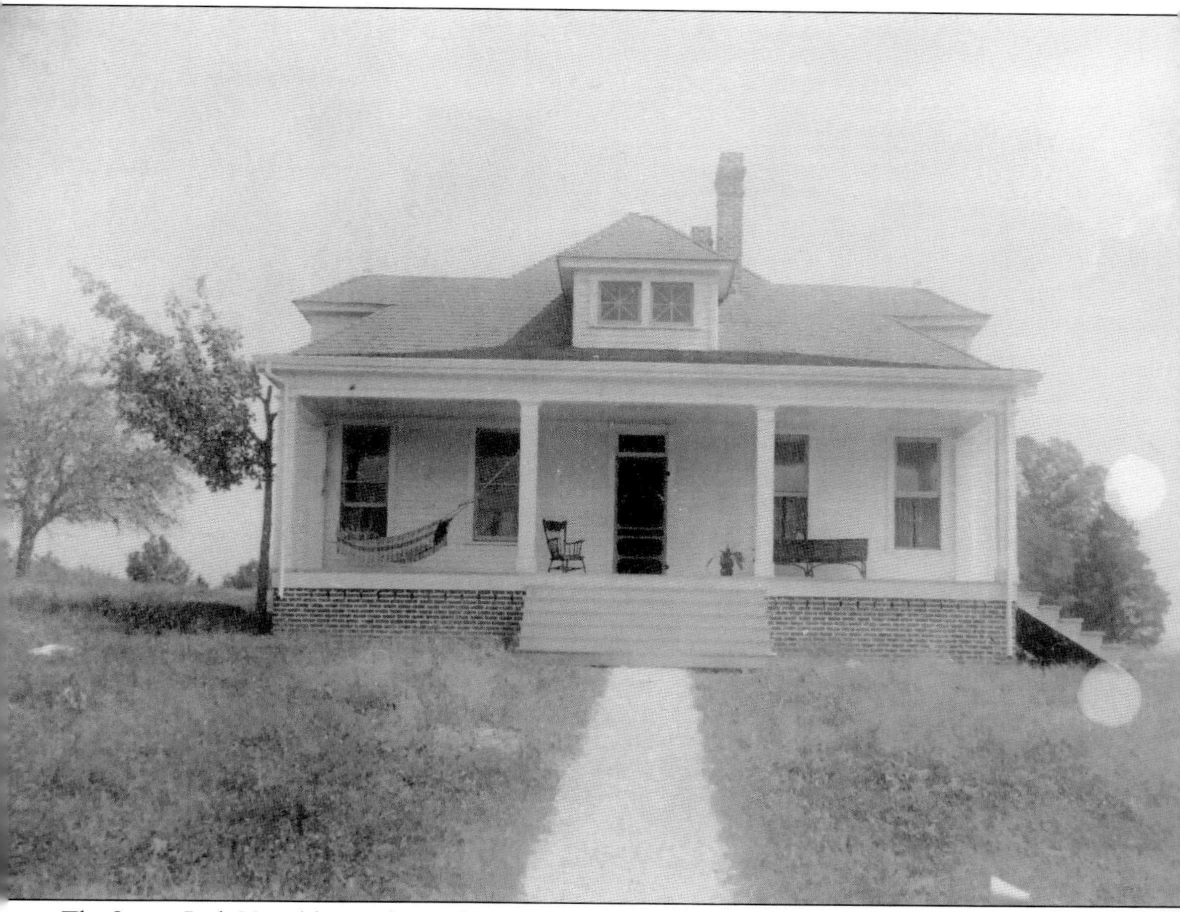

The James Park Vestal home, located on Martin Mill Pike, was purchased on March 25, 1905, for $1,200. (Courtesy of the Vestal family.)

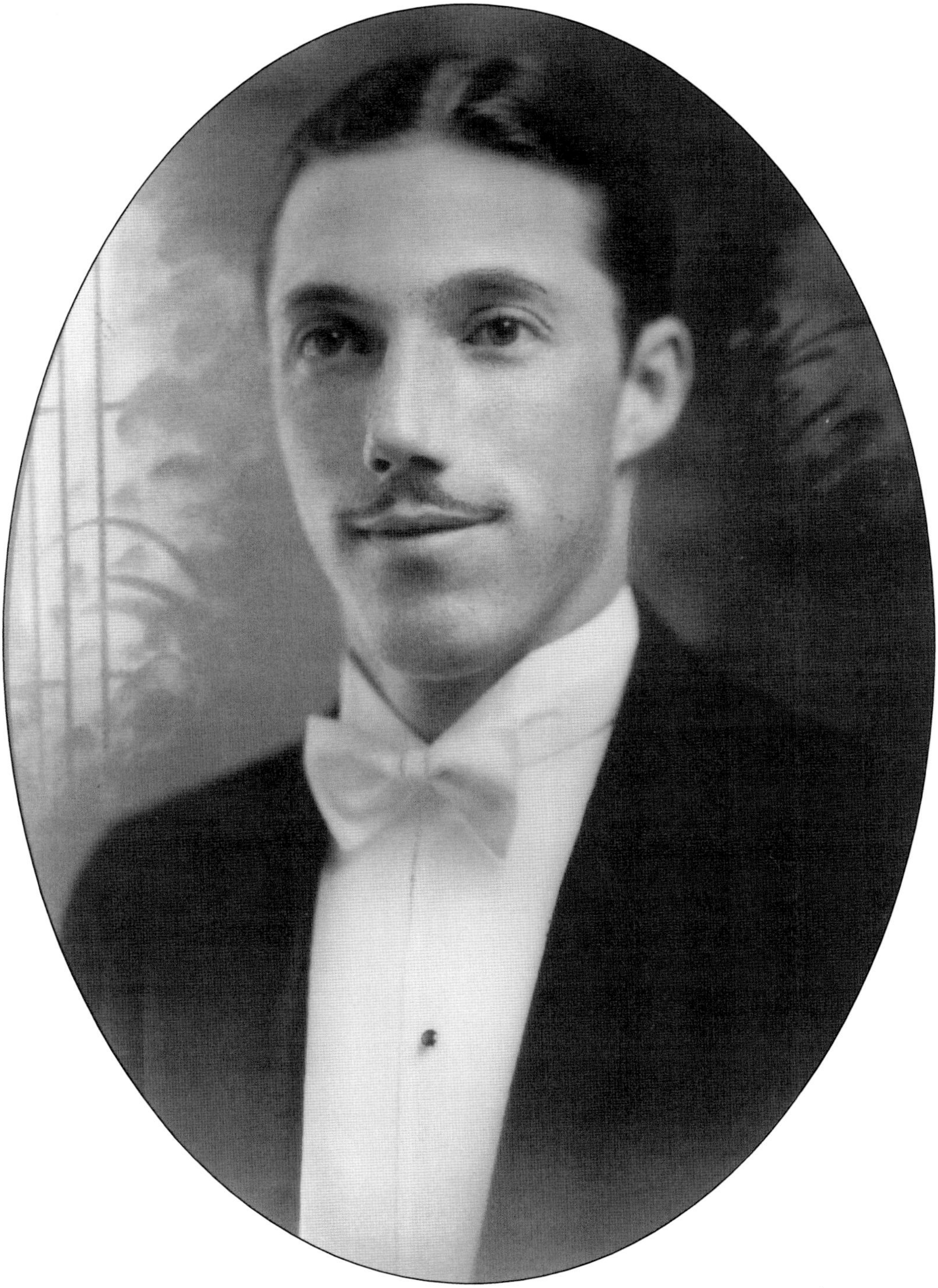

This is a photograph of Park G. Vestal in a friend's wedding in 1931. He was a merchant marine seaman in his youth; however, he was given an ultimatum to come home to the family lumber business. In 1929, he did so, and worked for the family business in North Carolina, Arkansas, Louisiana, and Kentucky before returning to Knoxville in 1946 as the vice president and secretary of Vestal Lumber & Manufacturing Co. (Courtesy of the Vestal family.)

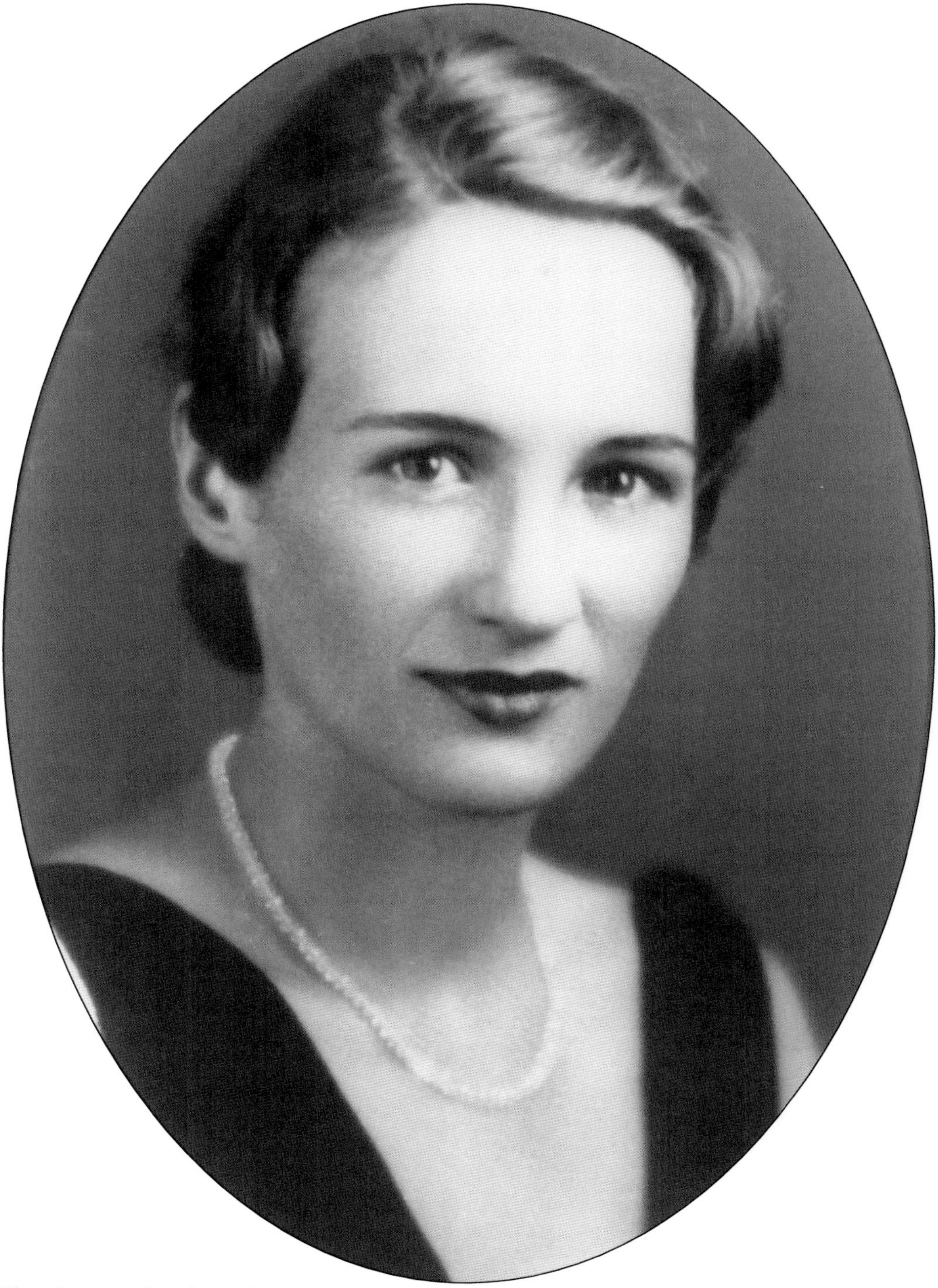

This photograph is from the wedding announcement of Elizabeth Koella to Park Gibbs Vestal in 1933. (Courtesy of the Vestal family.)

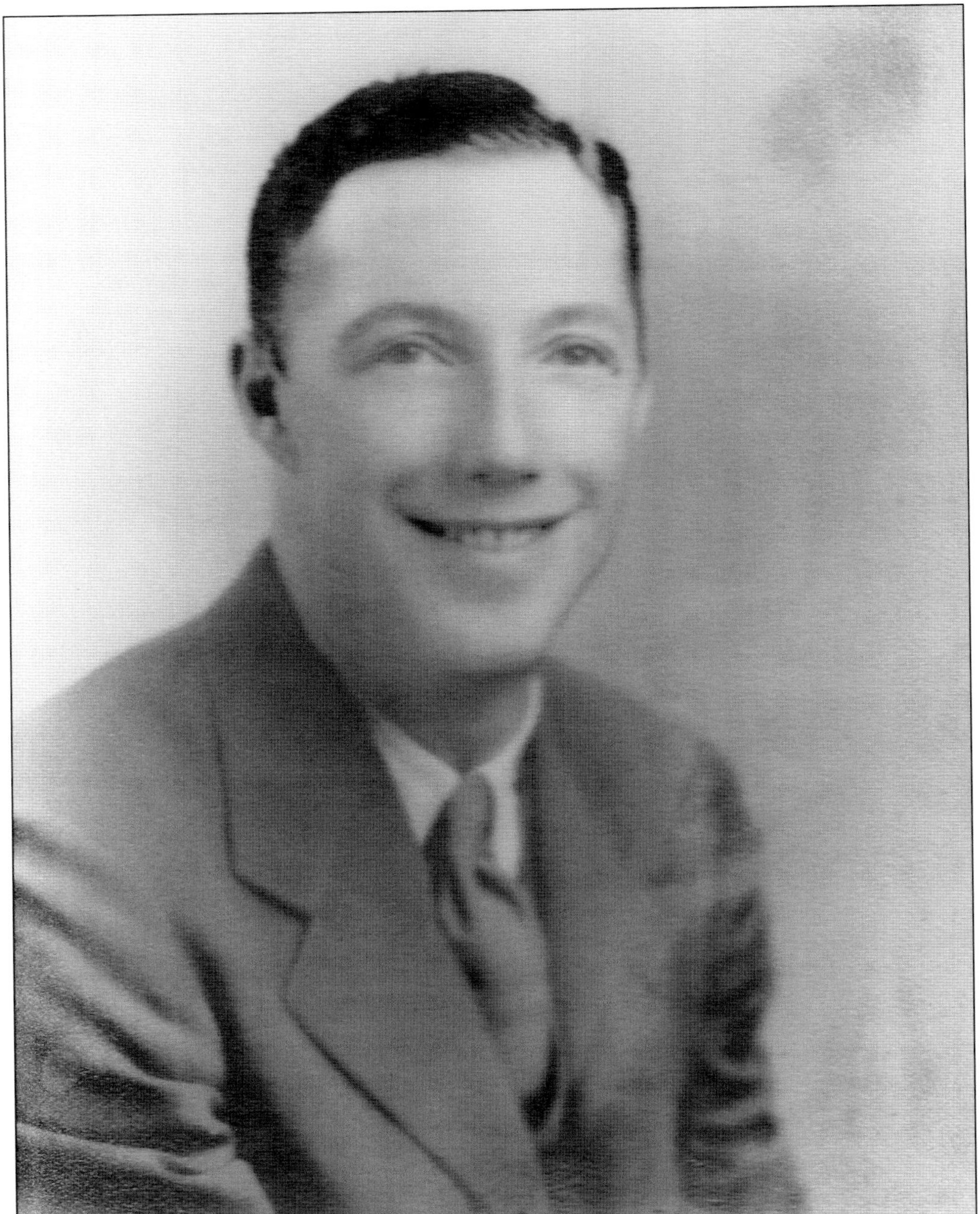

In 1951, Park Gibbs Vestal became president and treasurer of the Vestal Lumber & Manufacturing Co., with mills in Knoxville and Erwin, Tennessee; Sardis, Georgia; Columbia, South Carolina; Madisonville, Kentucky; and Buena Vista, Virginia. In 1961, when the Vestal company became a division of the Atlantic Lumber Co., Park became vice president of Atlantic Lumber Company. Both companies ceased existing in 1970, and a portion of land was donated to the Vestal Boys Club, now the site of the South Knoxville Community Center. (Courtesy of the Vestal family.)

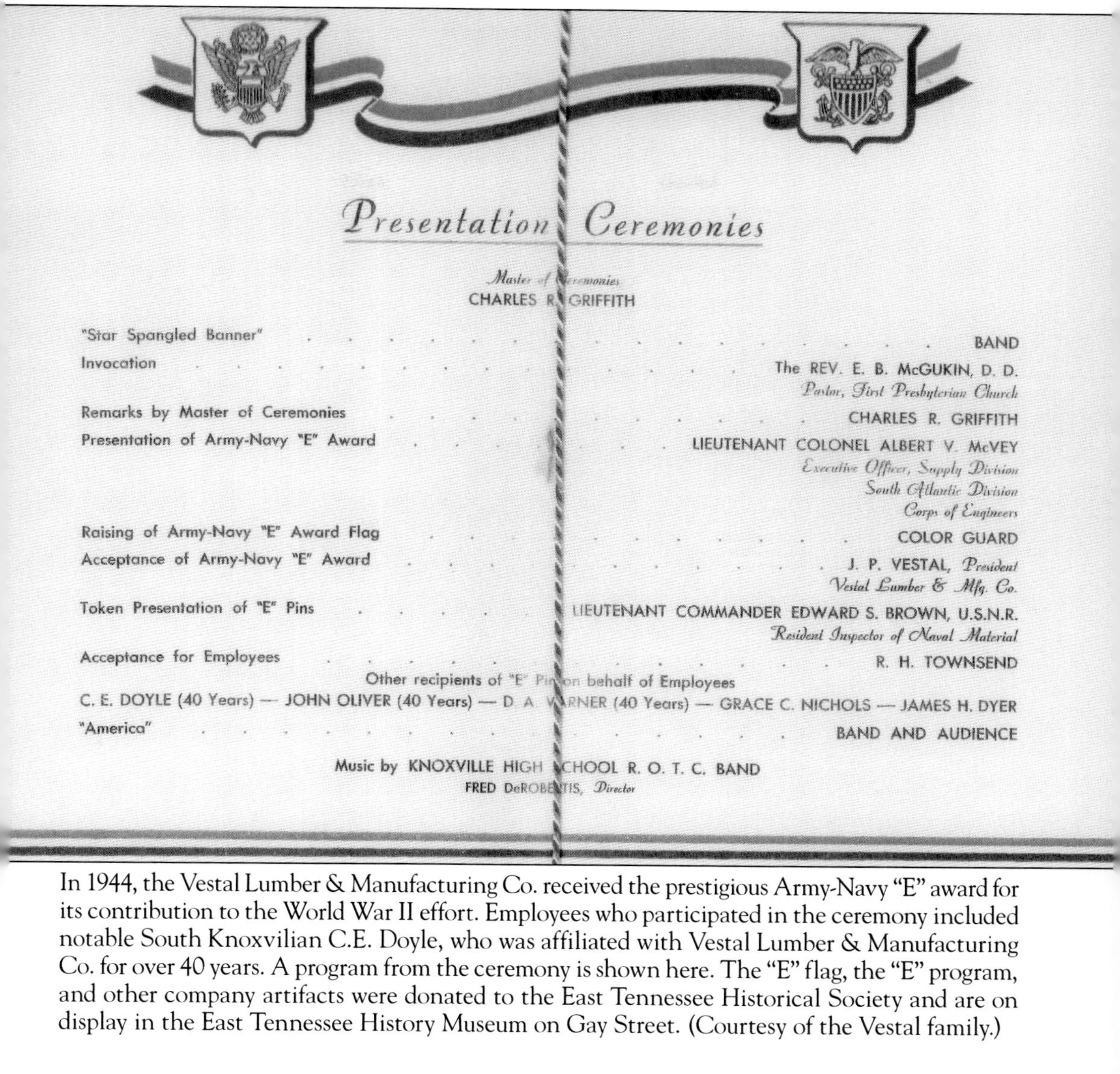

Presentation Ceremonies

Master of Ceremonies
CHARLES R. GRIFFITH

"Star Spangled Banner"	BAND
Invocation	The REV. E. B. McGUKIN, D. D. *Pastor, First Presbyterian Church*
Remarks by Master of Ceremonies	CHARLES R. GRIFFITH
Presentation of Army-Navy "E" Award	LIEUTENANT COLONEL ALBERT V. McVEY *Executive Officer, Supply Division* *South Atlantic Division* *Corps of Engineers*
Raising of Army-Navy "E" Award Flag	COLOR GUARD
Acceptance of Army-Navy "E" Award	J. P. VESTAL, *President* *Vestal Lumber & Mfg. Co.*
Token Presentation of "E" Pins	LIEUTENANT COMMANDER EDWARD S. BROWN, U.S.N.R. *Resident Inspector of Naval Material*
Acceptance for Employees	R. H. TOWNSEND

Other recipients of "E" Pin on behalf of Employees
C. E. DOYLE (40 Years) — JOHN OLIVER (40 Years) — D. A. VARNER (40 Years) — GRACE C. NICHOLS — JAMES H. DYER

"America"	BAND AND AUDIENCE

Music by KNOXVILLE HIGH SCHOOL R. O. T. C. BAND
FRED DeROBERTIS, *Director*

In 1944, the Vestal Lumber & Manufacturing Co. received the prestigious Army-Navy "E" award for its contribution to the World War II effort. Employees who participated in the ceremony included notable South Knoxvilian C.E. Doyle, who was affiliated with Vestal Lumber & Manufacturing Co. for over 40 years. A program from the ceremony is shown here. The "E" flag, the "E" program, and other company artifacts were donated to the East Tennessee Historical Society and are on display in the East Tennessee History Museum on Gay Street. (Courtesy of the Vestal family.)

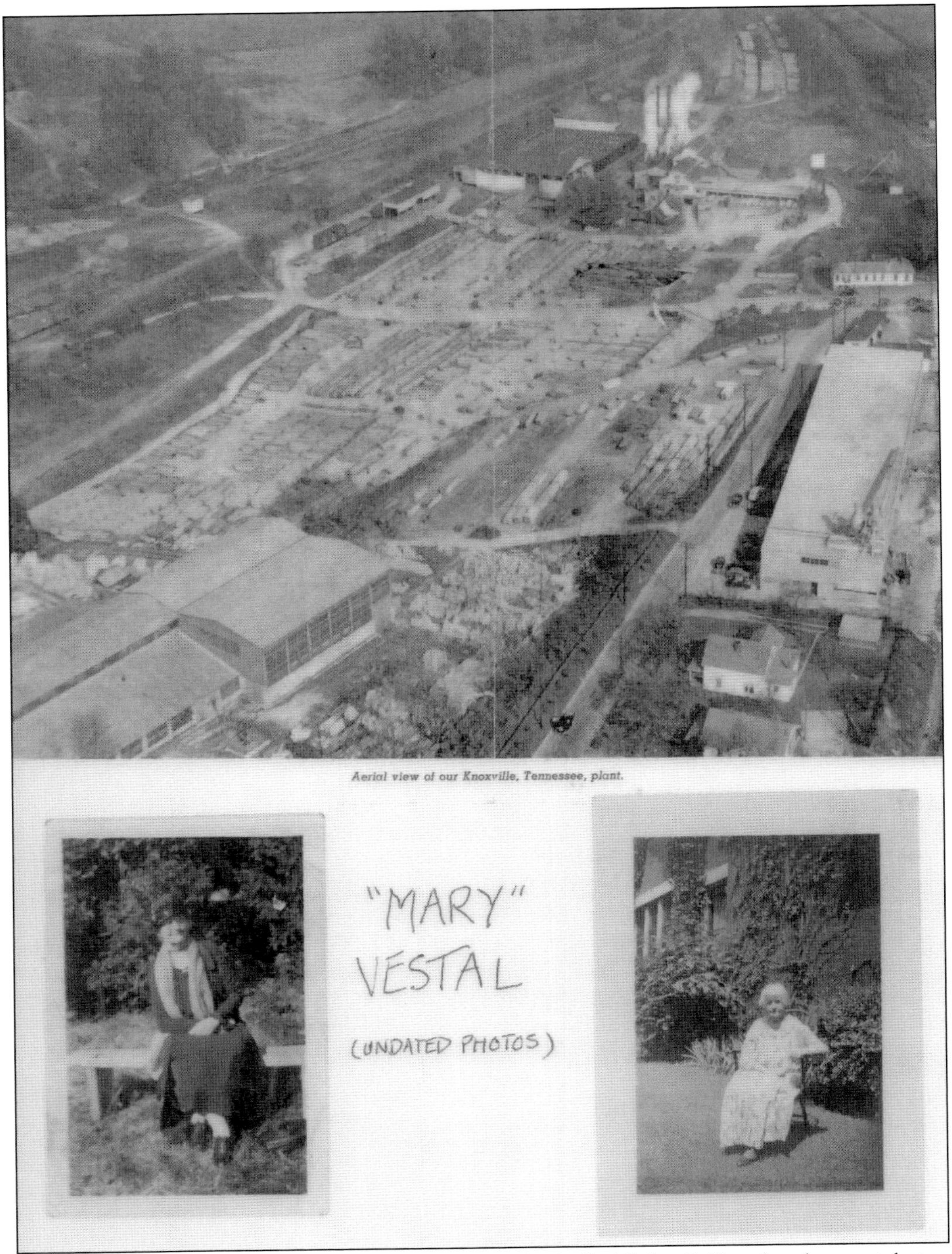

These are undated photographs of Anna Maria Gredig (called "Mary") Vestal and an aerial view of the Vestal plant taken from personal family scrapbooks. Mrs. Vestal, mother of the brothers who founded the Vestal Lumber & Manufacturing Co., was honored after her death in 1939 by former mayor George Dempster who named the small city park on Maryville Pike for his longtime Sunday school teacher. (Courtesy of the Vestal family.)

Four

EDUCATION

South Knoxville is home to the region's only academic hospital, the University of Tennessee Medical Center. The University of Tennessee was originally founded in 1794 as Blount College, which makes it one of the oldest institutions of higher education in the United States. Local institutions of higher education initially struggled to survive due to lack of support; however, by the 1840s, the importance of higher education had become realized in Knoxville. The University of Tennessee Memorial Research Center and Hospital became part of Knoxville's rich educational heritage when it opened in South Knoxville in 1956. Located on the edge of South Knox County, Johnson Bible College, now Johnson University, also plays an important role both in the area's educational past and future.

As South Knoxville began to significantly develop in the early 19th century, remote individual communities began to spring up. As a result, early schools in South Knoxville were primarily community church-based schools.

Additionally, Tennessee School for the Deaf plays an important role in the community. The school was established in 1844 as the Tennessee Asylum for the Deaf and Dumb. The first students were enrolled in 1845. The school moved a couple of times—most notably to Summit Hill Drive and Broadway—after its founding and before moving to Island Home in South Knoxville in the 1920s.

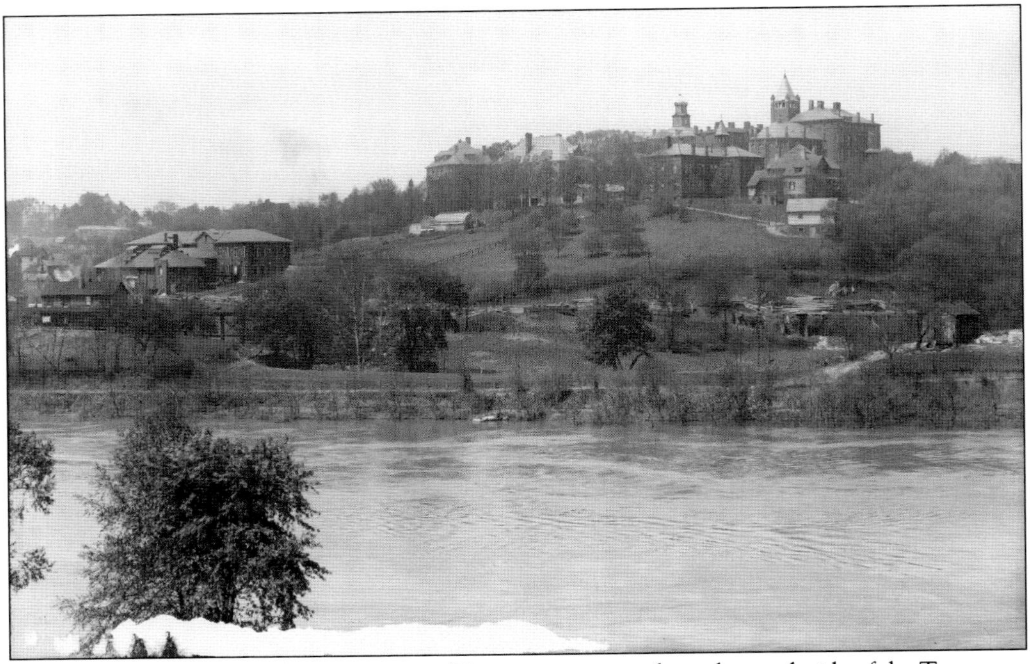

These photographs are of the University of Tennessee, as seen from the south side of the Tennessee River in 1903. (Courtesy of the Library of Congress.)

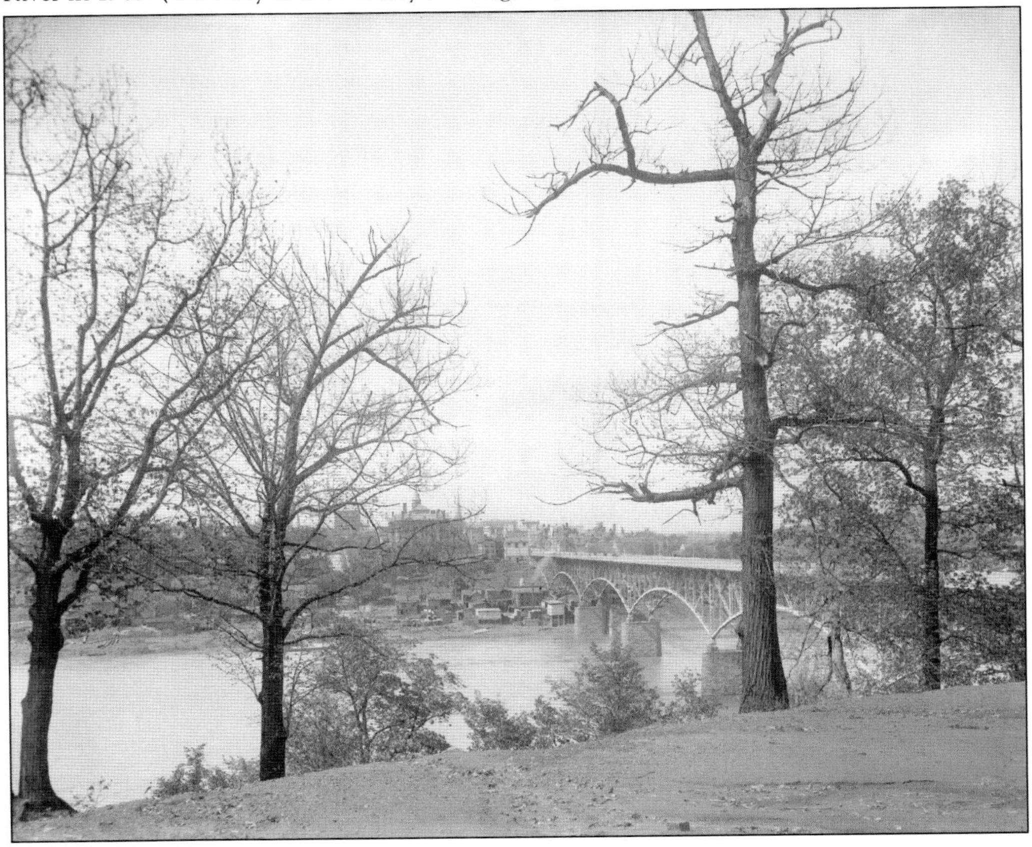

This photograph shows Flenniken School in 1902. The Flenniken community was one of the earliest South Knoxville communities to develop. The post office at Flenniken was established in 1881, and Martha Berry was the first postmaster. The post office operated until 1902. Flenniken was still listed as a separate community on the Rand McNally Railroad Guide until 1914. (Courtesy of the Berry family.)

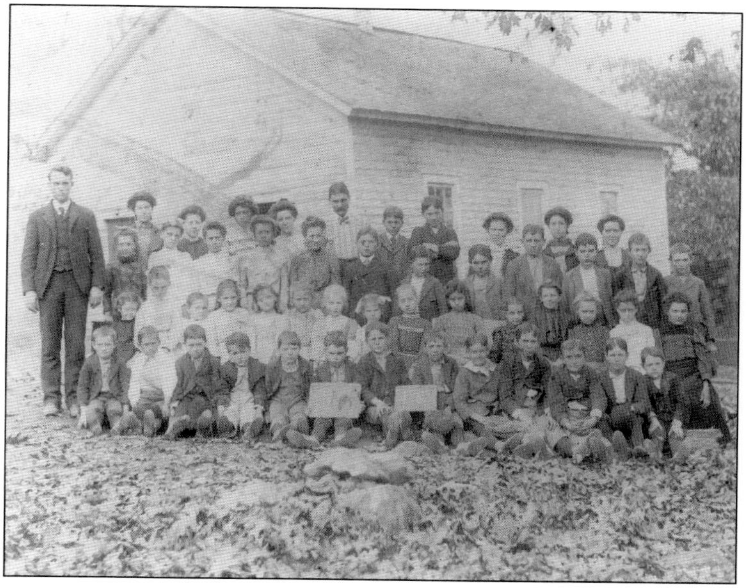

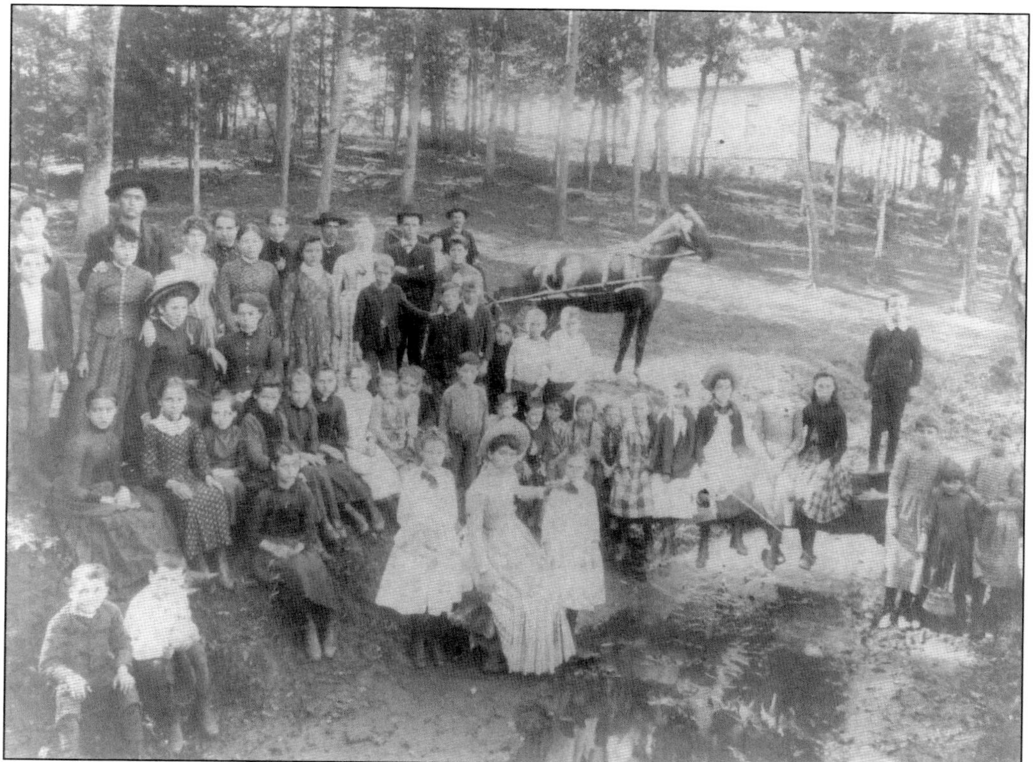

The Flenniken School became a county school in 1888 and a city school in 1917. The school on Sims Road was originally a one-room log structure. (Courtesy of the Berry family.)

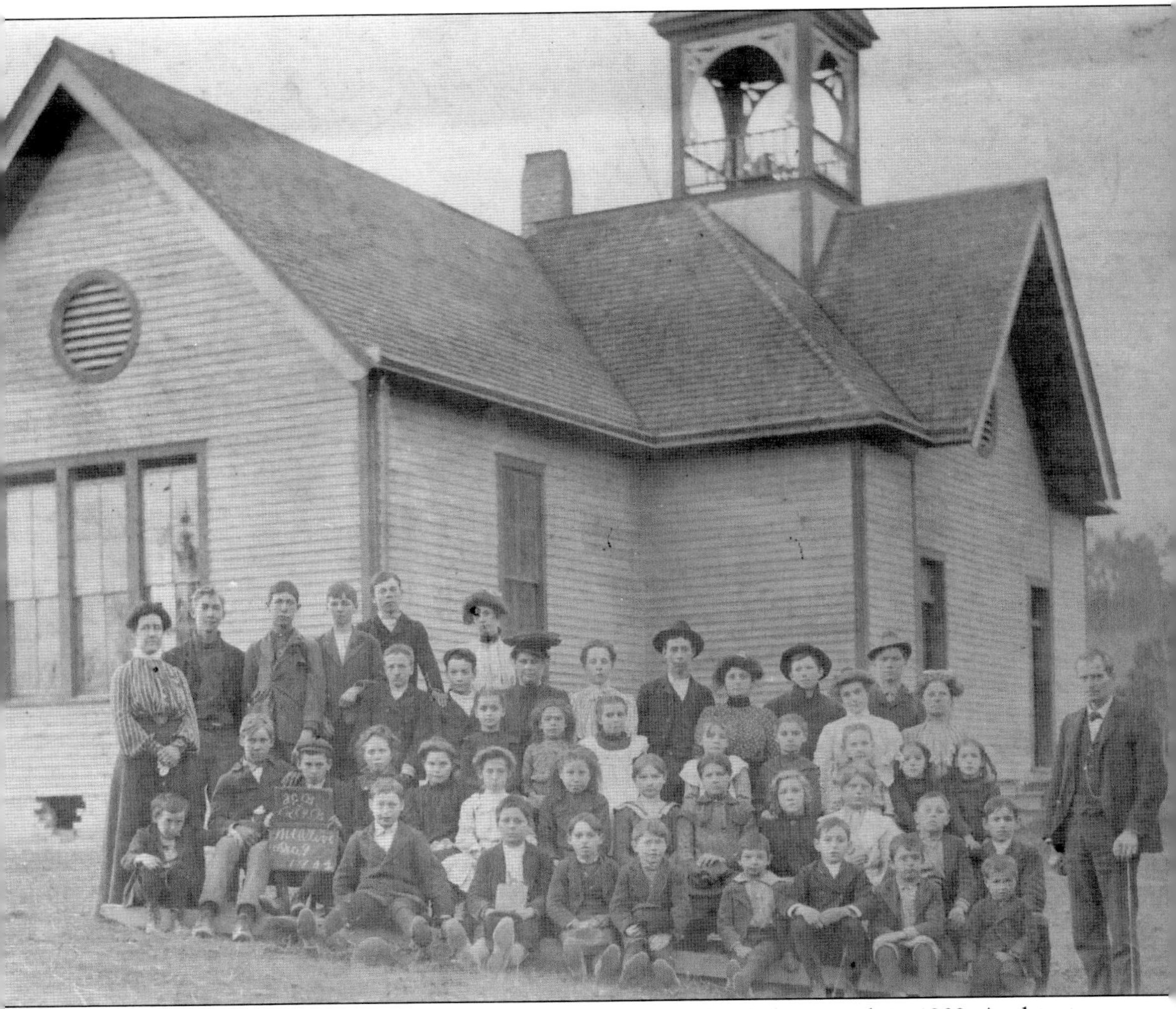

Students of Mount Olive School are shown sitting for a school photograph in 1902. At this time, the school building was a wooden two-room structure. The students are, from left to right, (first row) Clifton McCarrell, Sam Edwards, Alex McCarrell, Joe McCarrell, Bud King, Willie Flenniken, Jim Flenniken, Burl McCarrell, and Cowen Brown (principal and teacher); (second row) Tom Curry, Bish Ford, Charlie Baily, Ina Harris, Lula Large, Nora Curry, Roberta Edwards, Hessie Simpson, Ina Berry, Anna Mae Ford, Delmora Edwards, John Flenniken, and Tom Flenniken; (third row) Ruth Flenniken, Nina Edwards, Carrie Harris, Bessie Harris, Ethel King, Jessie Simpson, Maude Flenniken, and Mabel Flenniken; (fourth row) Ben Stager, John Wells, Dora Edwards, Eva Harris, Roy Berry, Lee McCarrell, Ottie Franklin, Agey Bruce, Bess Simpson, and Flora Edwards; (fifth row) Pearl Berry (primary teacher), Arthur Ford, Carl Berry, Clum Franklin, George Harris, and Lilly Baily. (Courtesy of the Berry family.)

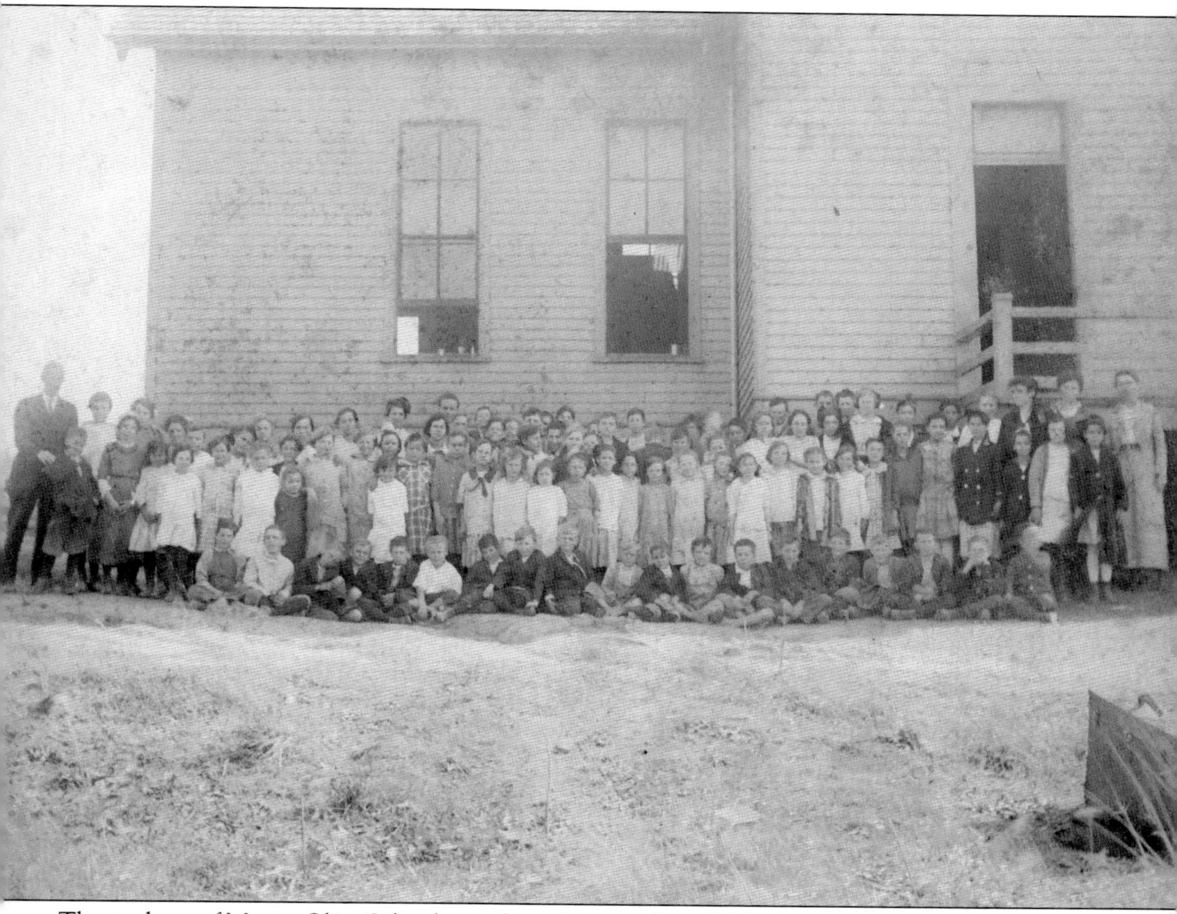

The students of Mount Olive School pose for a photograph in 1913. (Courtesy of the Berry family.)

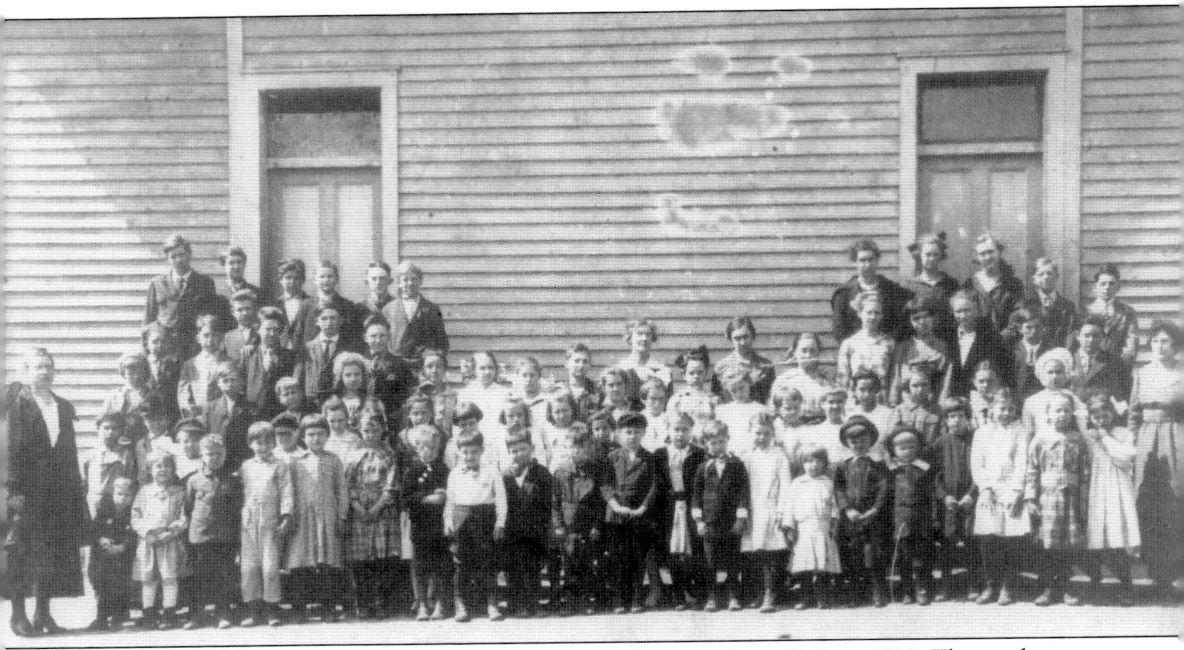

The students of Mount Olive School pose for a photograph in 1918 or 1919. The students are, from left to right, (first row) Anna Rudder (teacher), Otto Davis, Margaret Goff Cruze, Conanza Rudder, Frank Davis, unidentified, Gladys White, Mildred Goforth, Mack Davis, Theodore King, Fred Berry, Fred Rudder, Bill Rudder, Cane Rudder, William Berry, Mary Rogers, Leola White Berry, Theodore Rudder, Grover Rudder, Edith White Foster, Bonita Rodgers, Mae Goff, Grace Rudder, and Blanche Shumake (teacher); (second row) Joe McCarroll, the Manis twins, Ernest Rudder, unidentified, Roy Rudder, Pearl Elliot Linden, Lillian White, Clara Berry Bolin, Nellie Franklin Eggers, Geneva Gentry, Hattie Goff Hall, Anna Lee Davis, Mary Johnson Woodall, Thelma Berry Ford, Lib Hannah, Ada Ford, Myrtle Sims, Bella Mae Davis, Pearl Pate, and Kathleen King; (third row) Delmas Childress, Boyd Rudder, Calvin White, Robert Jackson, Howard Rudder, Cecil Moore, Albert Rudder, Ruby Rudder, Gladys Franklin Marshall, Hazel Rudder Jones, Cora White Day, ? Lane (teacher), Herman Lane, Lidia Medlin, Mamie Elliot Hudson, Eddie Rudder Ballard, Tommie Hannah, Mary Rudder Henry, Ernest Johnson, and Richard Miller; (fourth row) Tom Elliot, Bill Medlin, Jim Davis, Clarence Franklin, Edward Maxey, Larry Gentry, Willie McCarrell Coile, Helen Kidd, Maude Ford, Cletus Goforth, and Elmer White. (Courtesy of the Berry family.)

A program from Mount Olive School's 1912 commencement exercises is pictured here. (Courtesy of the Berry family.)

Commencement Exercises

To be Held at

Mount Olive School

TUESDAY, MARCH 26th, 1912

Program

Piano Solo .... Emma Foote
Invocation ....
Vocal Solo, "The Swallows" .... Annette Scarlett
Oration, "Pleasure of Life" .... Mabel Flenniken
Piano Duet, "Robin's Return"
.... Anna Thurman and Emma Foote
Oration, "Our Waking Dreams" .... Jessie Neubert
Music .... Dixie Quartette
Class Poem .... Maud Flenniken
Vocal Solo .... Kathryn Ghormley
Valedictory .... Anna Thurman
Piano Duet, "Moonlight Reverie"
.... Maud and Mabel Flenniken
Address .... Dean J. D. Hoskins
Vocal Solo .... Jennie Haddox
Presentation of Diplomas, Supt. M. W. Wilson
Cornet Solo .... George Ogle

CLASS ROLL

MOUNT OLIVE

Anna Thurman — Mabel Flenniken
Jessie Neubert — Maude Flenniken

ANDERSON SCHOOL

Raymond McCall — Neva May Johnson
Verna Wrinkle

STOCK CREEK SCHOOL

Geneva Brown

The students and teachers of Stock Creek School pose for a photograph in 1913. The students are, from left to right, Anna Thurman, Lawrence Goddard, Raymond Goddard, Albert French, Charlie Morgan, Horace Brownlow French, Earnest Johnson, Roy Rule, Billie Reagan, Helen Johnson, Lucille Goddard, Helen Johnson, Cecil Morgan, Dave Johnson, Ella Rule, Nell Rule, Kate Morgan, two unidentified, Bob Goddard, Pearl Goddard, Abe Shelley, Mossie Goddard, Howard Goddard, unidentified, Gib Goddard, Virgil Davis, Fred Jett, Loy Goddard, French Goddard, Lucy Johnson, Elmer French, Martha Johnson, Marsh French, and Jett Rondo. (Courtesy of the Berry family.)

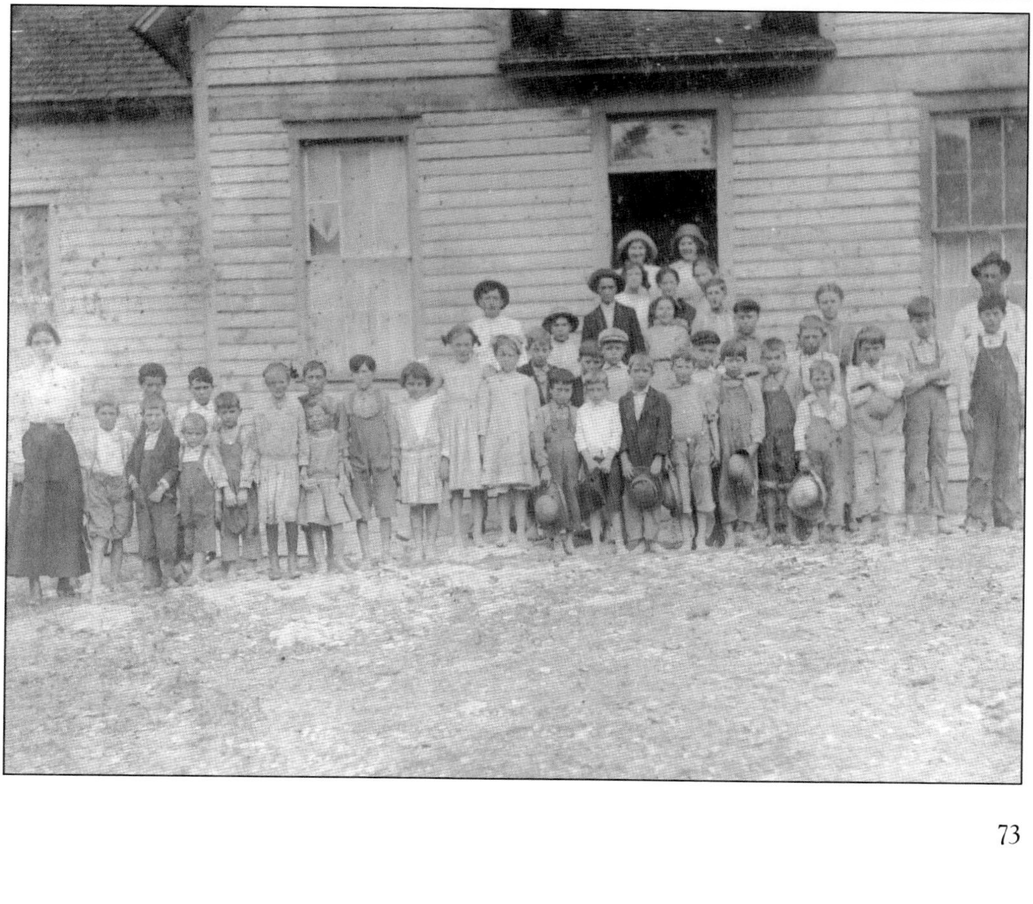

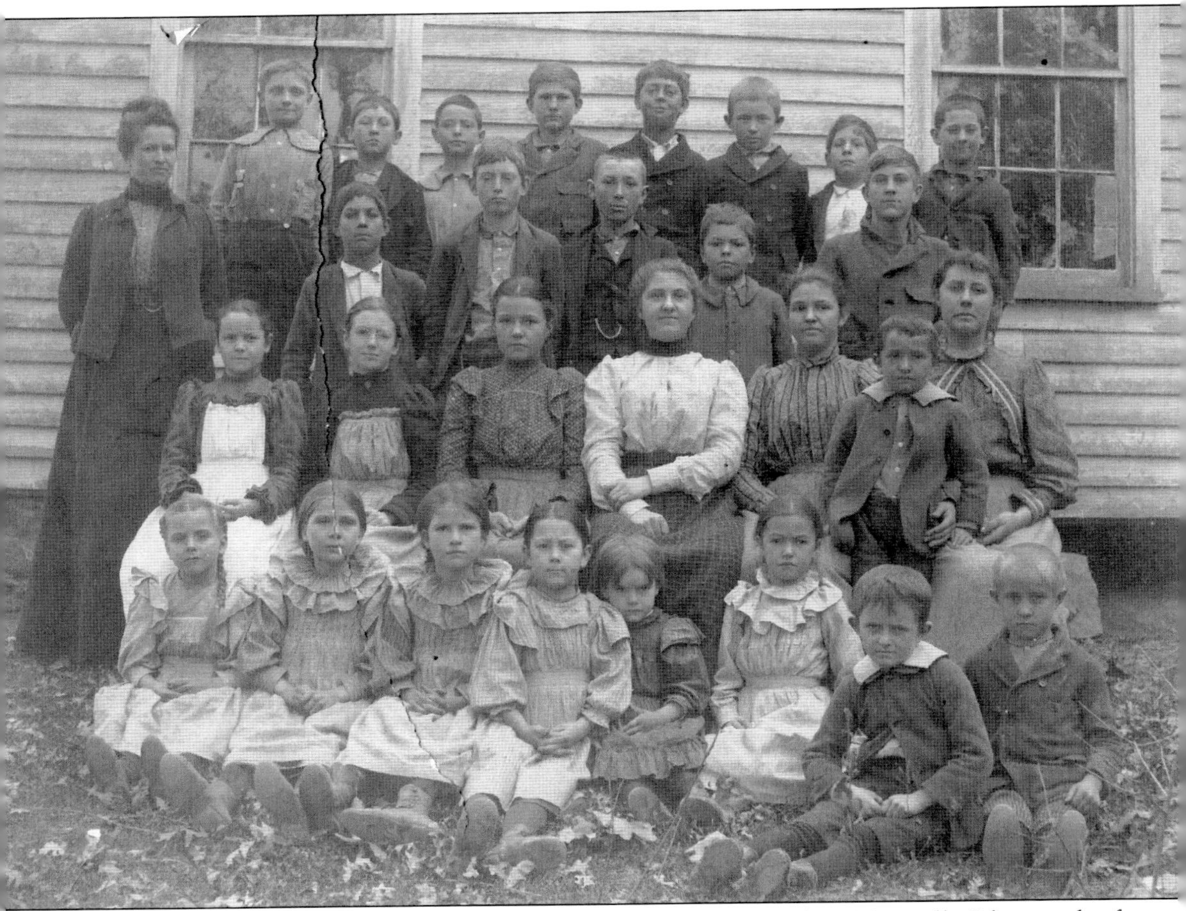

Students of Tipton School pose in 1902. The school was located on Maryville Pike, north of Flenniken and Tipton Station Roads. The students are, from left to right, (first row) Anna Thurman, Celia Rose, Letia Rose, unidentified, Etta Thurman, Florence Pickens, ? McBath, and ? Taylor; (second row) Nellie Pickens, Lona Berry, Linnie Pickens, Viola Rose, Leutia Pickens, and Mary Roper; (third row) unidentified, Carrie Thurman, Walter Cupp, Frank Pickens, and John Rose; (fourth row) Mamie Goddard, three unidentified, Paul Rose, Charlie Gibson, ? McBath, two unidentified, and Jett Rondo. (Courtesy of the Berry family.)

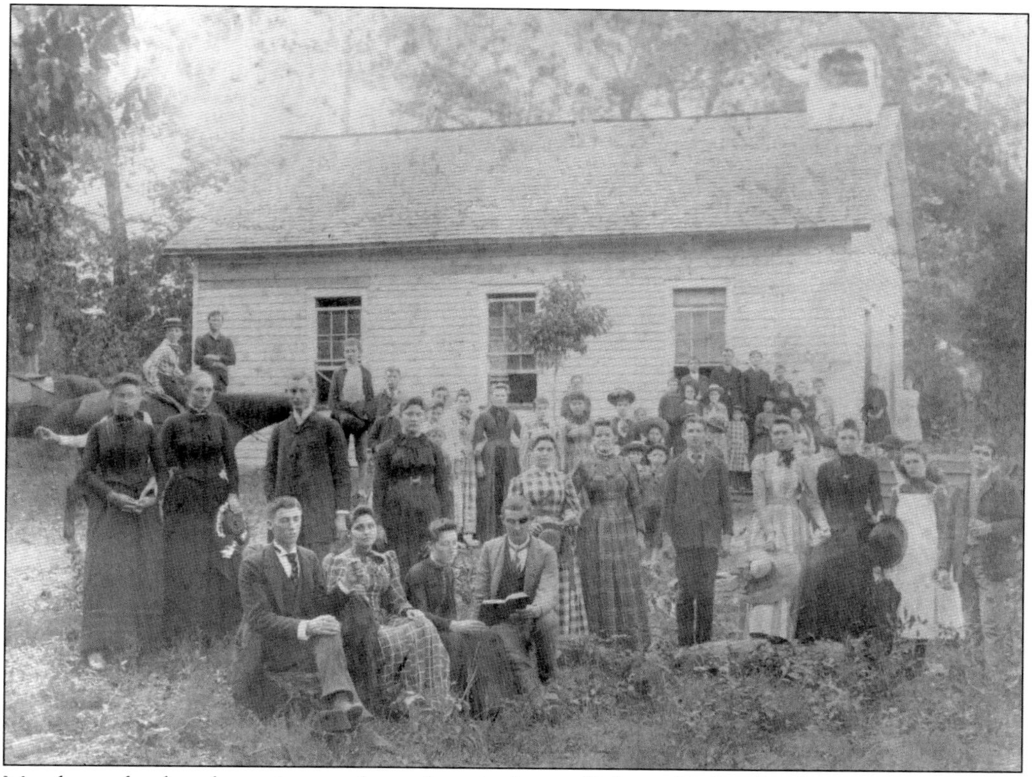

Members of a church service are shown here in front of Liberty Hall School in 1890. The school was located west of Maryville Pike, approximately two miles south of the Tennessee River, probably close to what is now Alcoa Highway. Among those pictured are Will Brakebill, Emmal McCarrell, Lillie Brakebill, Hugh Maloney, Pearl Maloney, Sallie Maxey, Hatie McCarrell, Milton McCarrell, Gordon McCarrell, John Brakebill, Mattie Hawkins, Alby Franklin, and Minnie McCarrell. (Courtesy of the Berry family.)

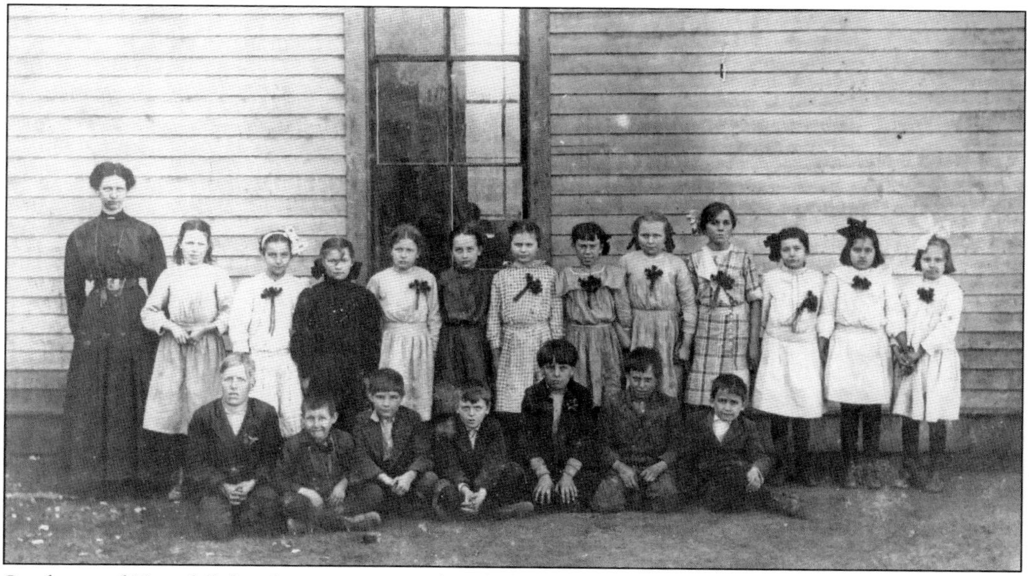

Students of Vestal School pose in an undated photograph. (Courtesy of the Berry family.)

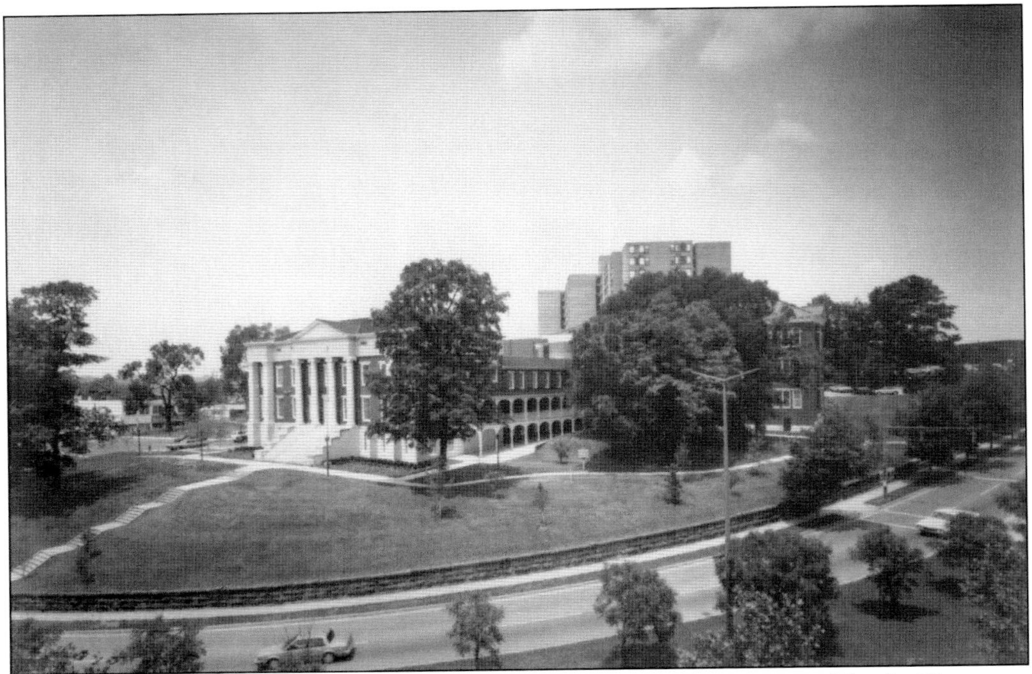

The building complex shown here in the late 1930s was originally constructed for the Tennessee School for the Deaf (TSD) and was occupied by TSD until 1924, when the City of Knoxville purchased the complex for office use. (Courtesy of the Library of Congress.)

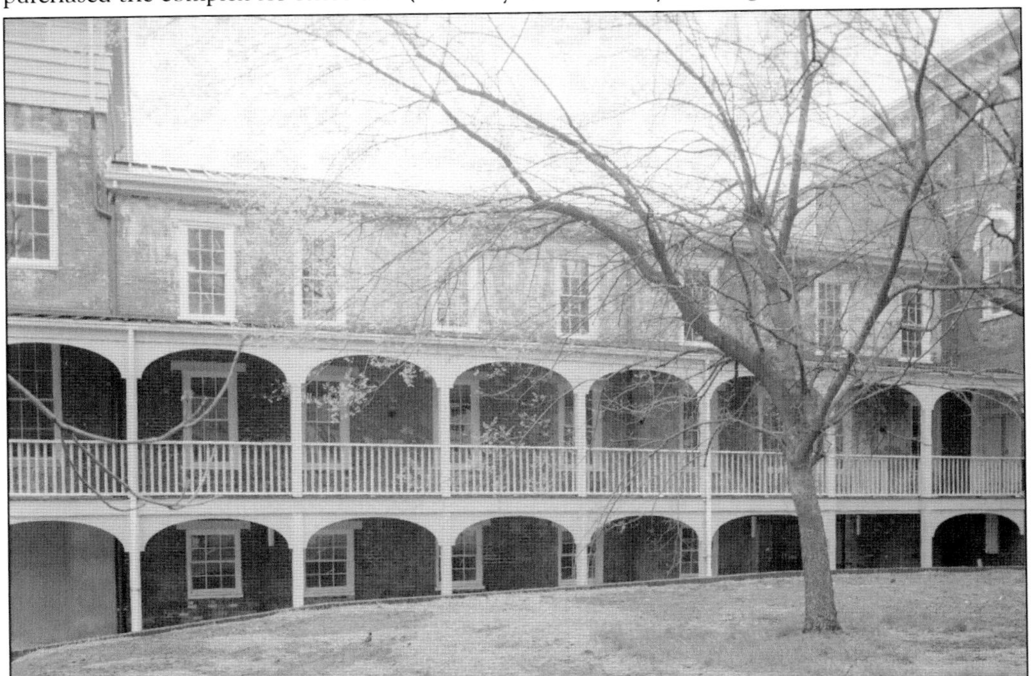

Another major historical use of the location occurred during the Civil War, when the buildings were used as a hospital by both the Confederate and Union armies. (Courtesy of the Library of Congress.)

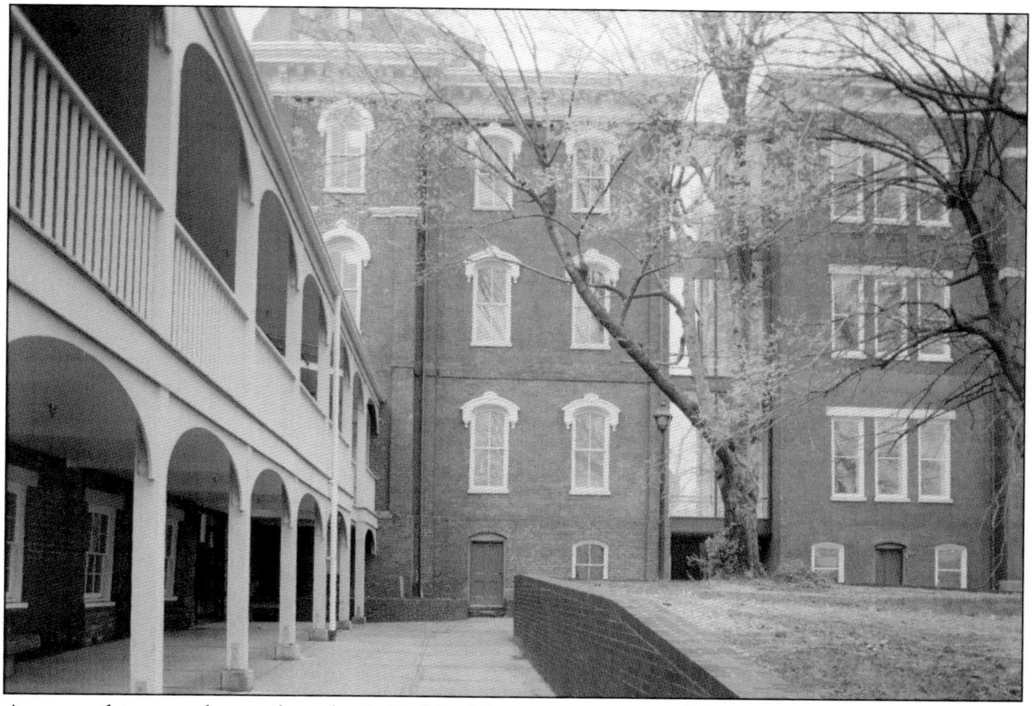

As an architectural complex, the initial building group is one of the few surviving major Greek Revival structures in East Tennessee and the only one in Knoxville. (Courtesy of the Library of Congress.)

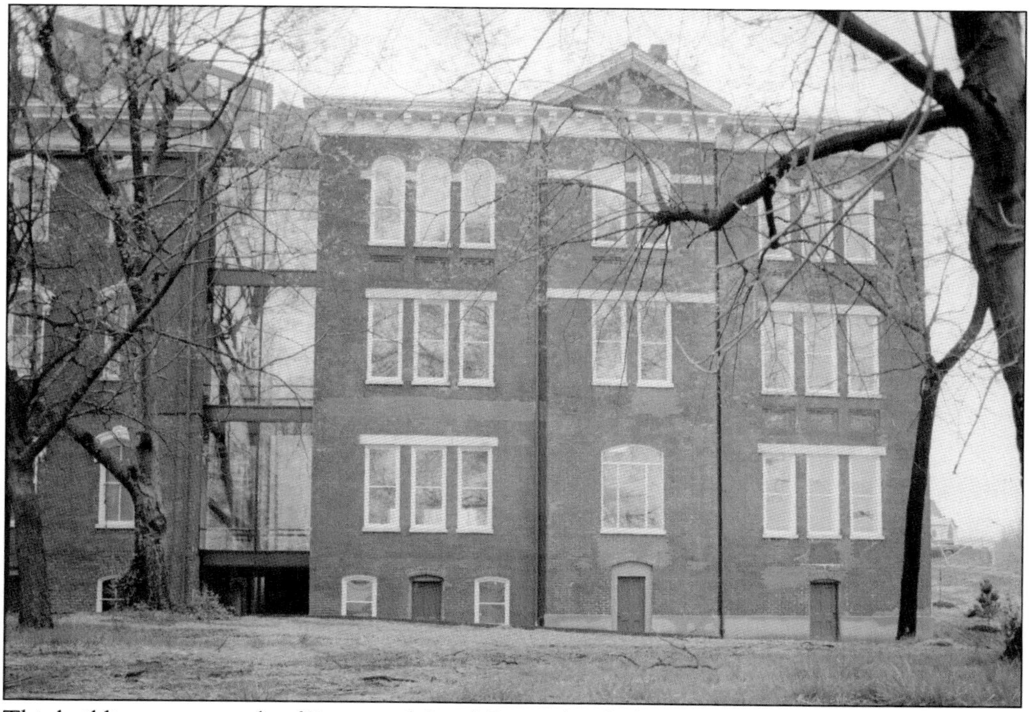

This building, an example of Provincial Greek Revival style, has had a variety of late-19th-century units added. (Courtesy of the Library of Congress.)

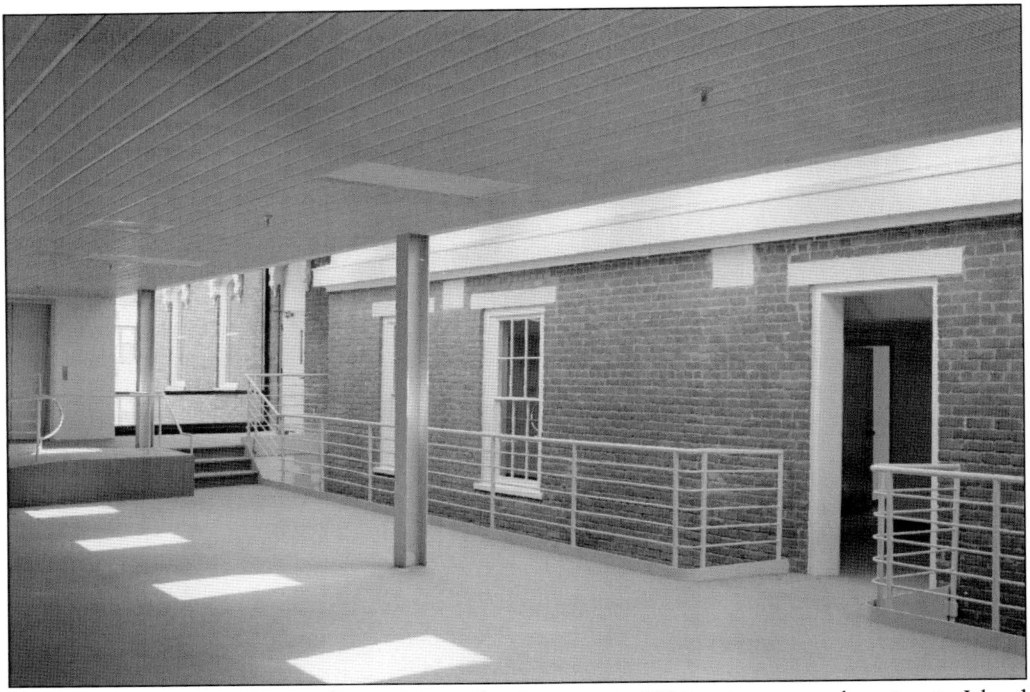

Tennessee School for the Deaf moved from this location in 1924 to its current location in Island Home in South Knoxville. (Courtesy of the Library of Congress.)

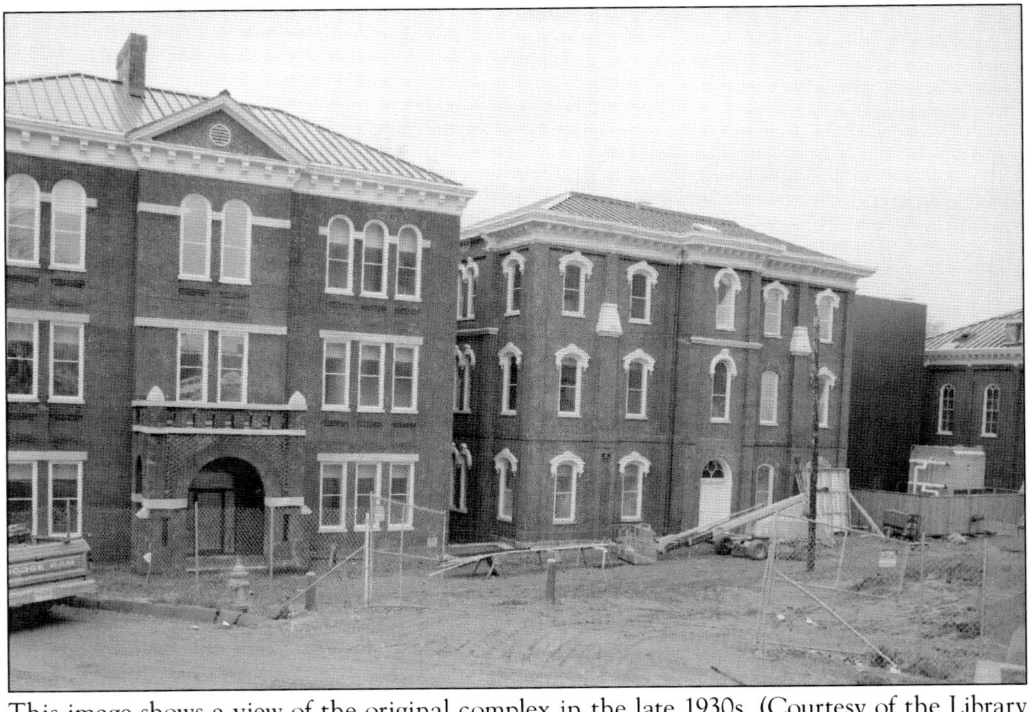

This image shows a view of the original complex in the late 1930s. (Courtesy of the Library of Congress.)

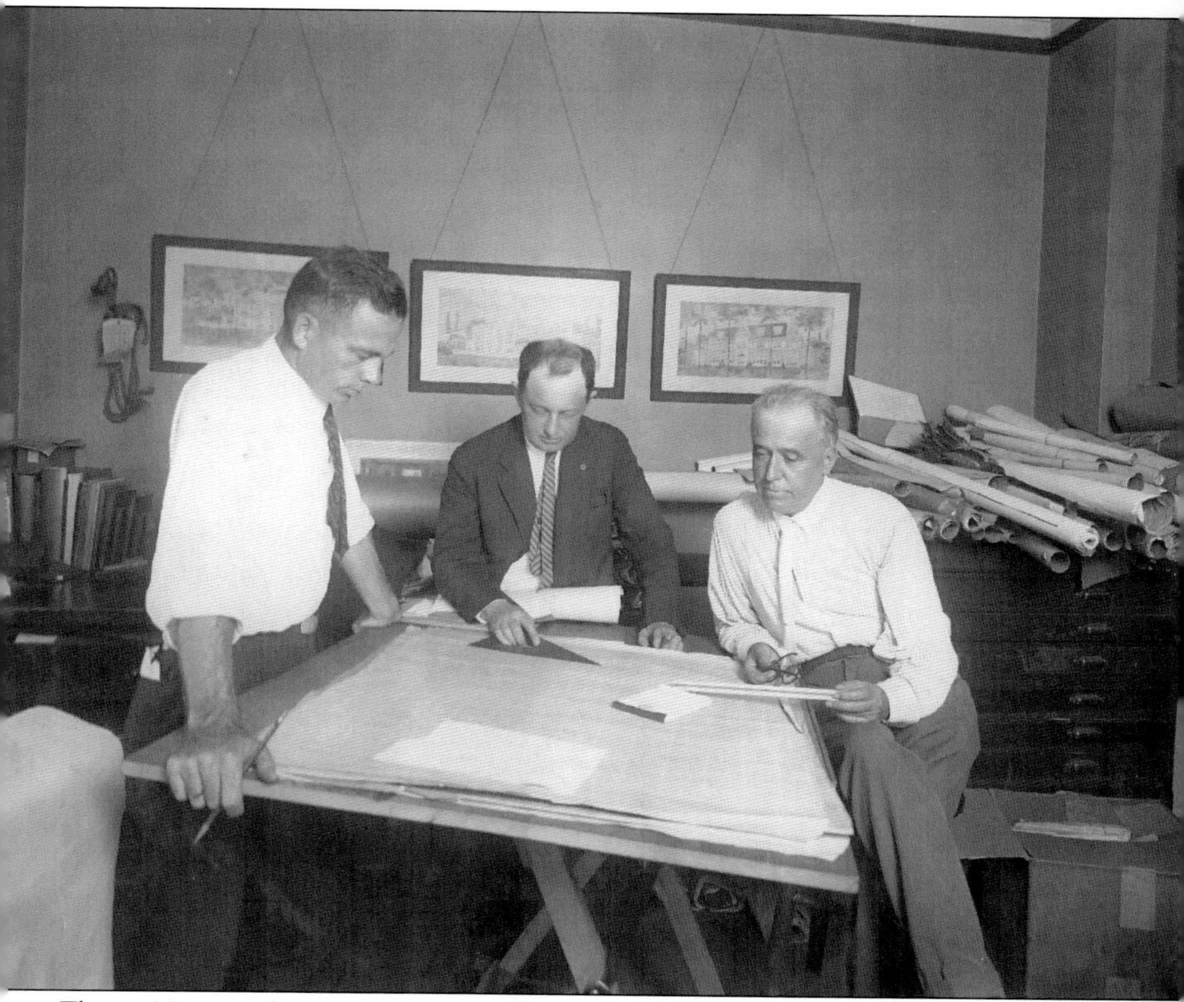

Thomas Marr, seen here reviewing design plans for Tennessee School for the Deaf's Island Home campus, was an accomplished Nashville-based architect, as well as an alumnus of TSD and Gallaudet College. As an architect, Marr was especially noted for his sleek, elegant Art Deco designs. He was a generous benefactor to the deaf community, including Tennessee School for the Deaf, whose campus he considered his proudest achievement. Among his legacies is TSD's Marr Memorial Library. (Courtesy of Tennessee School for the Deaf.)

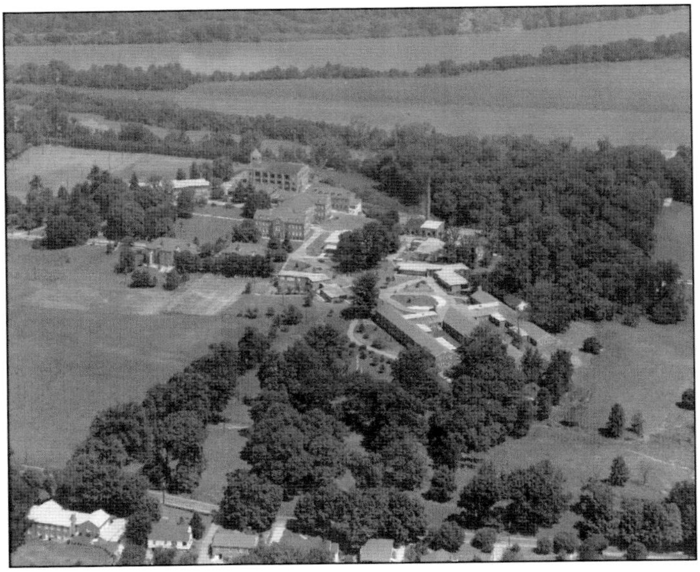

Tennessee School for the Deaf began operations in a rented house in downtown Knoxville and first enrolled students in 1845. The school moved to a Greek Revival building across from the University of Tennessee in 1848. The school established itself as one of finest schools for the hearing impaired and, following strong growth, moved to the Island Home campus in 1924. A 1957 aerial shot of the Island Home campus is shown. (Courtesy of Tennessee School for the Deaf.)

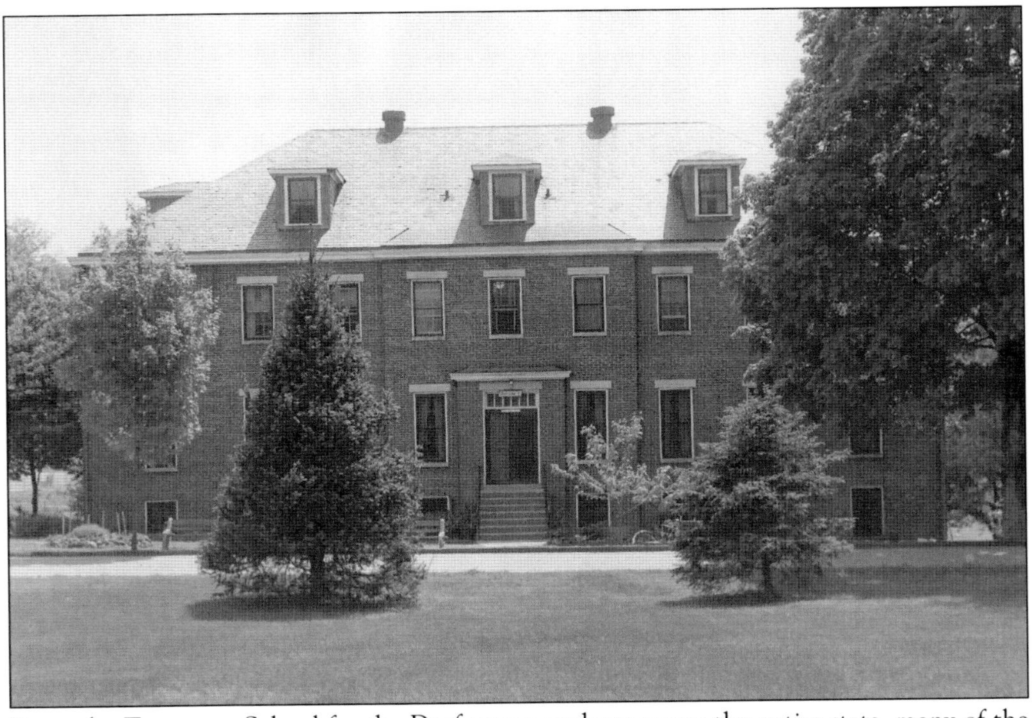

Since the Tennessee School for the Deaf serves students across the entire state, many of the students reside on campus in small cottages and dormitory-style residences. Cottage A, or Poore Hall, was designed by Marr and Holman and was completed in 1924. (Courtesy of Tennessee School for the Deaf.)

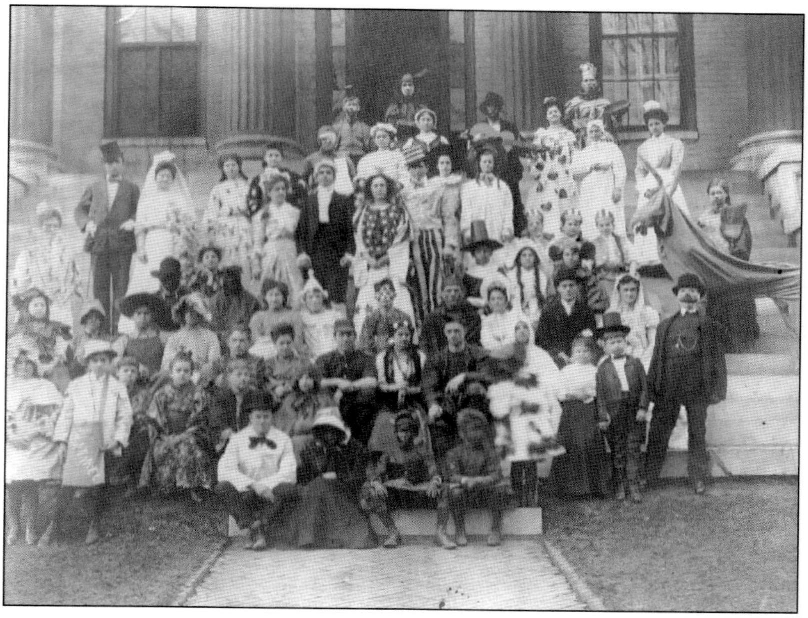

Over its more than 160 years of operation, the school has strived to foster a sense of community where students learn to live, work, and play. These students are dressed for a play outside of the downtown campus in the early 1900s. (Courtesy of Tennessee School for the Deaf.)

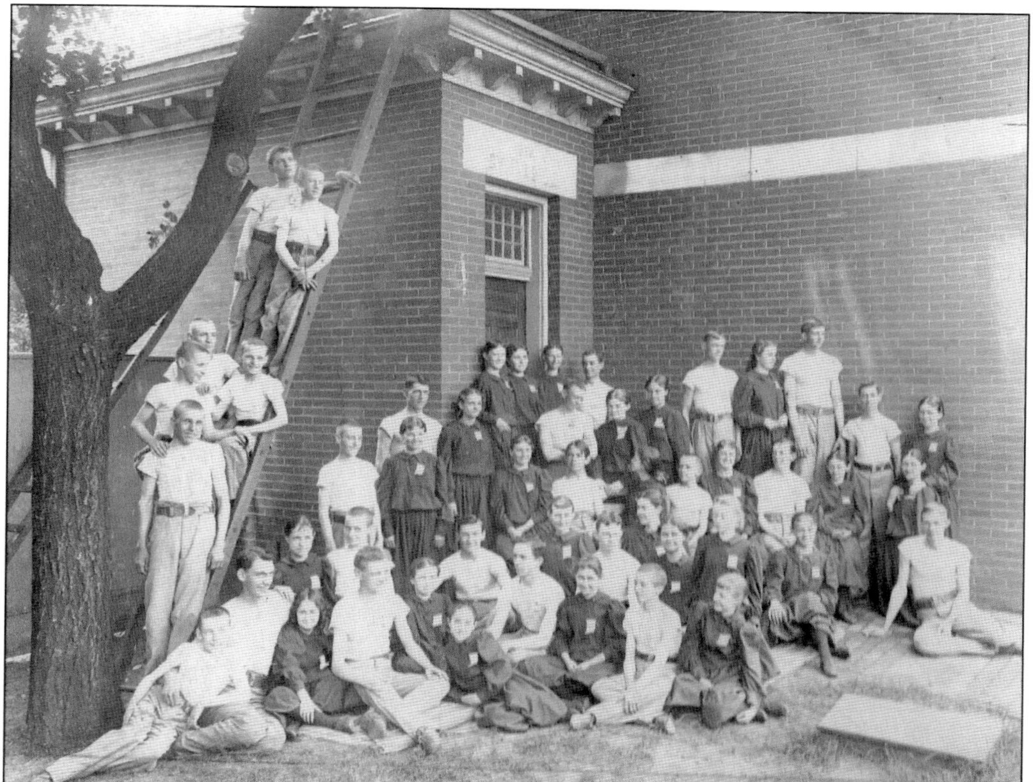

The school has long offered students opportunities to participate in extracurricular activities such as the physical education class shown here at the downtown campus in 1894. The school continues this tradition today by fielding athletics teams in several different sports. (Courtesy of Tennessee School for the Deaf.)

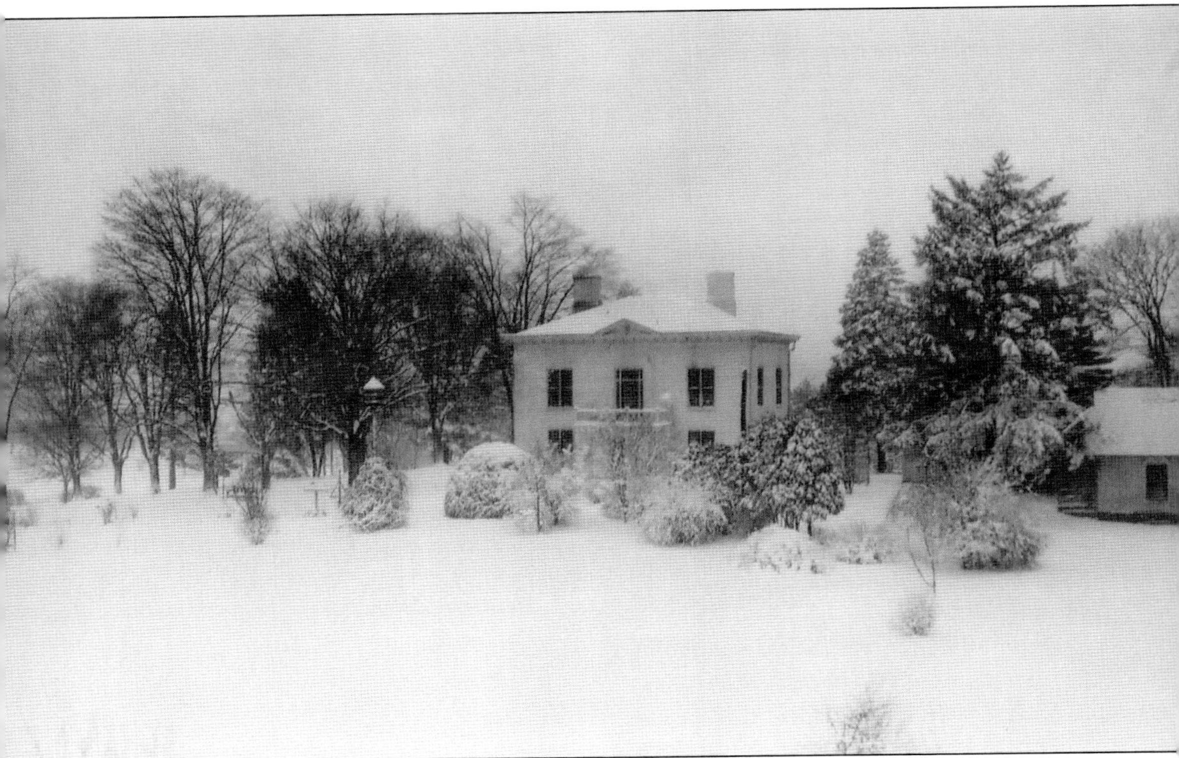

The Perez Dickinson Home is shown here in the winter on land that would eventually become the Tennessee School for the Deaf's Island Home Campus. Beloved Knoxville resident Col. Perez Dickinson, cousin of poet Emily Dickinson, built this home as a summer cottage in the mid-1800s. Perez, who maintained a large home in downtown Knoxville as his primary residence, used his island home as a summer cottage, a guest residence, and a horticultural center. Dickinson's house still exists on the grounds of the Tennessee School for the Deaf. The Island Home Park Historic District lies on land that formed the front approach to the grounds, and Island Home Boulevard follows the path established by the original drive to Dickinson's home. Dickinson was also a leading force behind the construction of the Gay Street Bridge. (Courtesy of Tennessee School for the Deaf.)

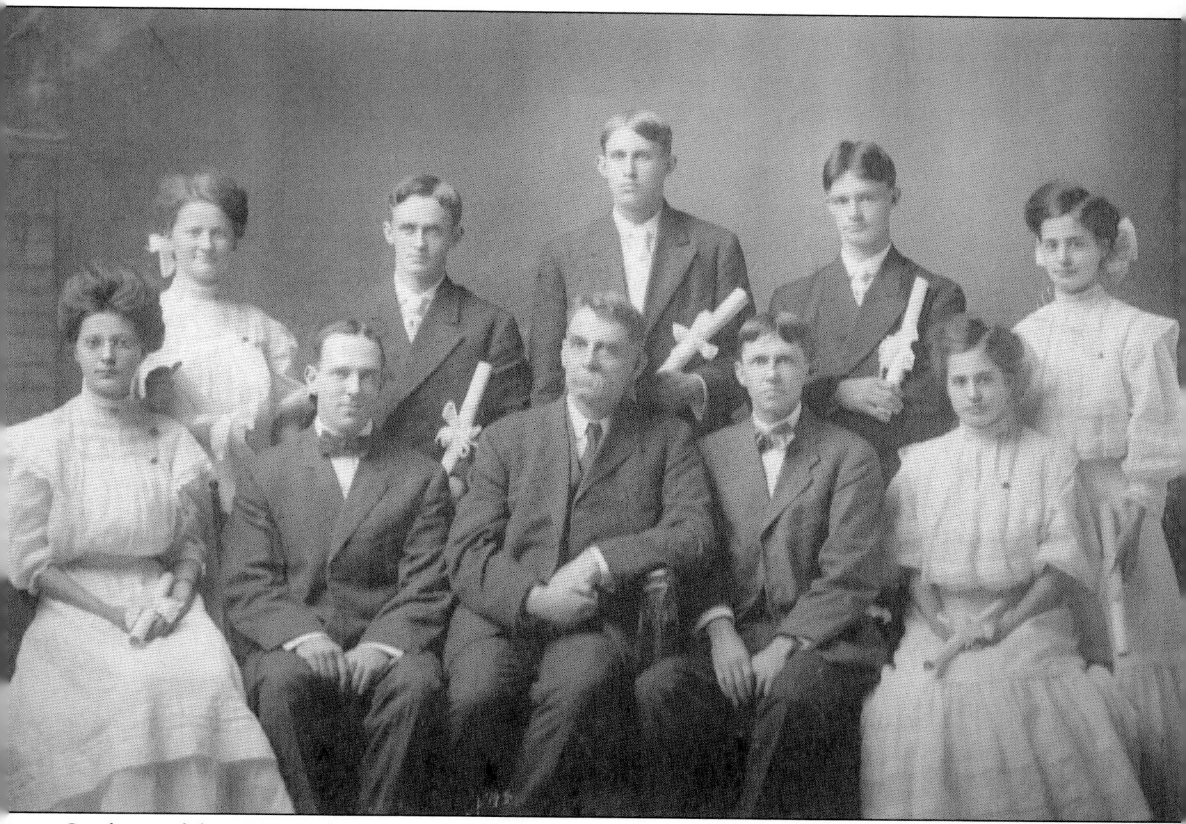

Students of the 1908 graduating class of Tennessee School for the Deaf pose for a portrait holding their diplomas. Pictured are, from left to right, (first row) Mollie Watson, W.H. Chambers, Supt. Thomas L. Moses, Horace E. Walker, and Ida Johnson; (second row) Jennie Hicks, Lonas Payne, William Dalton, Crockett Burgin, and Lida Johnson. (Courtesy of Tennessee School for the Deaf.)

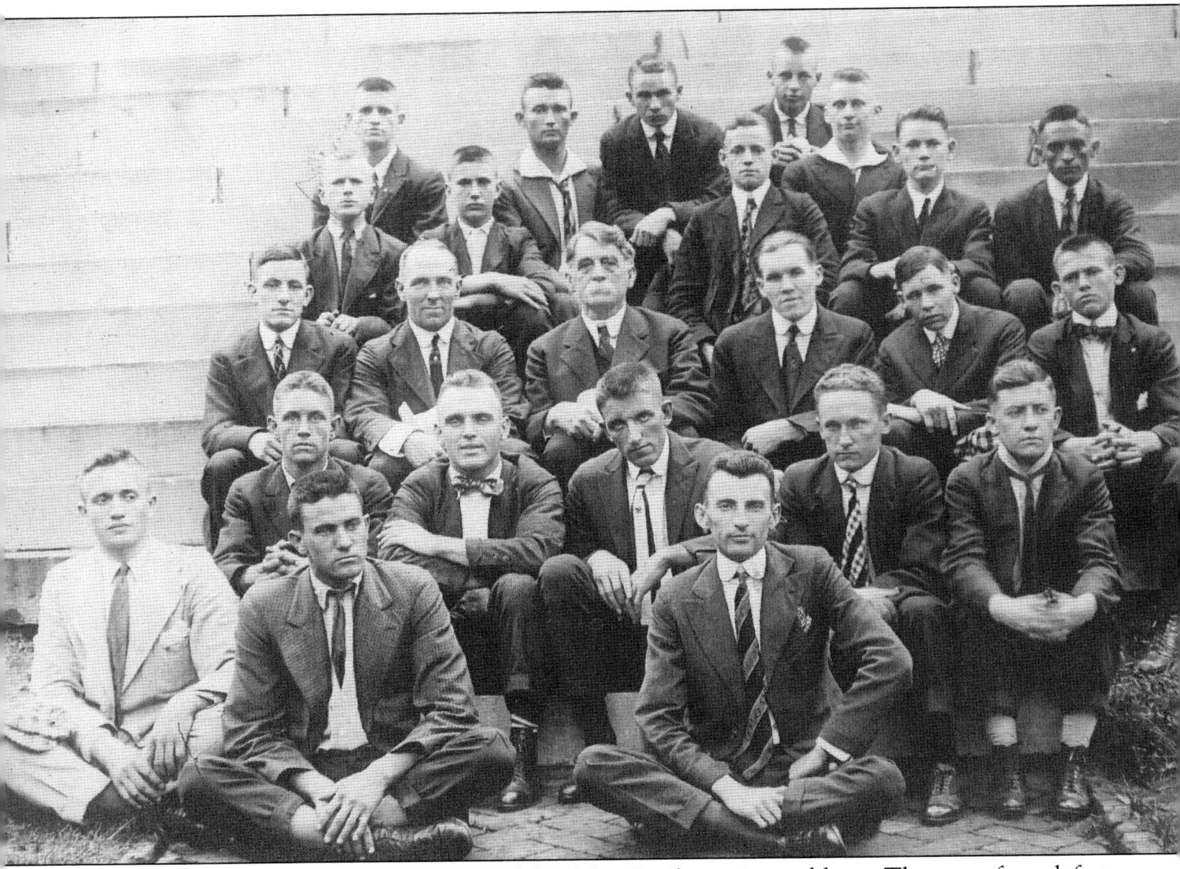

The members of the 1915–916 Boys Club of the Deaf are pictured here. They are, from left to right, (first row) Edgar Phelps, Oscar Duncan, and Jesse Cain; (second row) Andrew Sellers, Louie Davis, Arthur Blevins, Henry Sherrill, and Sanders Cowan; (third row) Luther Price, William Chambers, Supt. Thomas Moses, Russell Moore, Joe Carter, and Daniel Acuff; (fourth row) Luther Swindell, Cleo Andes, Prentis Lucado, Samuel Henry, and Hugh Bishop; (fifth row) Walter Hodge, Oliver Williams, James Bradshaw, Horace Bright, and Robert Condill. (Courtesy of Tennessee School for the Deaf.)

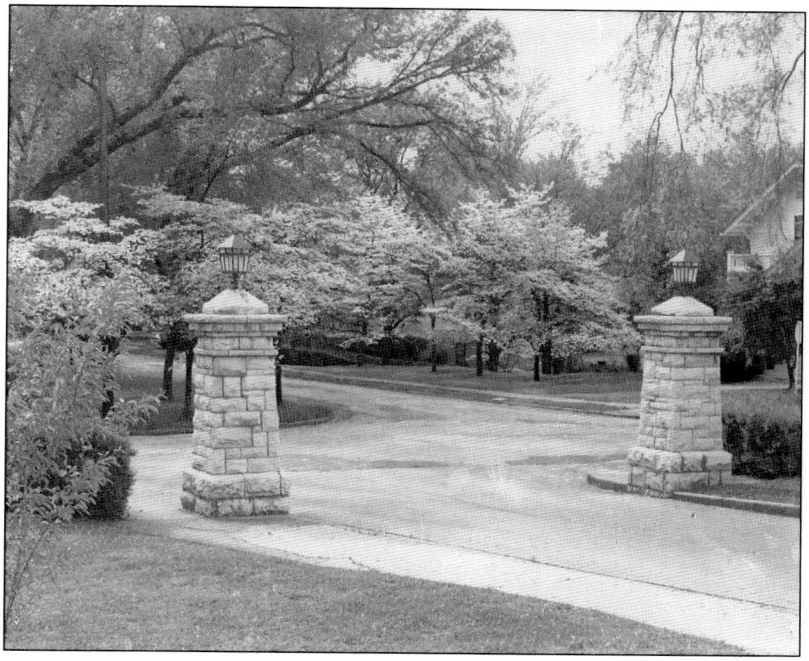

The entrance to the Tennessee School of the Deaf's Island Home campus is shown here in the 1950s. These markers still stand today at the entrance to the Island Home community. (Courtesy of Tennessee School for the Deaf.)

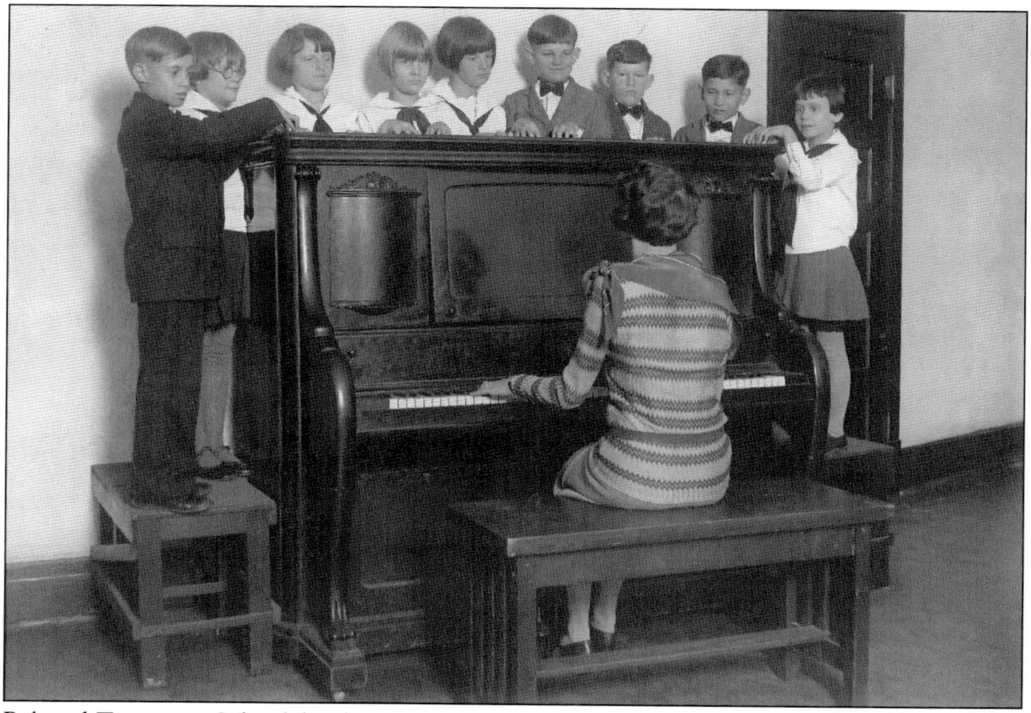

Beloved Tennessee School for the Deaf rhythm teacher Gladys Jane is shown here playing the piano with students. The students have placed their fingertips on the piano in order to feel the vibrations of the music. (Courtesy of Tennessee School for the Deaf.)

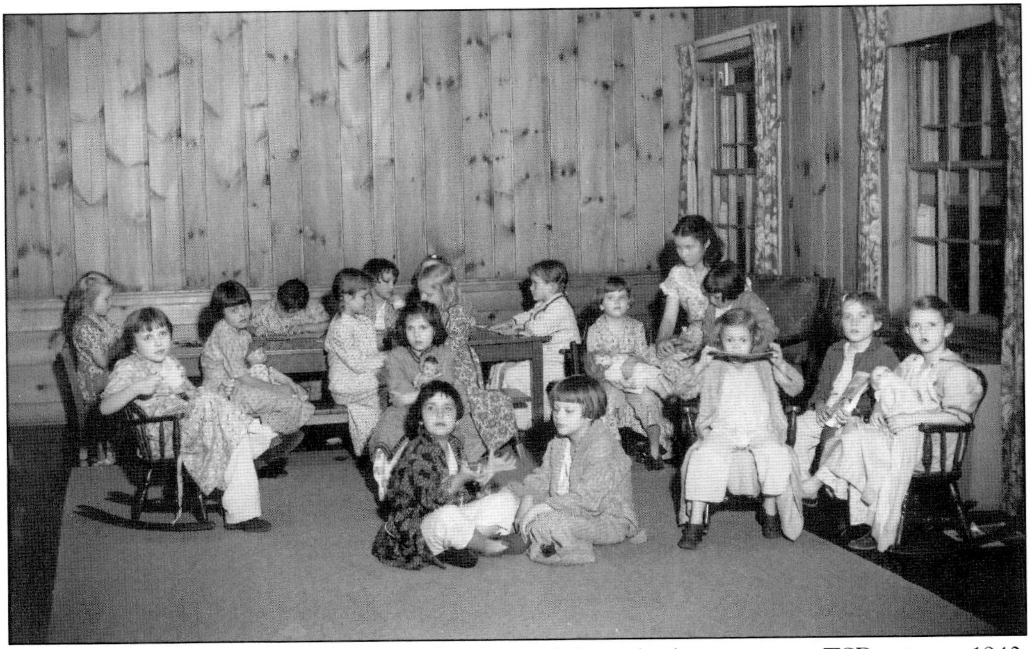

This photograph, which shows the inside of one of the girls' dormitories at TSD prior to 1940, provides a picture of life at the school. (Courtesy of Tennessee School for the Deaf.)

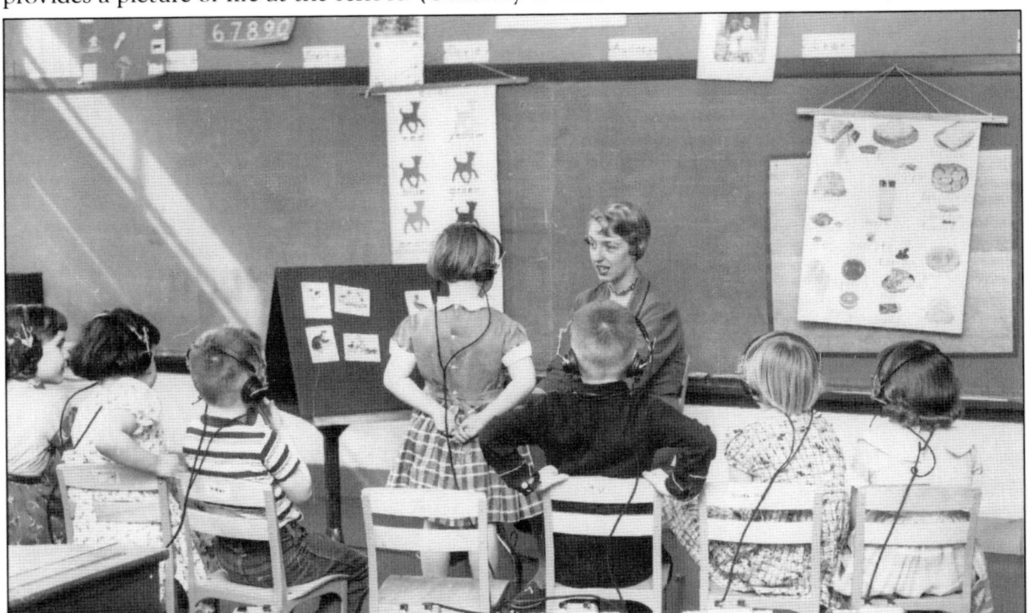

This is a photograph taken by a photography teacher of an elementary school class at TSD during the 1950s. (Courtesy of Tennessee School for the Deaf.)

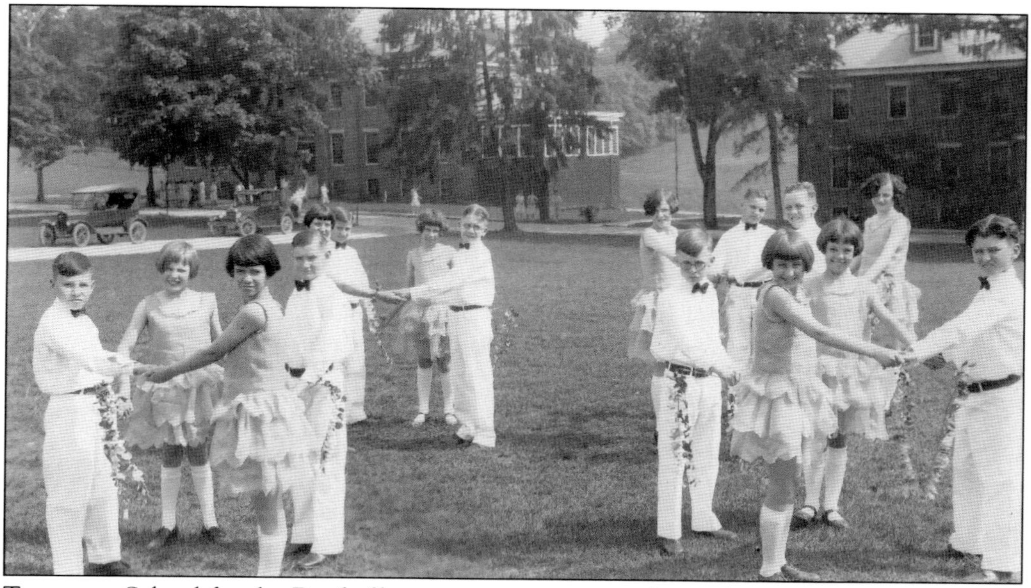

Tennessee School for the Deaf offers many opportunities for students to grow academically, vocationally, and socially. Here, students prepare for a spring pageant at TSD in 1927. (Courtesy of Tennessee School for the Deaf.)

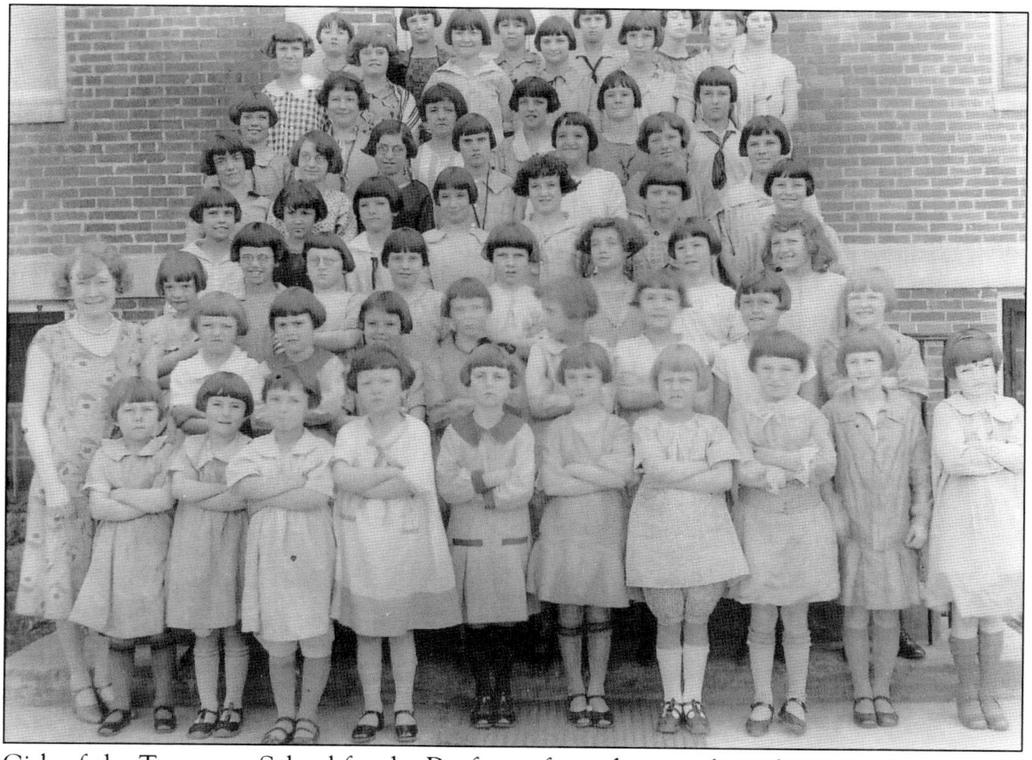

Girls of the Tennessee School for the Deaf pose for a photograph in the 1930s. (Courtesy of Tennessee School for the Deaf.)

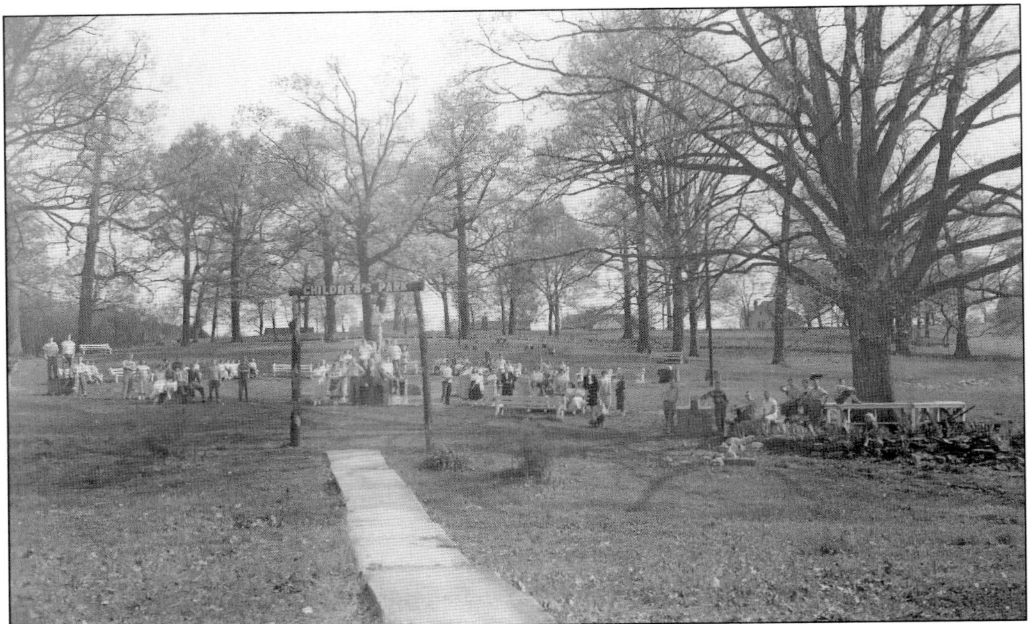

The pastoral and somewhat detached setting of the Island Home campus offers a unique locale for the school. For instance, the children's park playground, beloved to many students, is located at the center of Tennessee School for the Deaf's campus, shown here in the 1930s. (Courtesy of Tennessee School for the Deaf.)

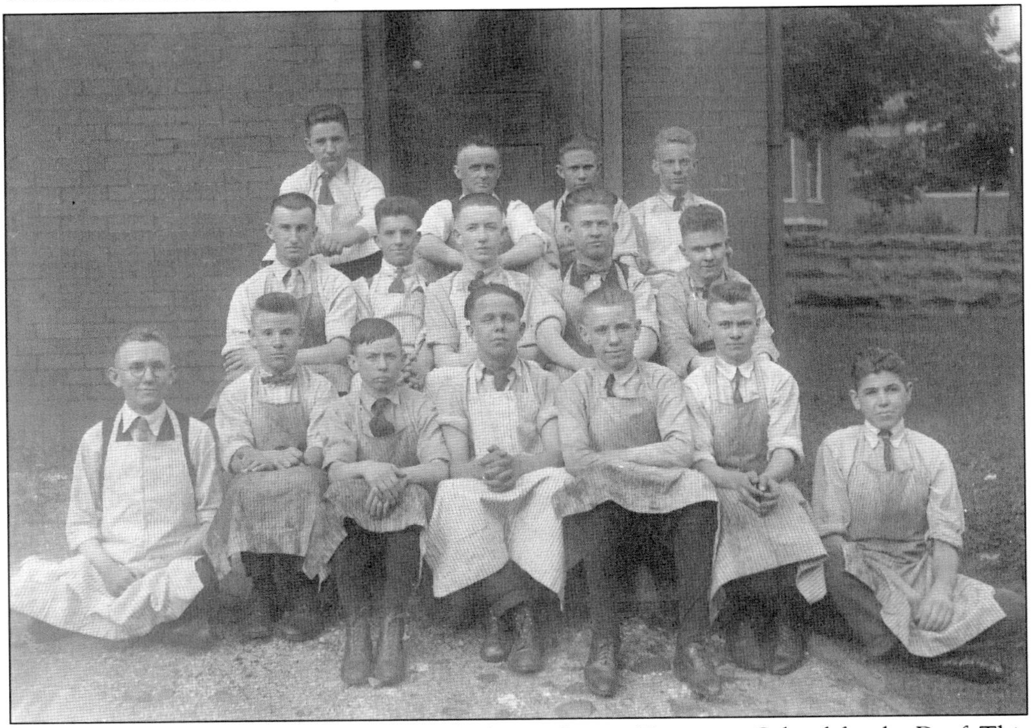

Shoe repair was one of the vocations taught by teachers at Tennessee School for the Deaf. This image shows a 1919 shoe repair class taught by Lonas Payne. (Courtesy of Tennessee School for the Deaf.)

Elementary-age boy students pose with faculty for a picture in the 1930s. From its inception to the present, Tennessee School for the Deaf has focused on providing its students with a holistic education. Students not only studied, but lived and were taught extensive life skills on the Island Home Campus. (Courtesy of Tennessee School for the Deaf.)

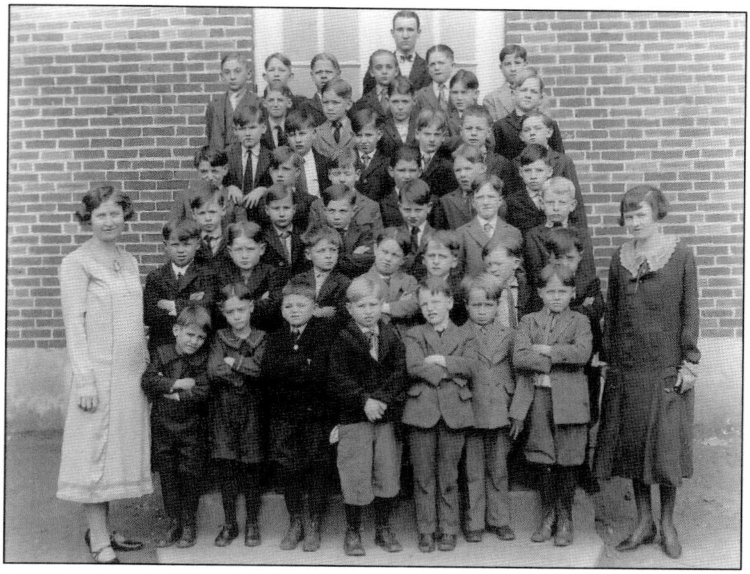

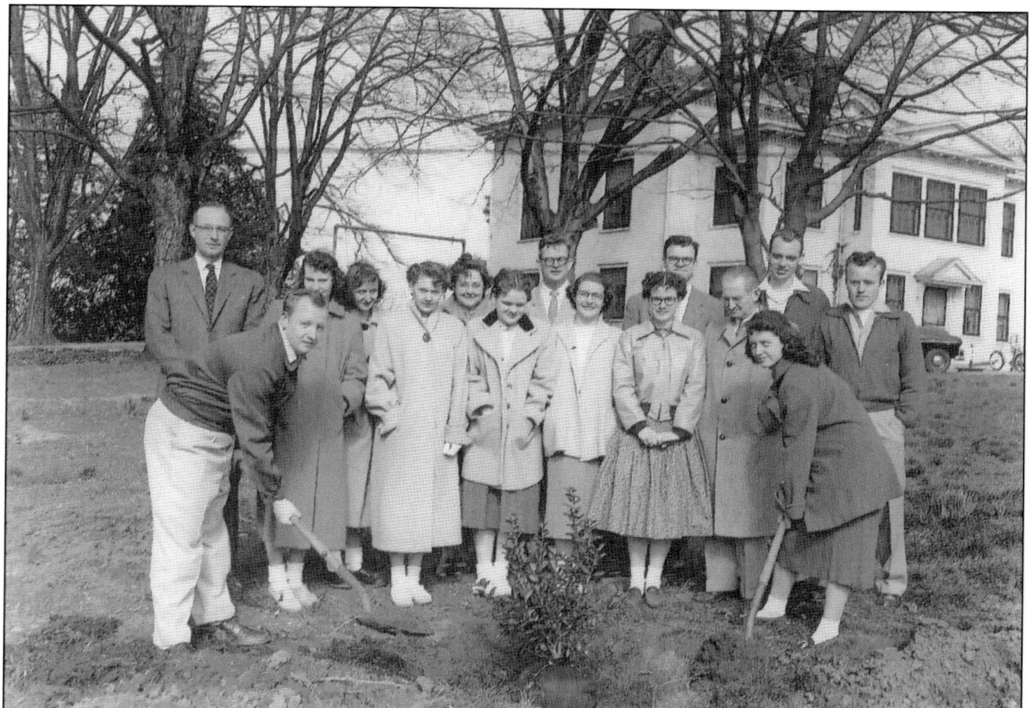

In this 1950s image, students plant flowers outside of the Perez Dickinson home, which is now the superintendent's home. (Courtesy of Tennessee School for the Deaf.)

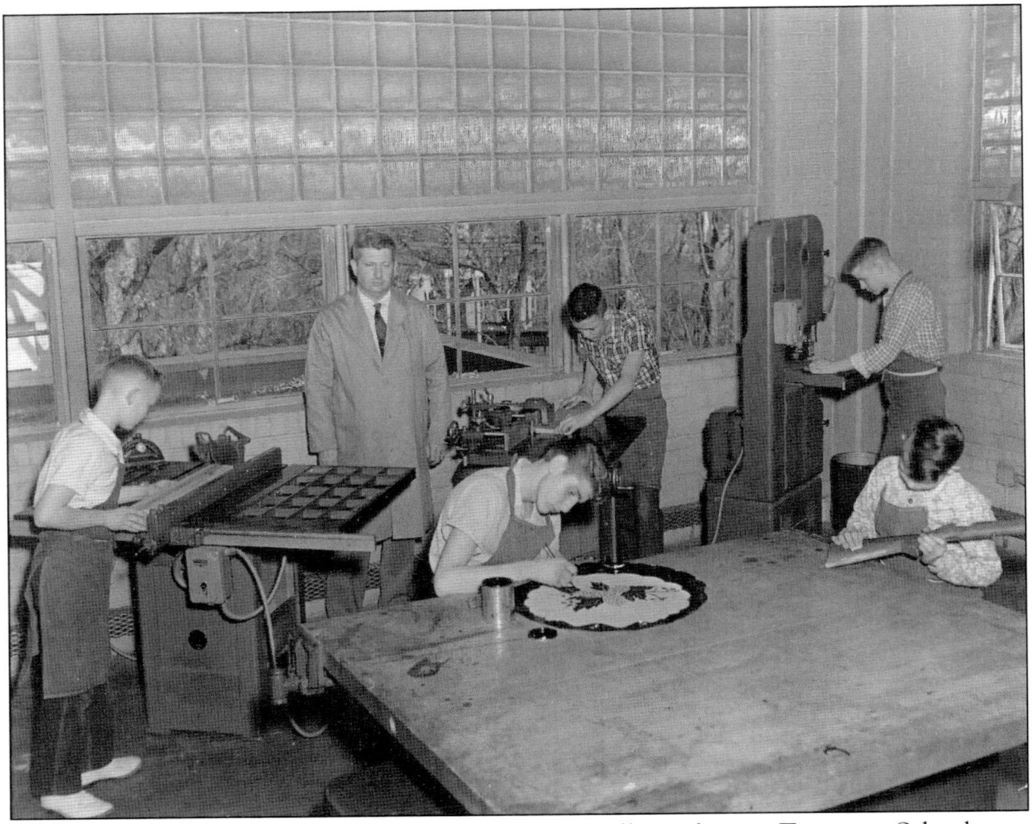

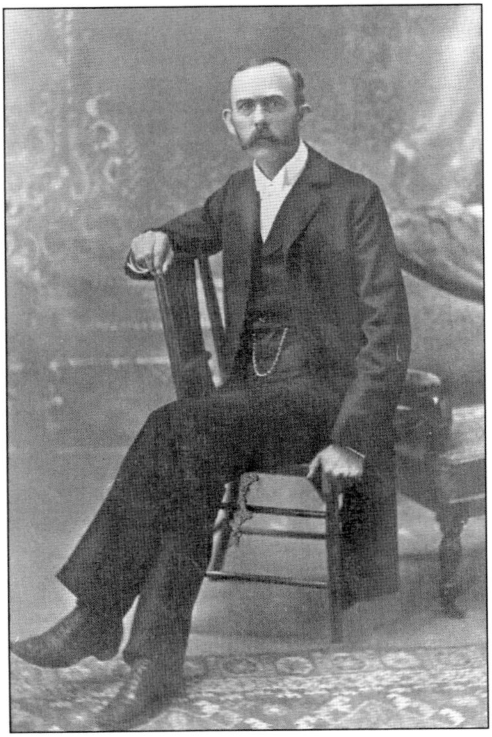

Historically, students at Tennessee School for the Deaf were trained in a variety of trades, such as printing, engraving, and agriculture. Above is a photograph of the print shop at TSD, a fairly common vocation for the deaf and hearing impaired during the mid-20th century. (Courtesy of Tennessee School for the Deaf.)

In 1893, Ashley S. Johnson (1857–1925) founded Johnson Bible College (now Johnson University), serving as president from 1893 to 1925. This portrait was taken in 1898. (Courtesy of Johnson University.)

Emma Elizabeth Johnson (1863–1927) cofounded Johnson Bible College with Ashley Johnson. She served as president from 1925 to 1927. This portrait was taken in 1898. (Courtesy of Johnson University.)

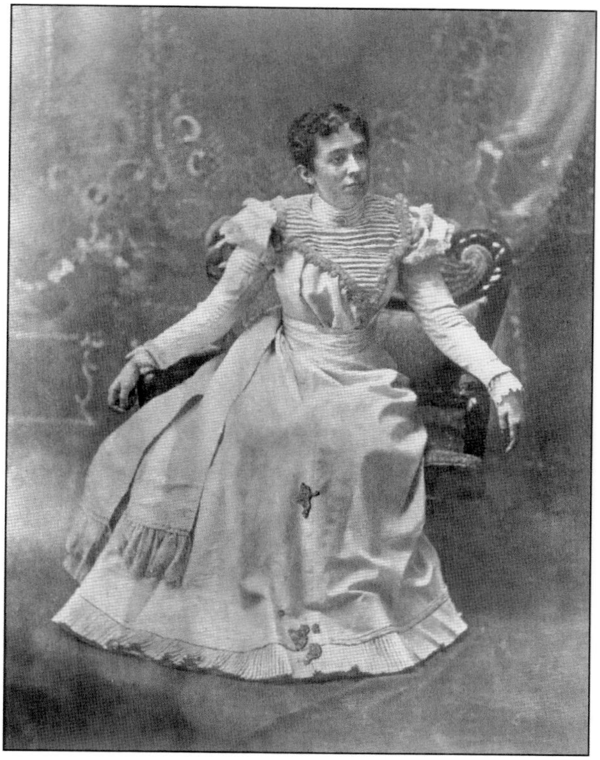

Ashley and Emma Johnson are photographed in 1899 overlooking the French Broad River from their home, the "White House," on the campus of Johnson University in Kimberlin Heights, Tennessee. (Courtesy of Johnson University.)

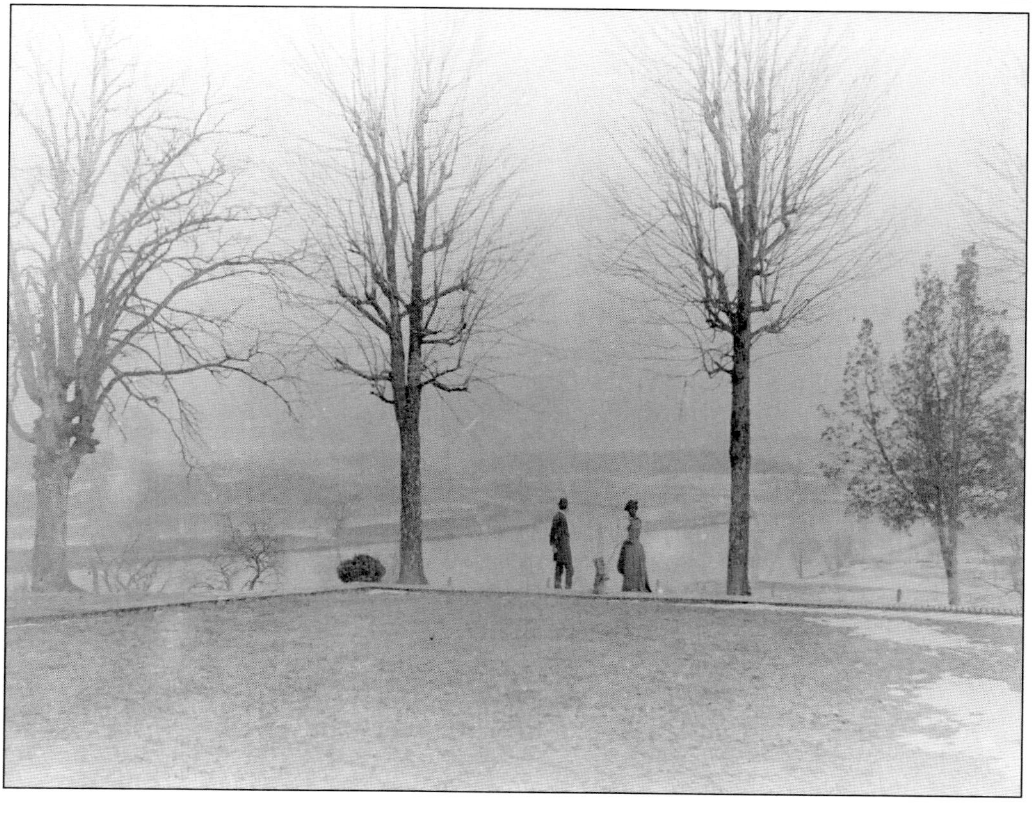

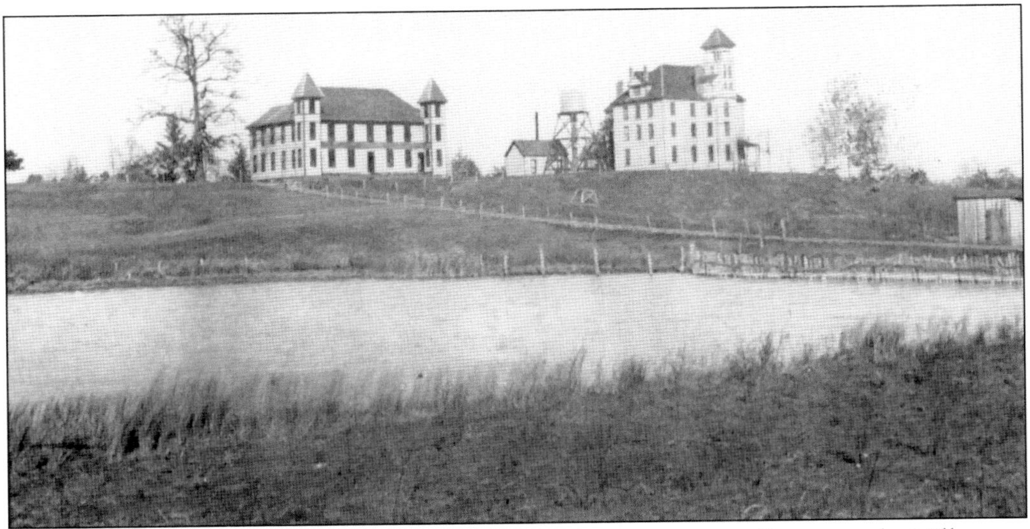

Known as the Hill, industrial hall and the main building are shown on the campus of Johnson University around 1900. (Courtesy of Johnson University.)

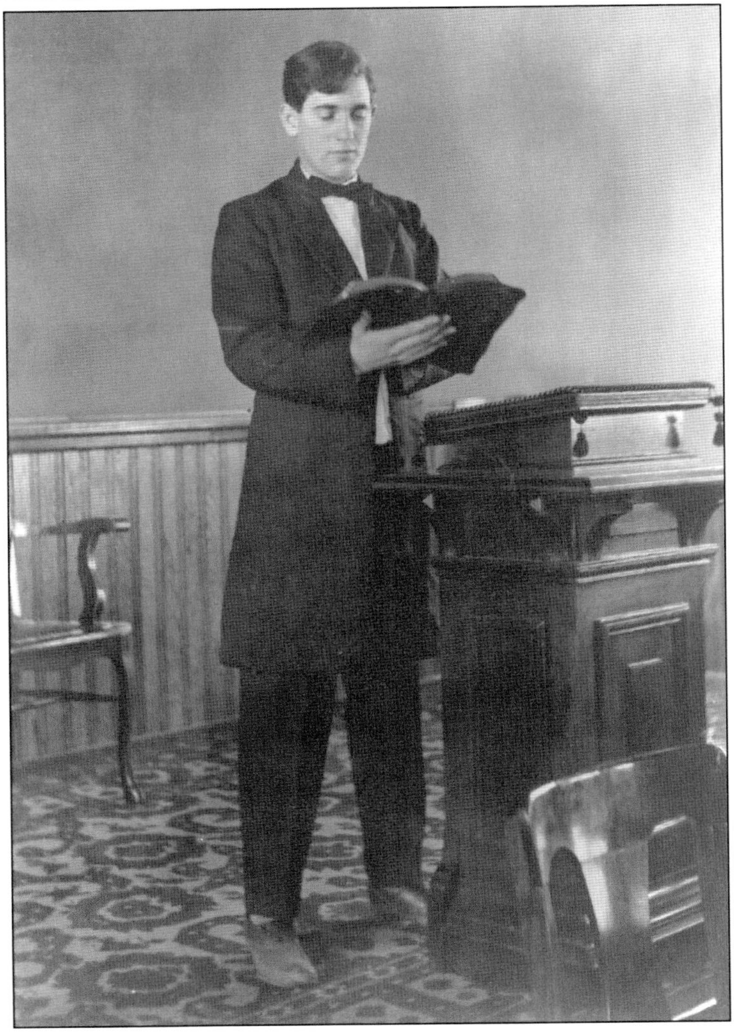

Walter G. Smith is seen at left student preaching in First Main Building on the campus of Johnson University around the early 1900s. (Courtesy of Johnson University.)

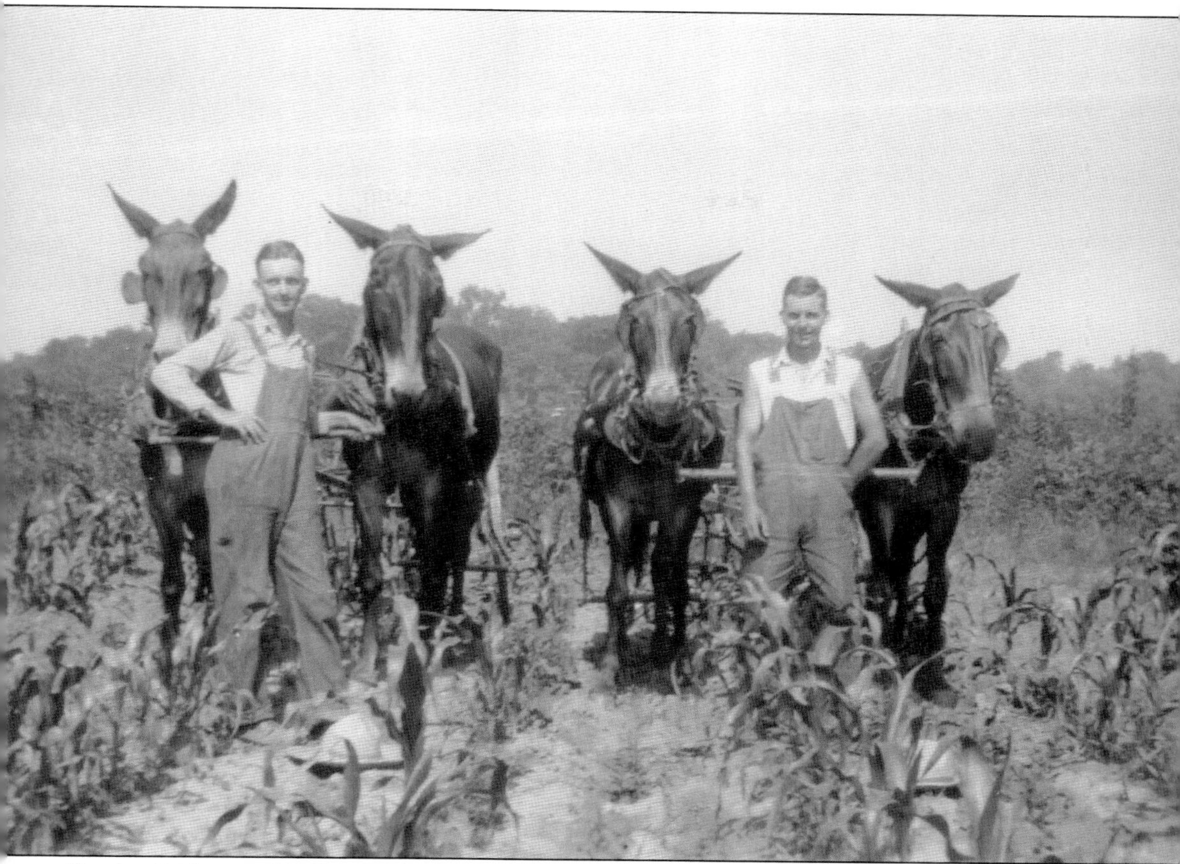

Charles Sublett and Wilbur Reid Sr. are shown plowing on the campus of Johnson University in 1932. (Courtesy of Johnson University.)

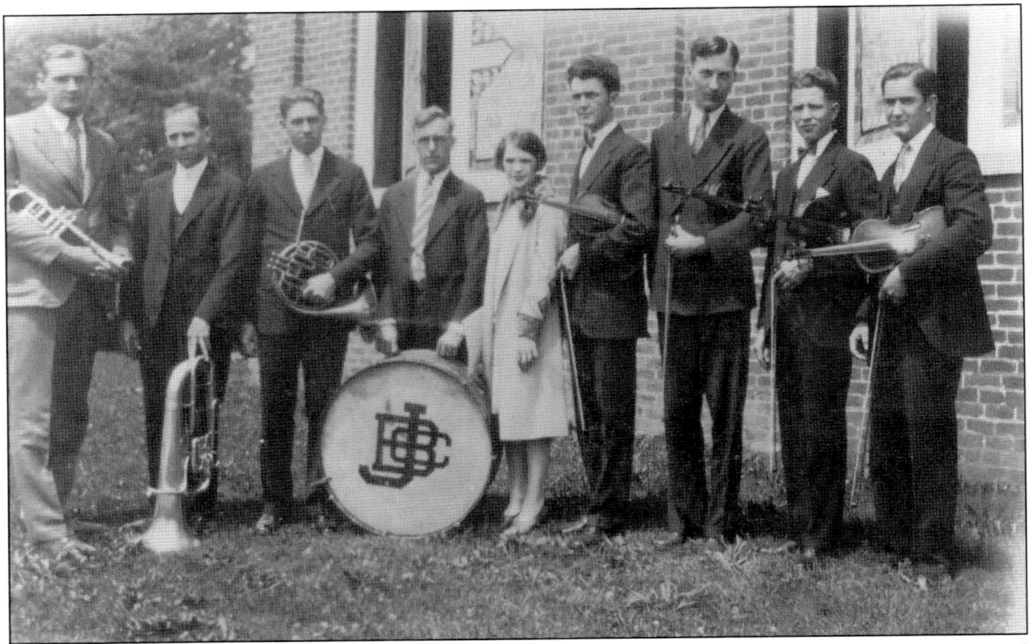

From the beginning, the mission of Johnson Bible College (now Johnson University) incorporated training for the family, college, and church into one complete system including opportunities for music ministry. This photograph shows the 1927–1928 Johnson Bible College student band. (Courtesy of Johnson University.)

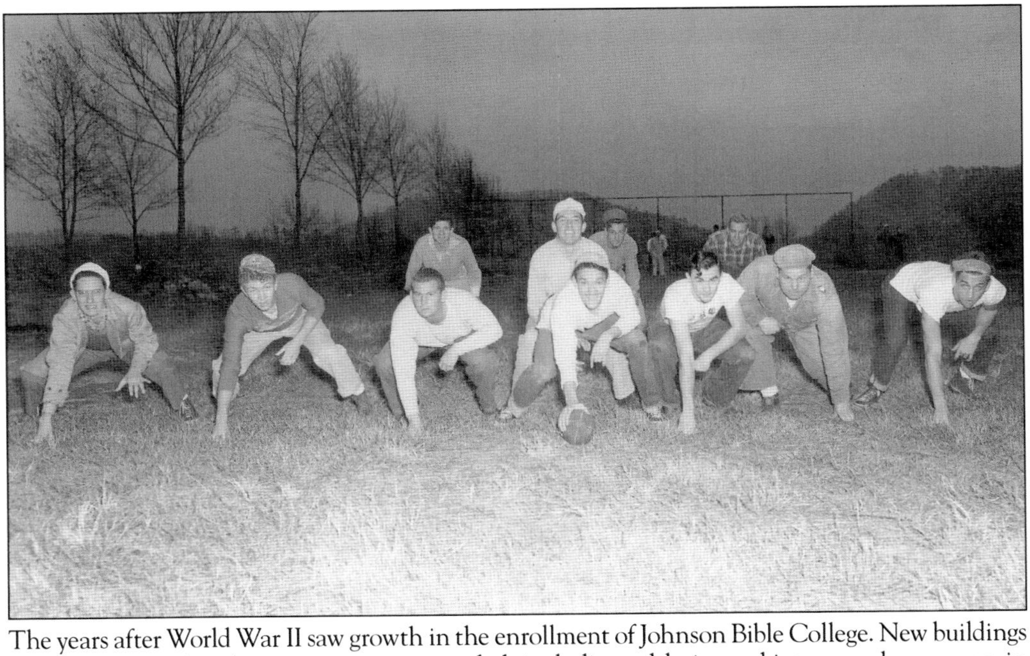

The years after World War II saw growth in the enrollment of Johnson Bible College. New buildings were constructed and programs were expanded, including athletics and intramural programs, in accordance with the mission of complete preparation for educated ministry. The 1949 intramural football team is shown here. (Courtesy of Johnson University.)

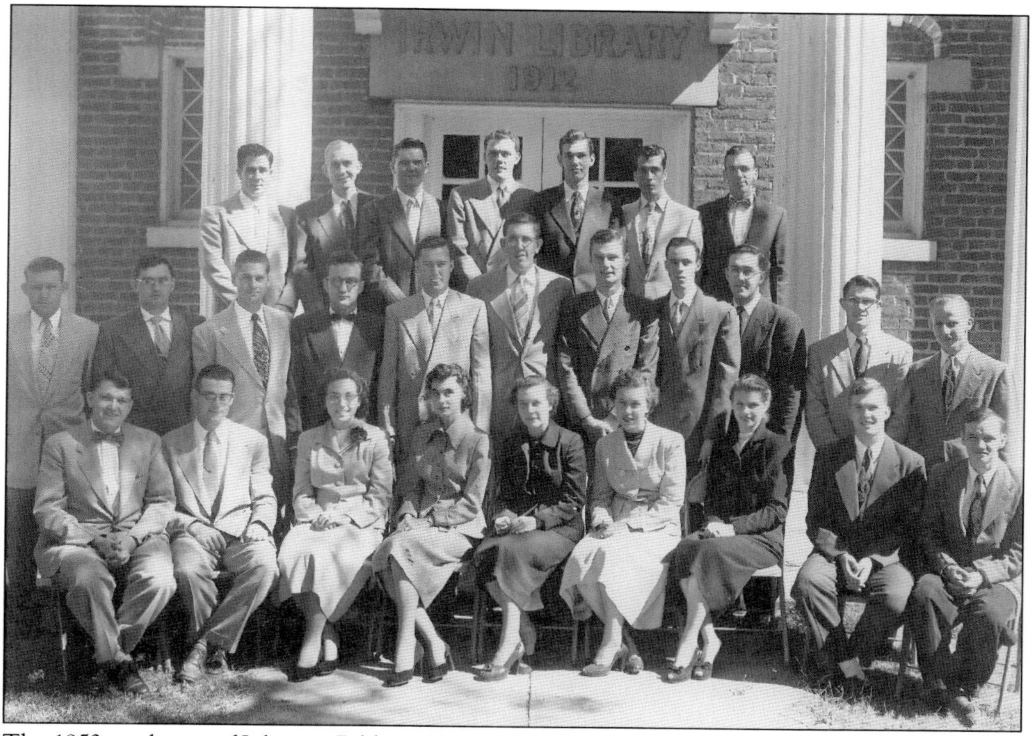

The 1953 graduates of Johnson Bible College pose for a photograph in front of the Irwin Library. (Courtesy of Johnson University.)

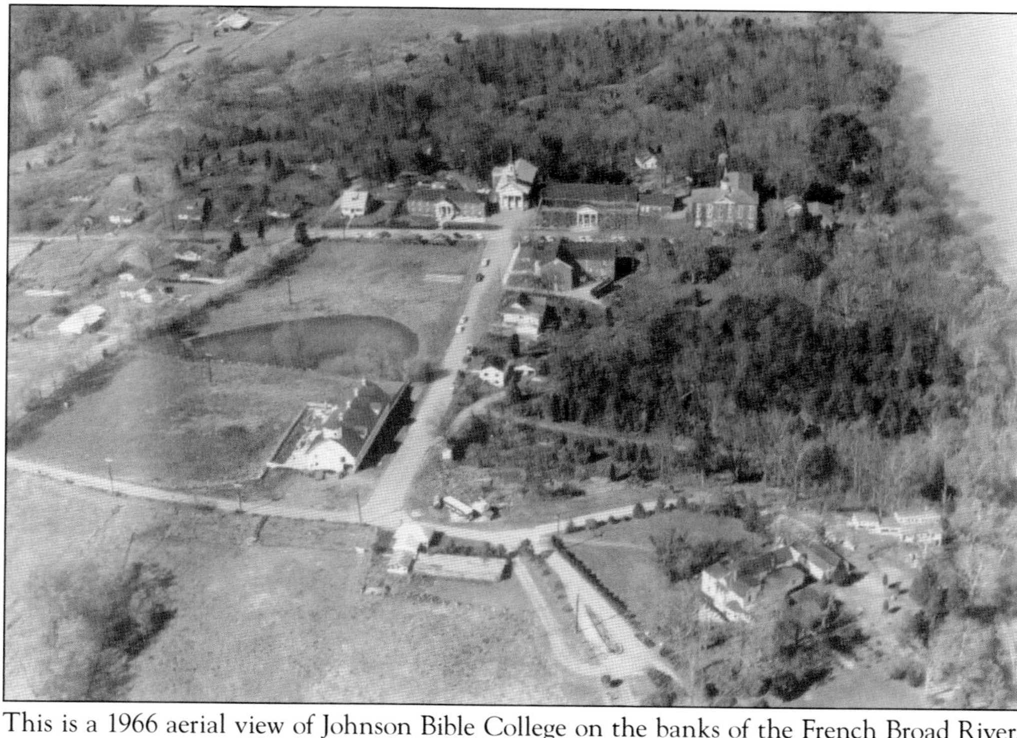

This is a 1966 aerial view of Johnson Bible College on the banks of the French Broad River. (Courtesy of Johnson University.)

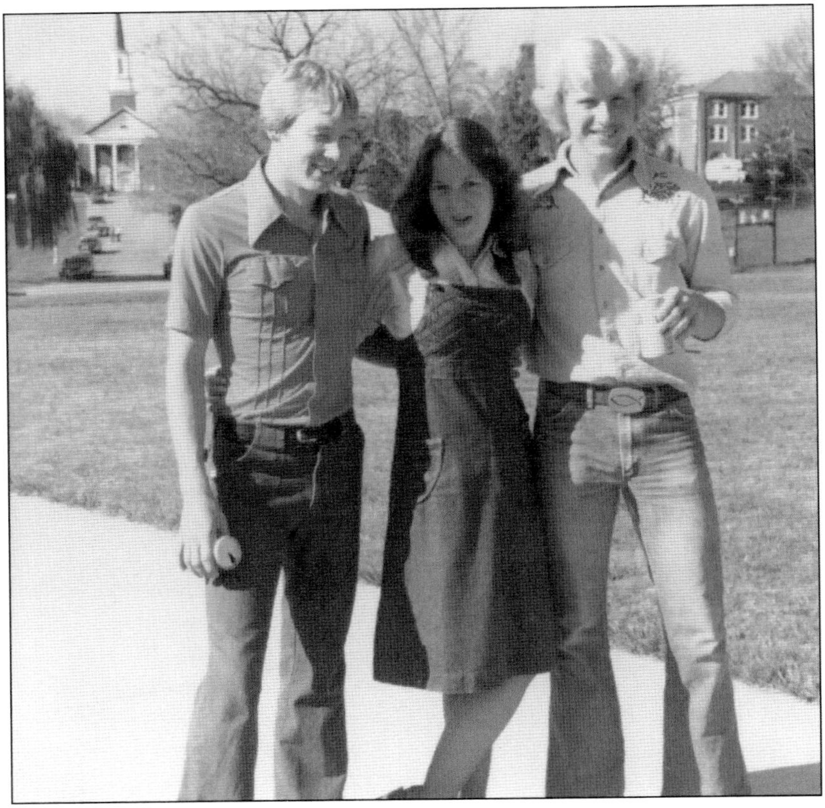

From left to right, students Don Hamilton, Brenda Davenport, and Kent Smith pose for a photograph at Johnson Bible College. (Courtesy of Johnson University.)

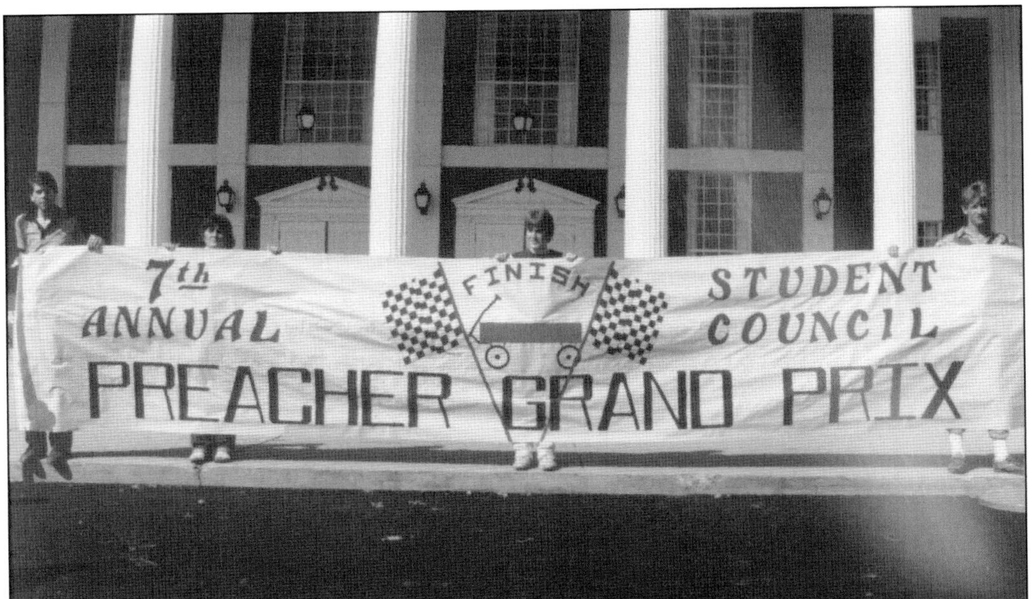

This photograph shows the seventh annual preacher Grand Prix soapbox derby at Johnson Bible College. (Courtesy of Johnson University.)

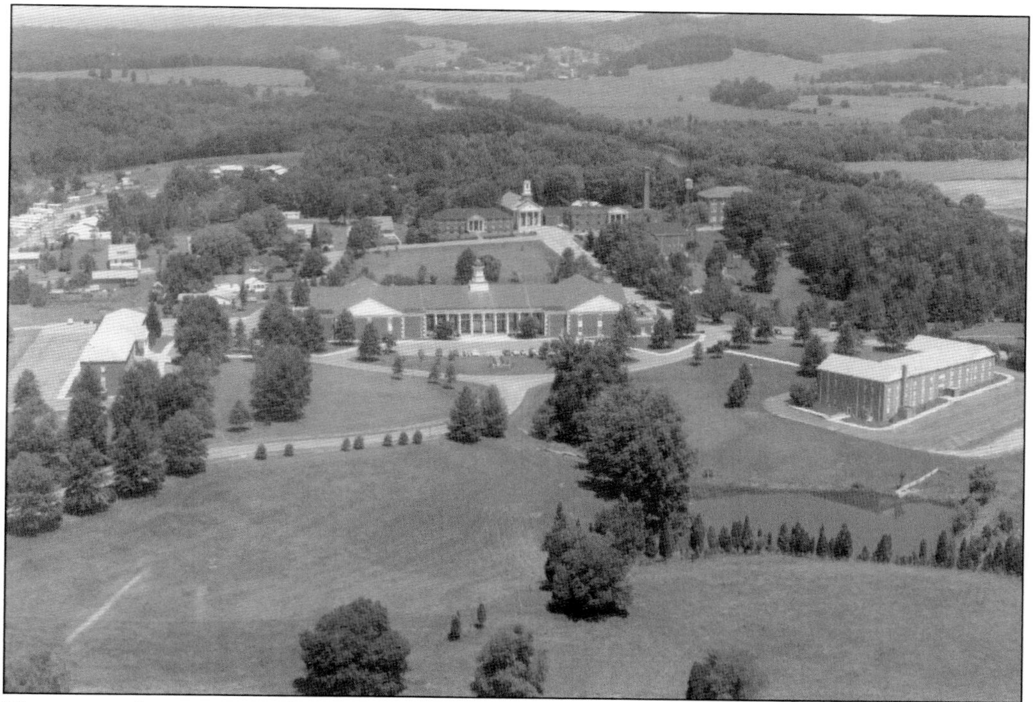

This image shows an aerial view of Johnson Bible College (now Johnson University). (Courtesy of Johnson University.)

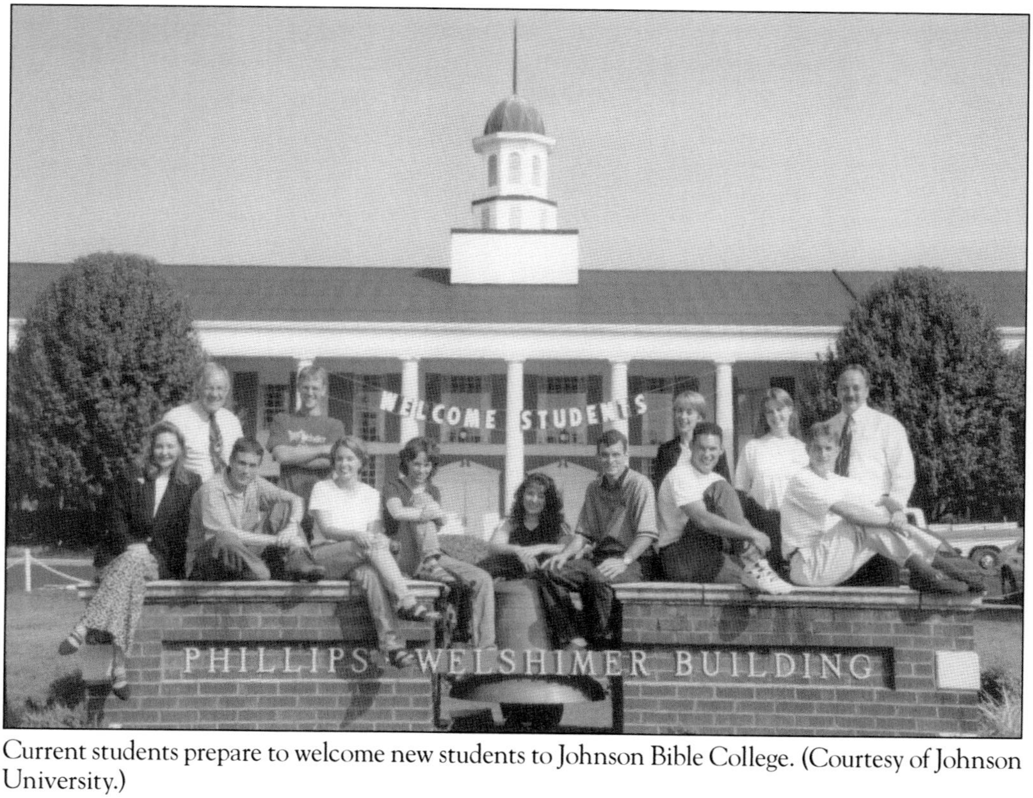

Current students prepare to welcome new students to Johnson Bible College. (Courtesy of Johnson University.)

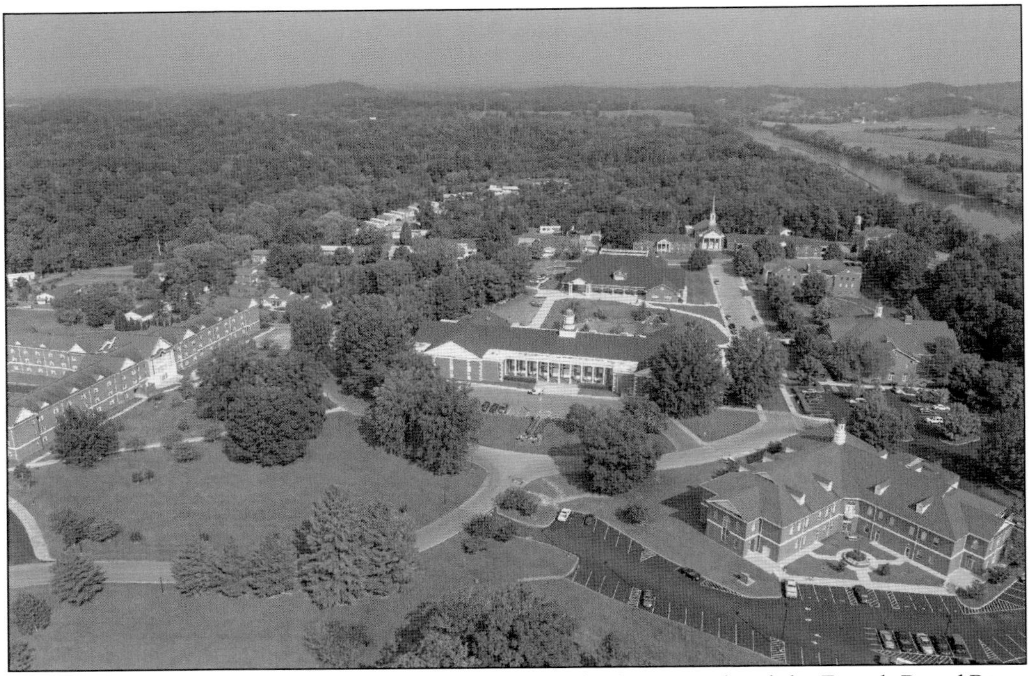

This view of Johnson University shows the college in the foreground and the French Broad River in the background. To the left is Johnson Hall, and Alumni Memorial Chapel is to the back, near the river. (Courtesy of Johnson University.)

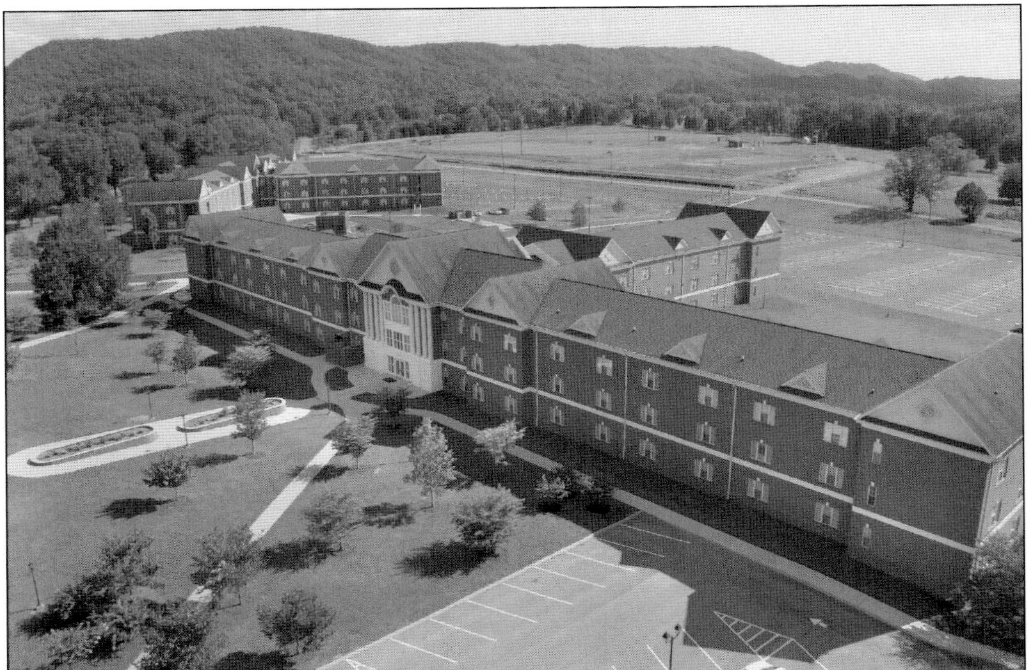

An aerial photograph of Johnson Hall on the campus of Johnson University is shown here. This dormitory was named in honor of Emma Johnson, co-founder and second president of the college, serving from 1925 to 1927. (Courtesy of Johnson University.)

Five

Religious Life

By the mid-19th century, Knoxville had gained the reputation of being "the city of churches." Churches began forming in the area as late as the 1770s, and in 2007, it was estimated that there were approximately 670 churches in Knoxville. Since its founding, religious life has played a significant role in the city of Knoxville, and this is no less true for South Knoxville.

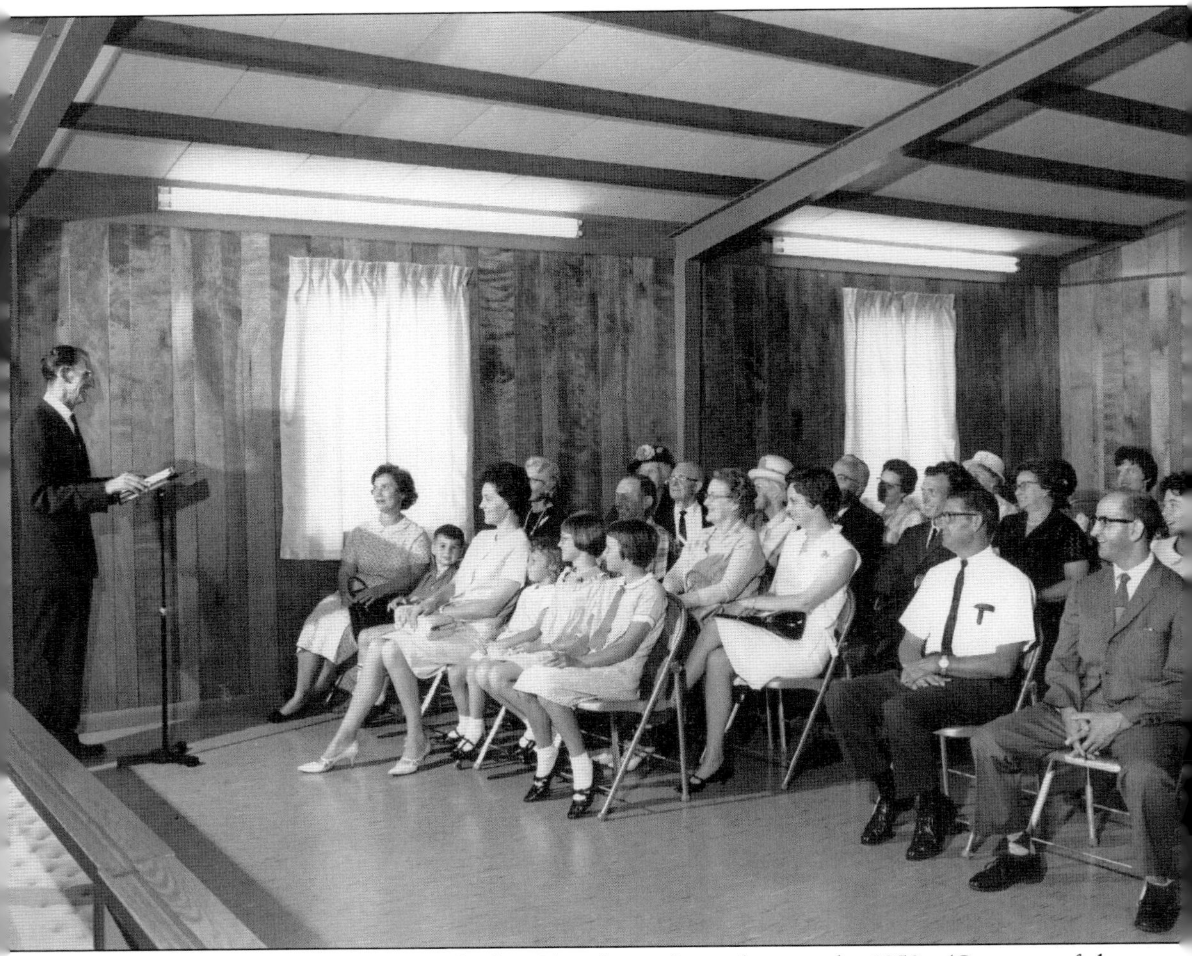

Members of the Arrowhead Methodist Church are shown here in the 1950s. (Courtesy of the Berry family.)

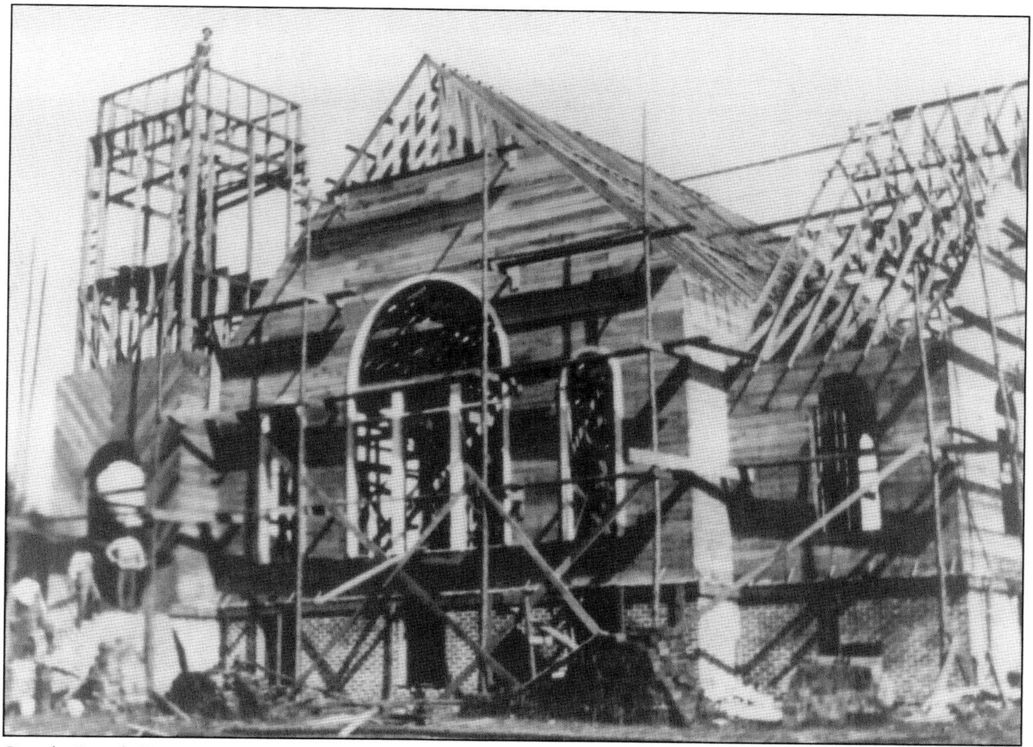

Stock Creek Baptist Church is shown above during construction and below in 1918. Stock Creek Baptist Church was founded in 1791. Throughout its early history the church persevered through the threat of Indian attack and the Civil War. In 1912, two brothers, listed as the Harris brothers in church minutes, donated a parcel of land for a new building in memory of their parents who were early church members. On October 29, 1916, despite the economic hardships of World War I, the first service was held in the new sanctuary built by a congregation of less than 40 members. (Both, courtesy of the Berry family.)

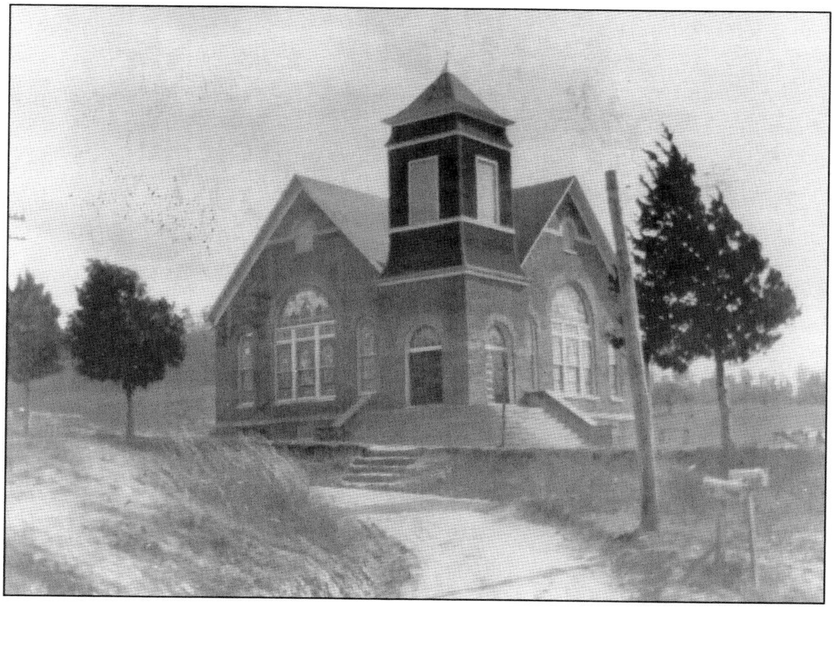

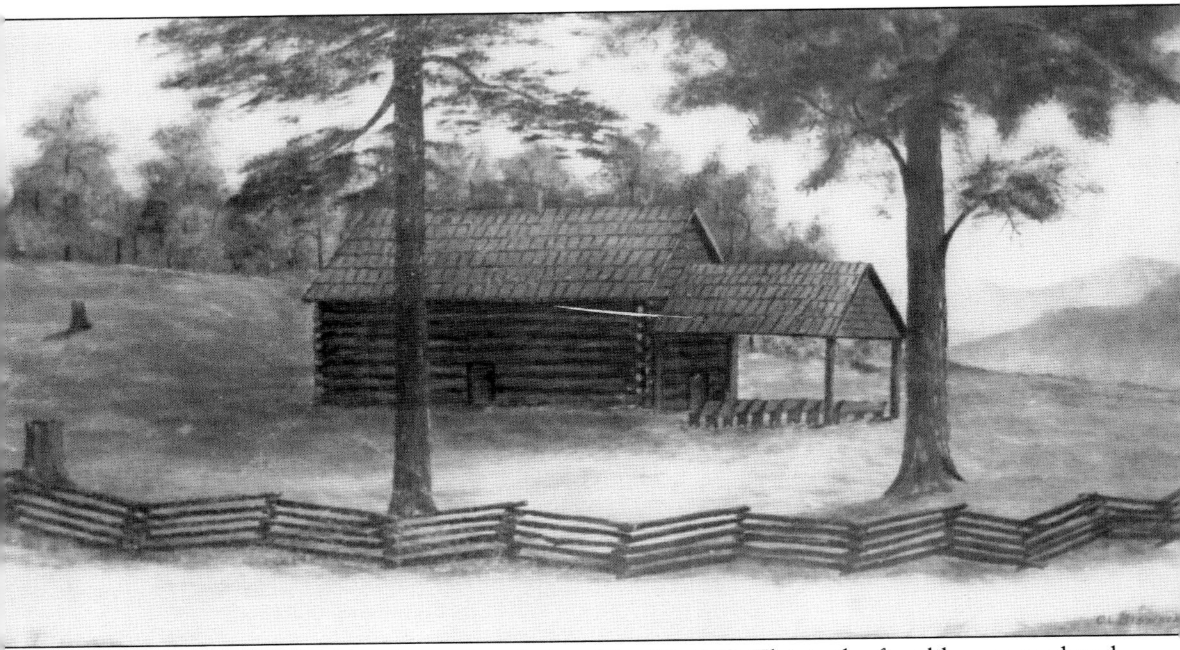

Mount Olive Baptist Church was founded on May 20, 1837. This is the first likeness produced of the original building in 1884. There are two paintings of the original church building at the Mount of Olives. One includes windows and the other does not (both are probably correct). Four of the first members were slaves belonging to families of the church. This particular building was sold to the highest bidder on the fourth Saturday in January in 1884 for $32.23. It was dismantled and rebuilt as a barn. (Courtesy of the Berry family.)

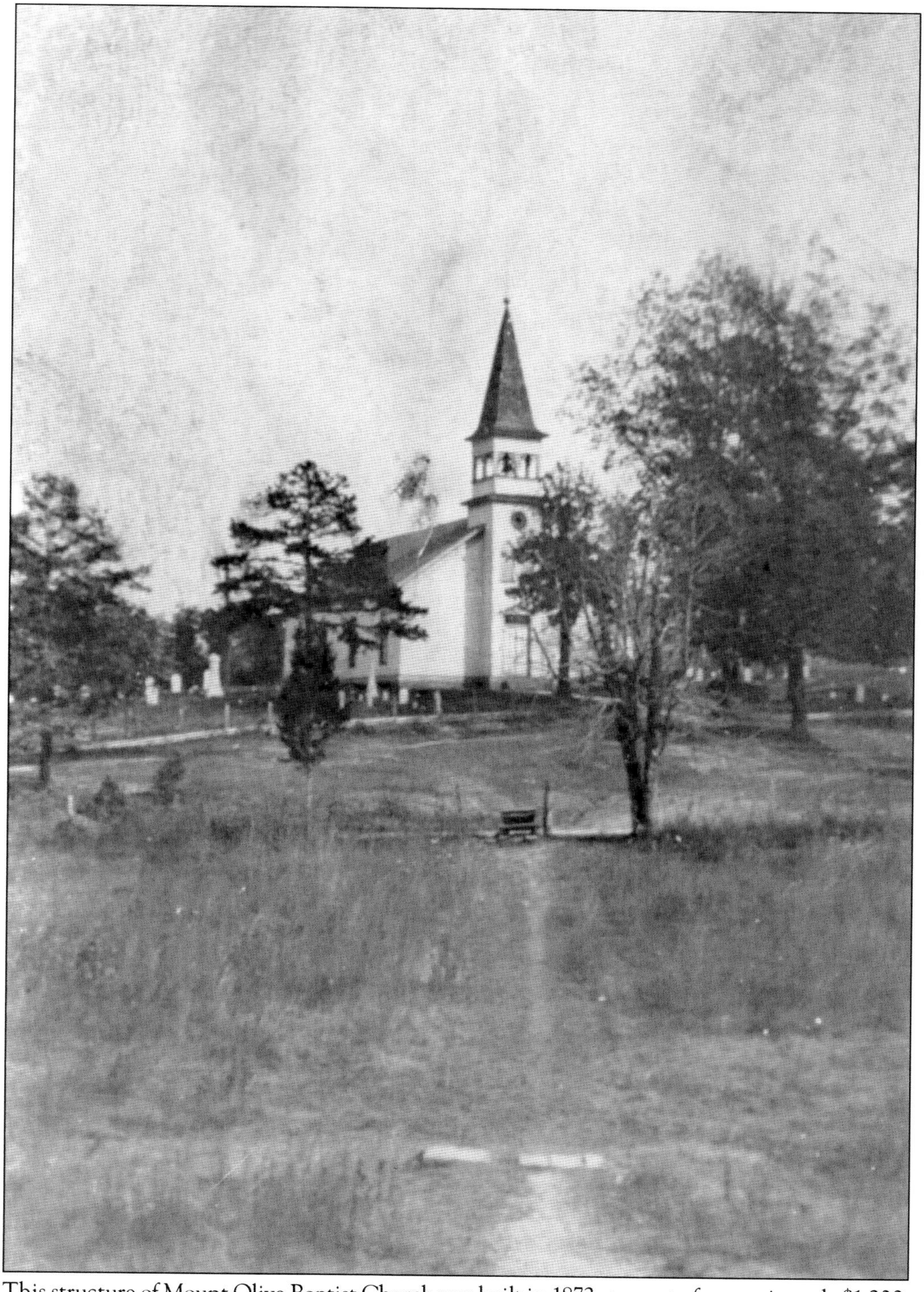

This structure of Mount Olive Baptist Church was built in 1872 at a cost of approximately $1,200. Church minutes state, "It was then moved and adopted that the dedication of the Mount of Olives Church House take place on the first Sabbath of September in 1872." The four foot by eight foot front and belfry was added in 1889 for $238.55. (Courtesy of the Berry family.)

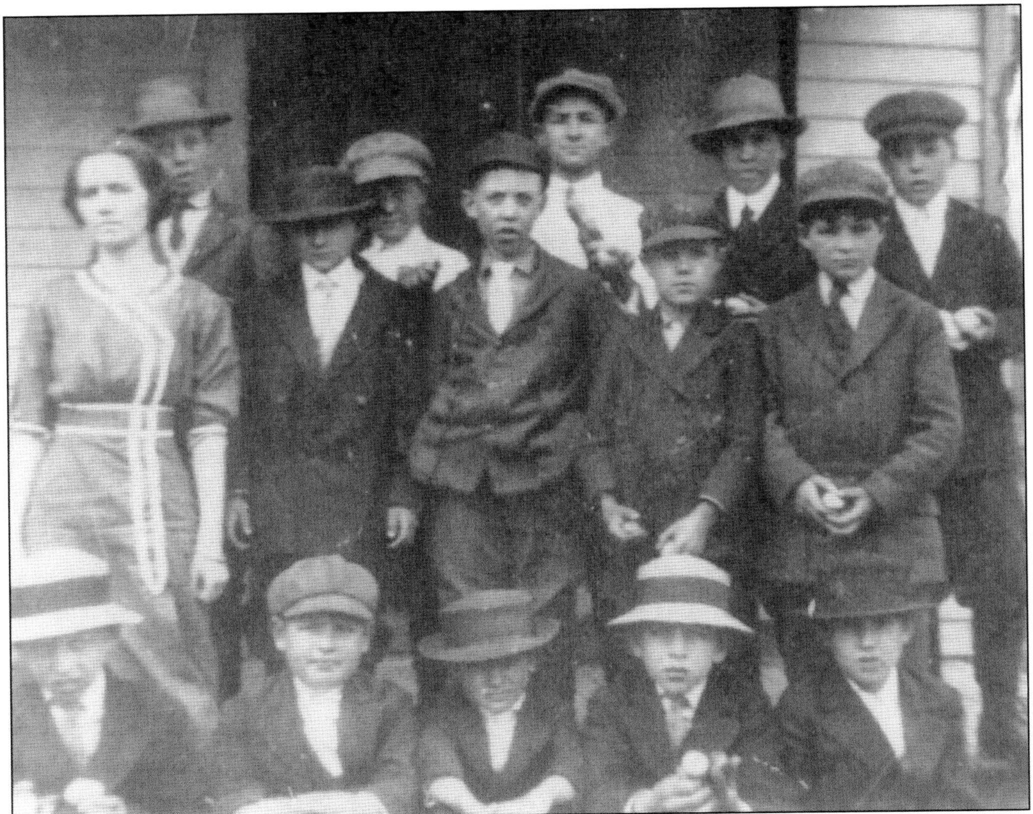

Members of a Mount Olive Baptist Church Sunday school Easter egg hunt pose for a photograph in 1912 with some of the boys modestly displaying the eggs that they found. (Courtesy of the Berry family.)

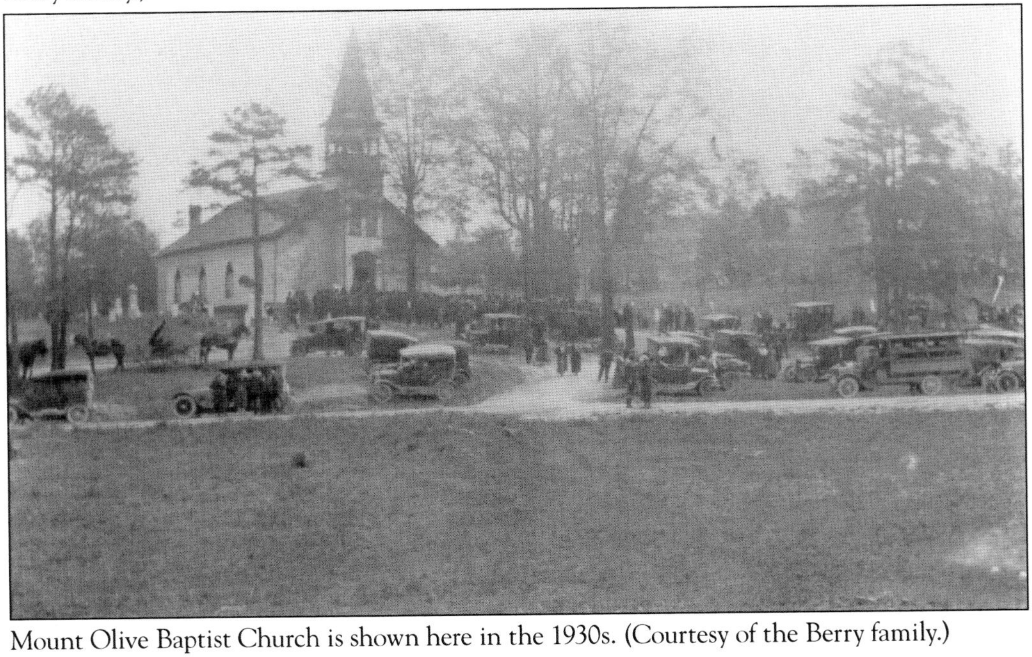

Mount Olive Baptist Church is shown here in the 1930s. (Courtesy of the Berry family.)

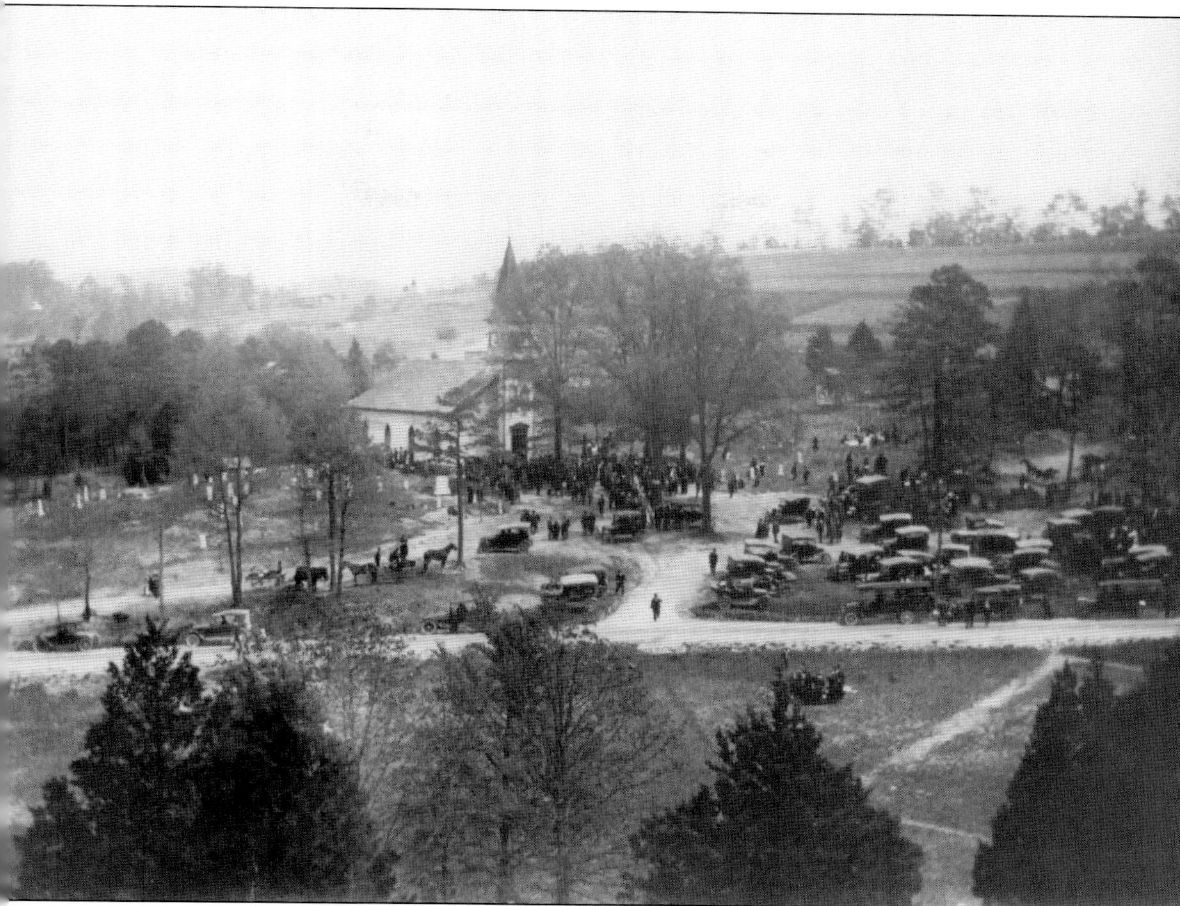

The survivors of the *Sultana* sinking, one of the worst maritime disasters in US history, continued to meet until their deaths. This is one of the meetings held at Mount Olive Baptist Church. (Courtesy of the Berry family.)

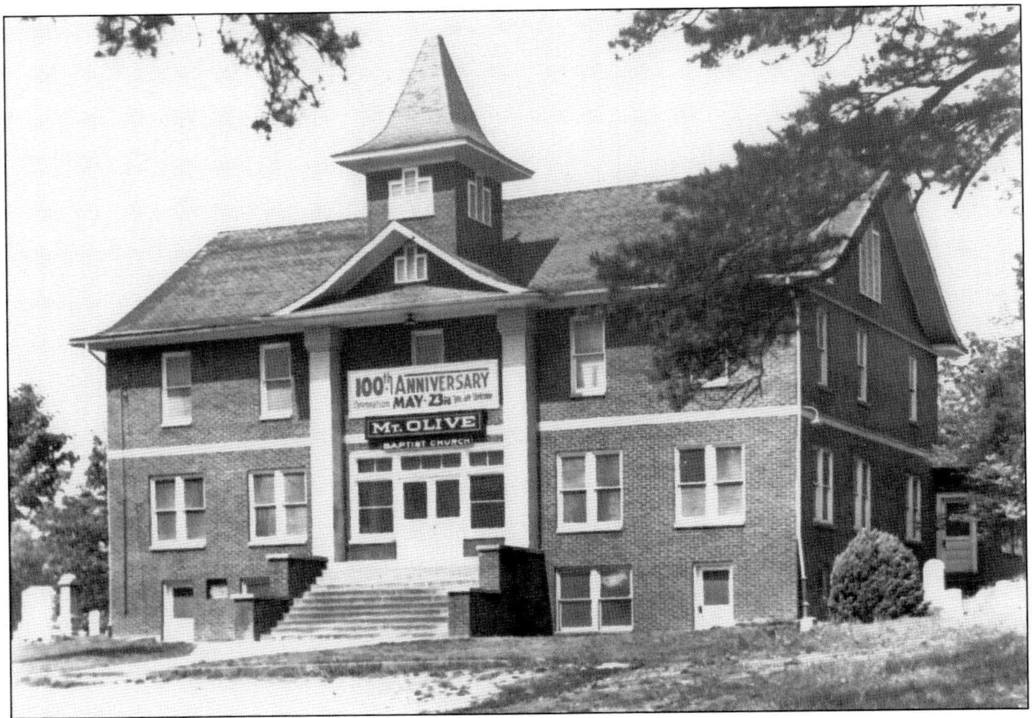

Mount Olive Baptist Church celebrated its 100th anniversary in 1937. (Courtesy of the Berry family.)

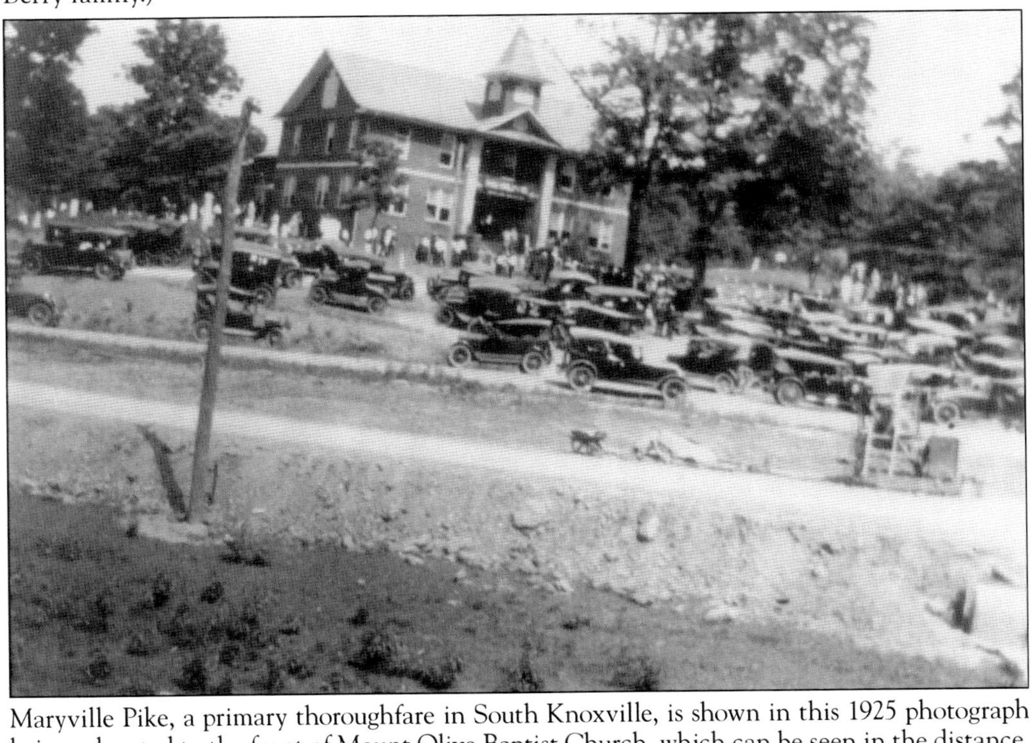

Maryville Pike, a primary thoroughfare in South Knoxville, is shown in this 1925 photograph being relocated to the front of Mount Olive Baptist Church, which can be seen in the distance. (Courtesy of the Berry family.)

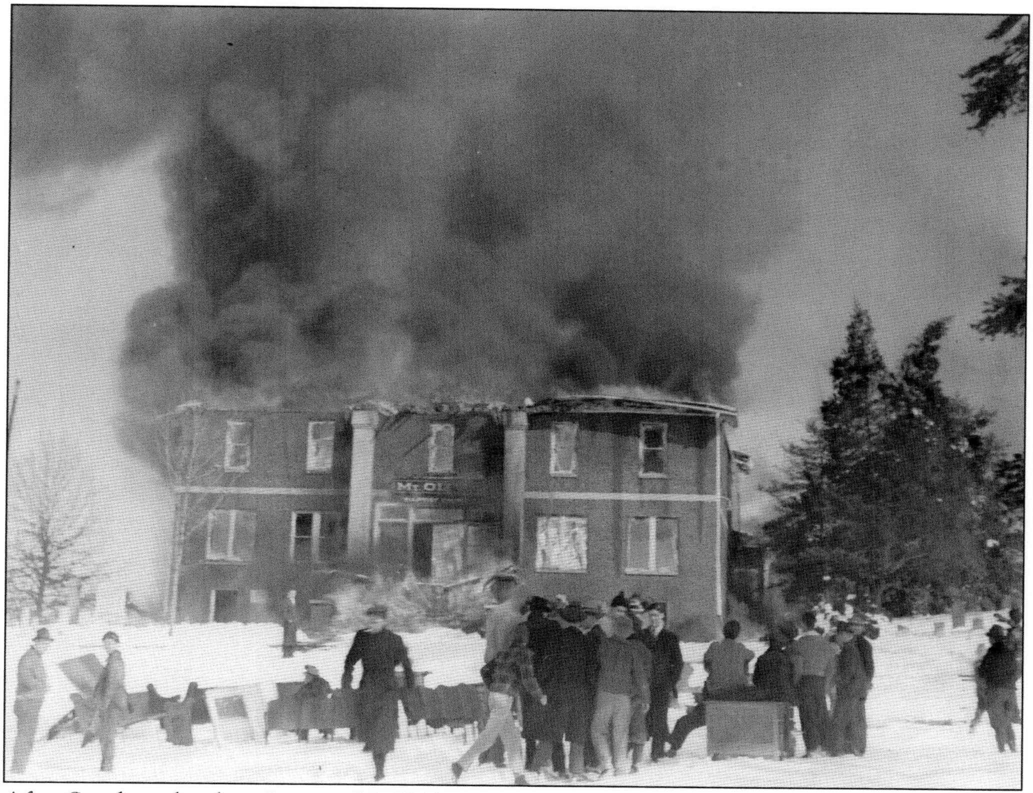

After Sunday school on January 28, 1940, Mount Olive Baptist Church caught fire and was totally destroyed. Members could only stand and watch as their sanctuary tragically burned. Many later recalled that the weather that day was one of the coldest in a long time, with a temperature of eight degrees below zero and eight inches of snow on the ground. (Courtesy of the Berry family.)

JANUARY 28, 1940
CHURCH MINUTES STATE
" THIS WAS THE COLDEST DAY IN YEARS, 8° DEGREES BELOW ZERO, AND ABOUT 100 GATHERED FOR SUNDAY SCHOOL AT THE CLOSE OF SUNDAY SCHOOL, OUR CHURCH CAUGHT FIRE AND COMPLETELY BURNED UP. THE LOSS WAS OVER 30,000 AND HAD 10,000 INSURANCE. PLANS ARE BEING MADE TO BUILD ANOTHER CHURCH. A LARGE PORTION OF THE FURNITURE WAS SAVED. THE ELECTRIC ORGAN WAS SAVED FROM THE FIRE."

THE CHURCH MET IN THE SCHOOL, ACROSS MARYVILLE HIGHWAY, WHILE A NEW CHURCH WAS BEING BUILT.

An excerpt from church minutes regarding the 1940 fire is shown here. It is compelling to see both the sadness and the hope and determination contained in the short note. (Courtesy of the Berry family.)

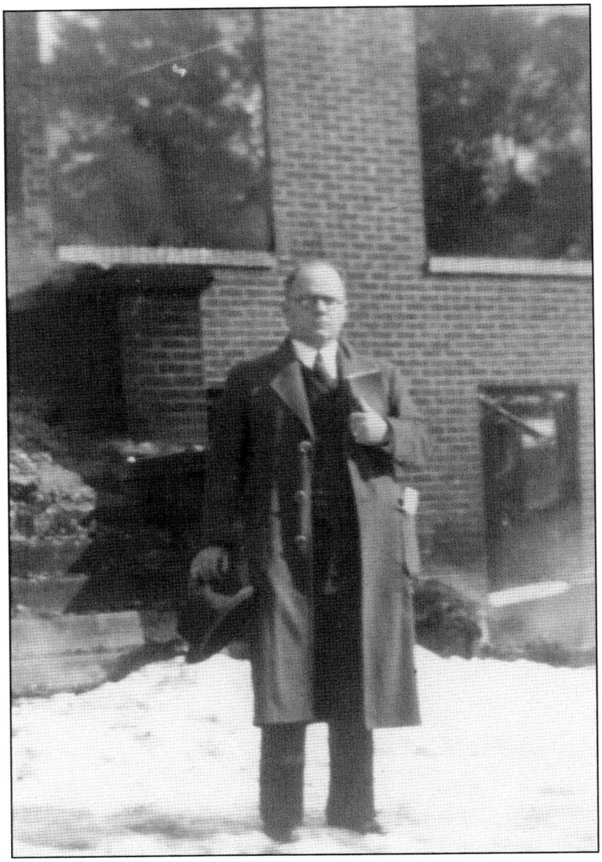

Reverend Grigsby, pastor of Mount Olive Baptist Church, is shown in this 1941 photograph. (Courtesy of the Berry family.)

After the fire, church members began the process of rebuilding Mount Olive Baptist Church. Mount Olive Elementary School allowed the church to hold services in their facility across the street for a period of one year while the building was constructed. The cornerstone for the building was laid on August 30, 1940. (Courtesy of the Berry family.)

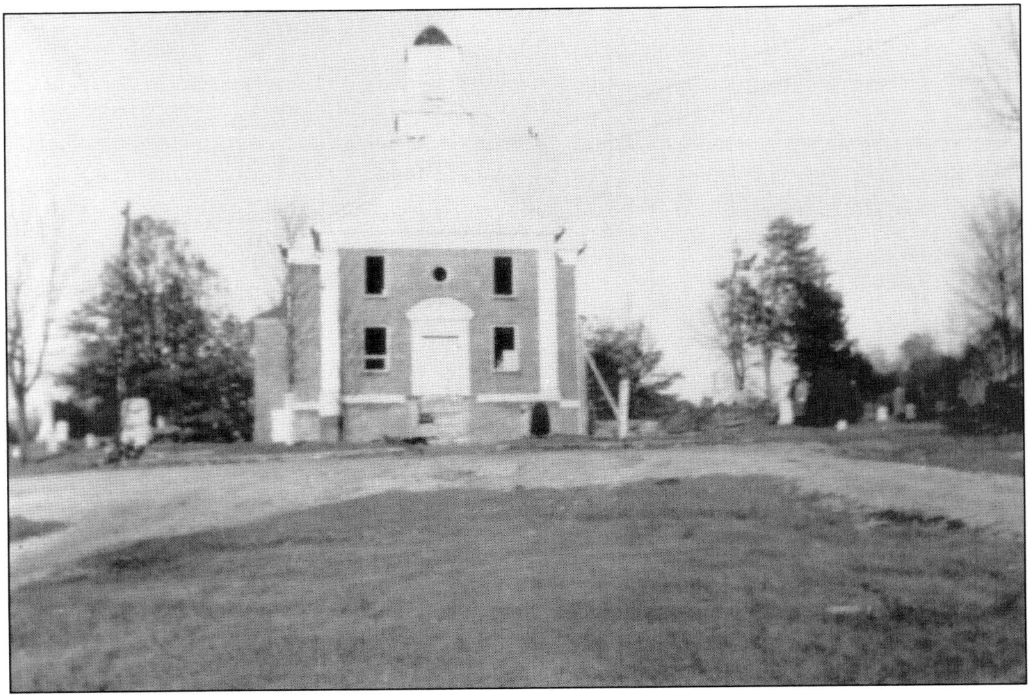

This image was taken after the completion of the fourth and current building of Mount Olive Baptist Church after the devastating fire consumed the previous building. The first service was held in this building on January 8, 1941. (Courtesy of the Berry family.)

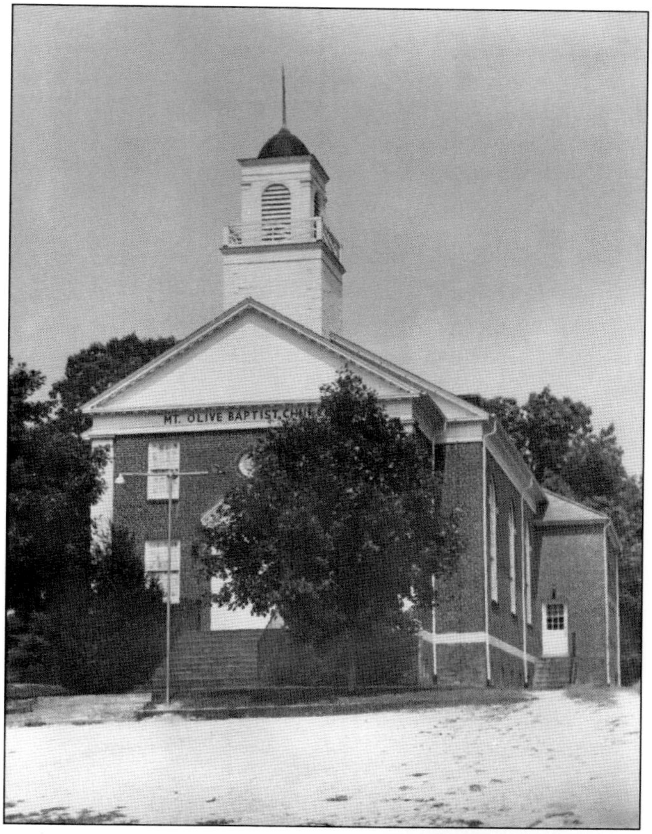

Vestal United Methodist Church is seen in this 1940s photograph. Vestal United Methodist was founded in 1875, and for the first three years, services were held in Flenniken School. The church was initially known as Jones Chapel, but the name was changed to Vestal United Methodist shortly after its current facility, seen here, was erected in 1925. (Courtesy of Knox County Two Centuries Photograph Project, McClung Historical Collection.)

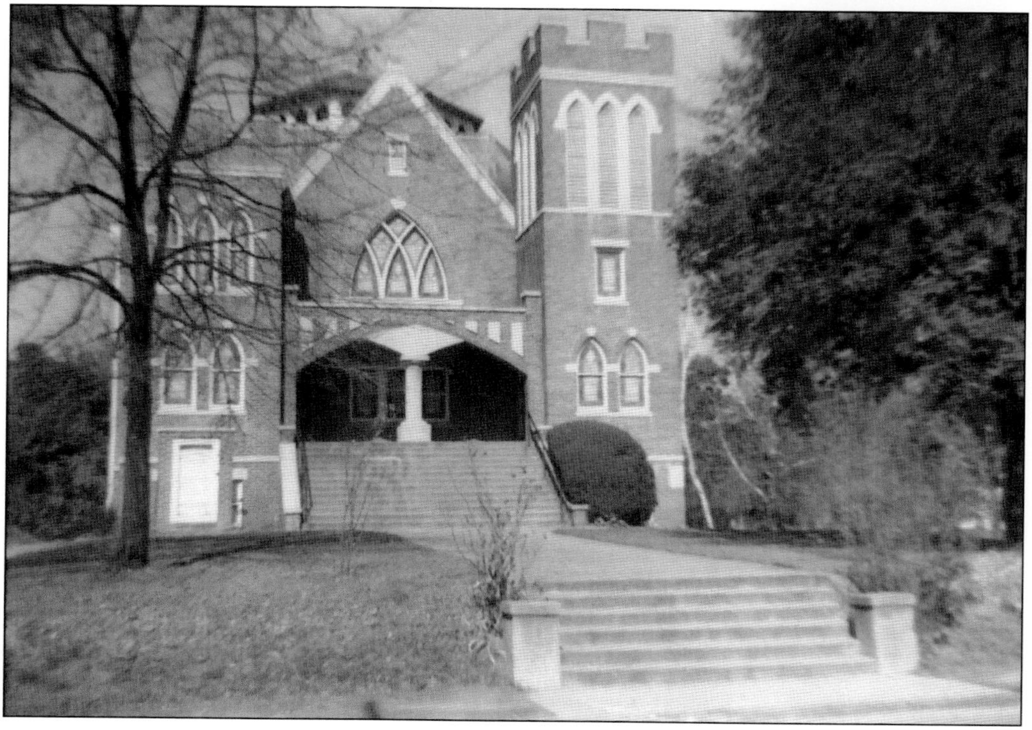

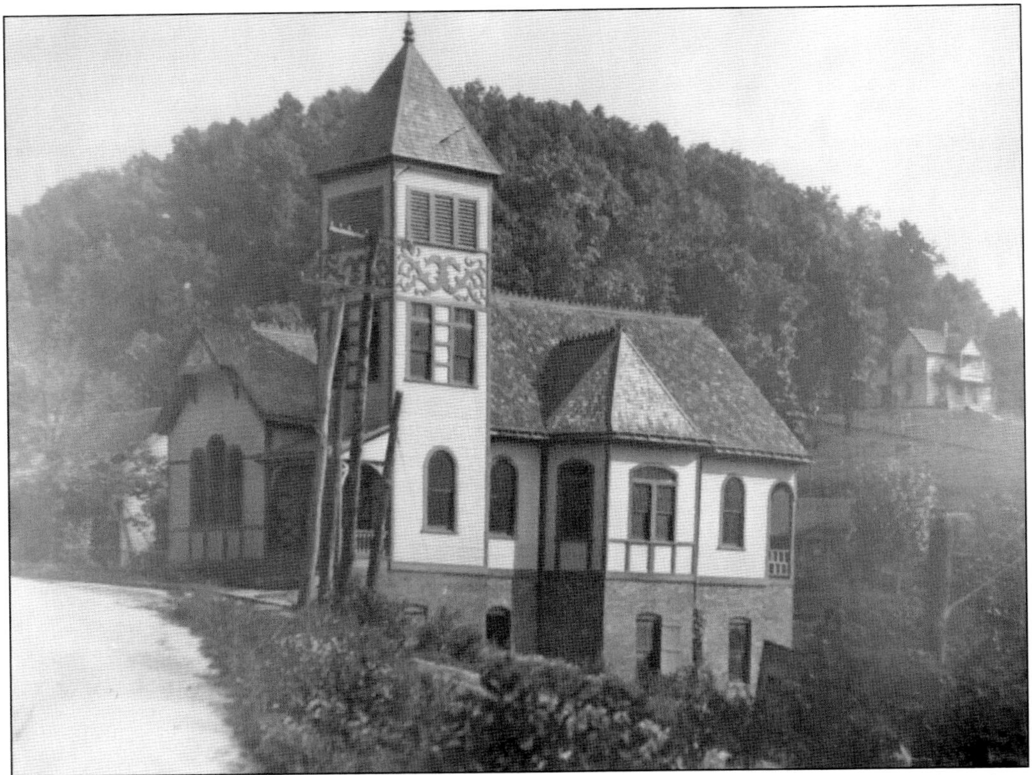

The South Knoxville Presbyterian Church on Martin Mill Pike (now Chapman Highway), is shown in 1890 near the current site of Kern's Bakery on Chapman Highway. The house on the right belonged to C.B. Gossett. (Courtesy of Knox County Two Centuries Photograph Project, McClung Historical Collection.)

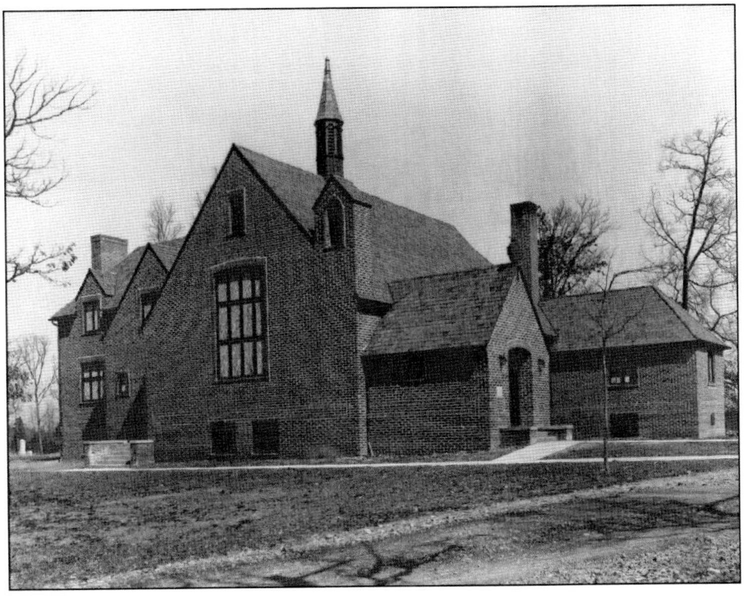

The New Prospect Presbyterian Church on Sevierville Pike in South Knoxville is shown. The church burned in 2005. (Courtesy of Thompson Photograph Collection, McClung Historical Collection.)

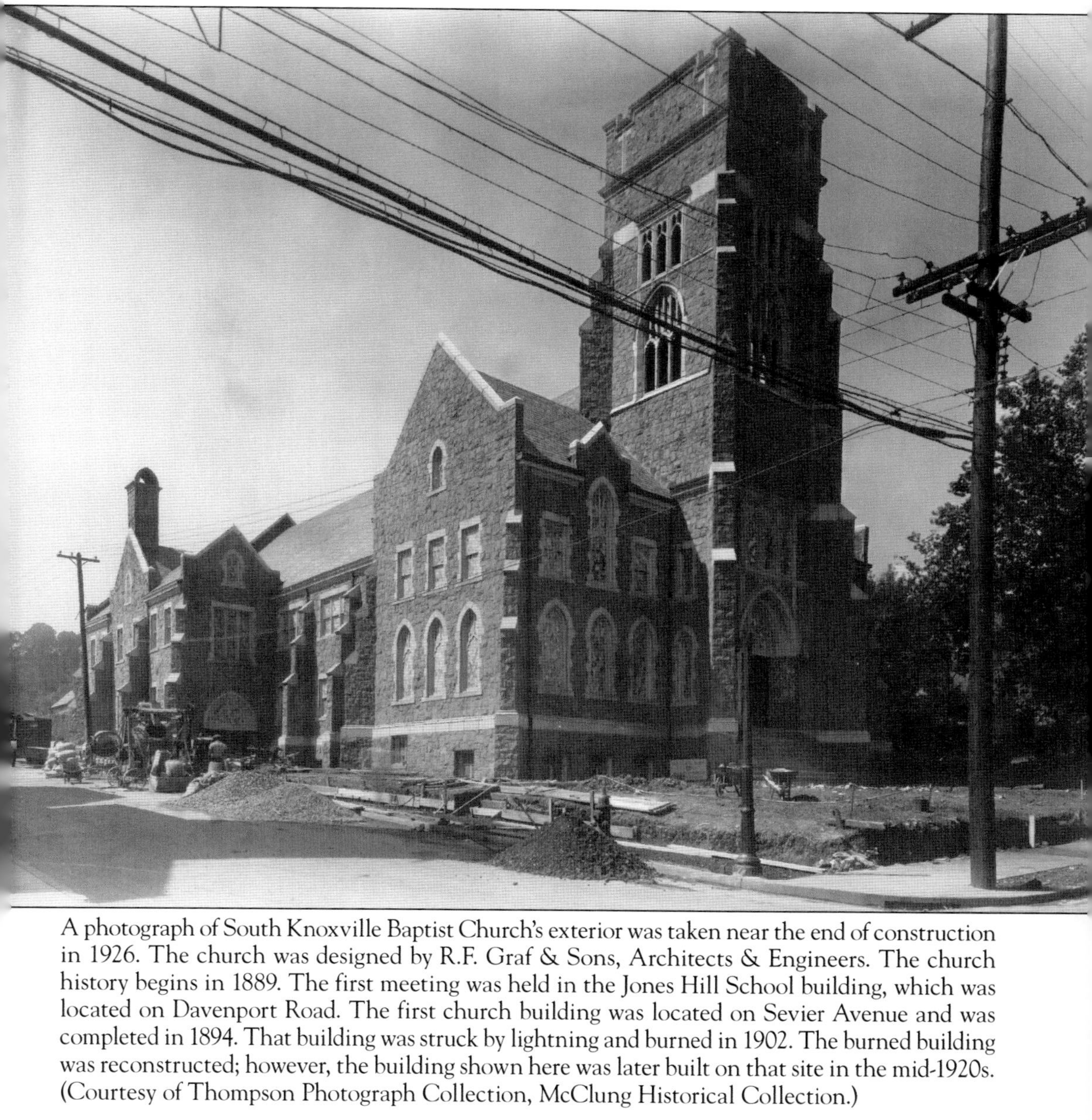

A photograph of South Knoxville Baptist Church's exterior was taken near the end of construction in 1926. The church was designed by R.F. Graf & Sons, Architects & Engineers. The church history begins in 1889. The first meeting was held in the Jones Hill School building, which was located on Davenport Road. The first church building was located on Sevier Avenue and was completed in 1894. That building was struck by lightning and burned in 1902. The burned building was reconstructed; however, the building shown here was later built on that site in the mid-1920s. (Courtesy of Thompson Photograph Collection, McClung Historical Collection.)

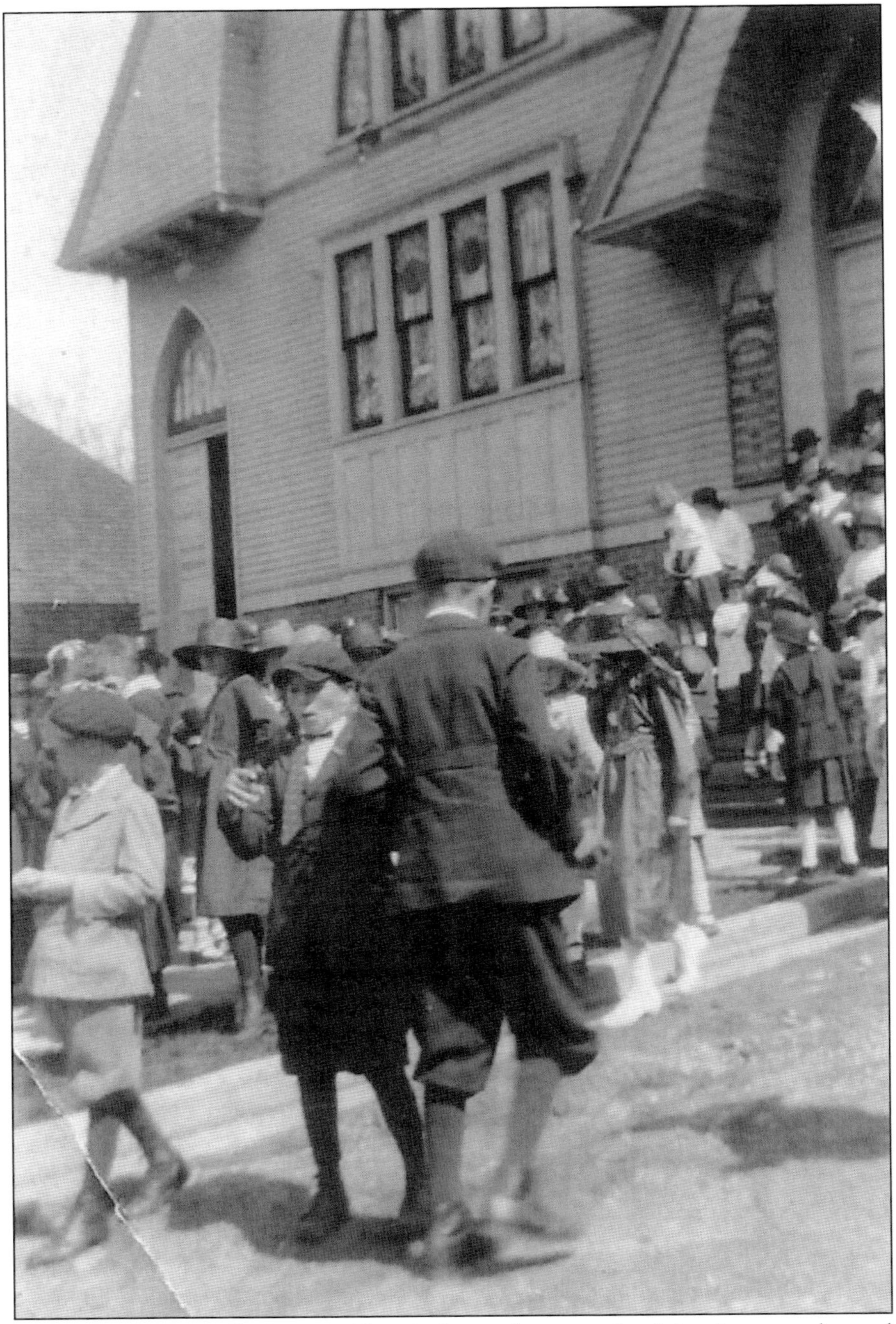

Members of South Knoxville Baptist Church, located just south of the river, are shown leaving a morning service. The building shown here housed the congregation from 1902 until 1927. (Courtesy of the Berry family.)

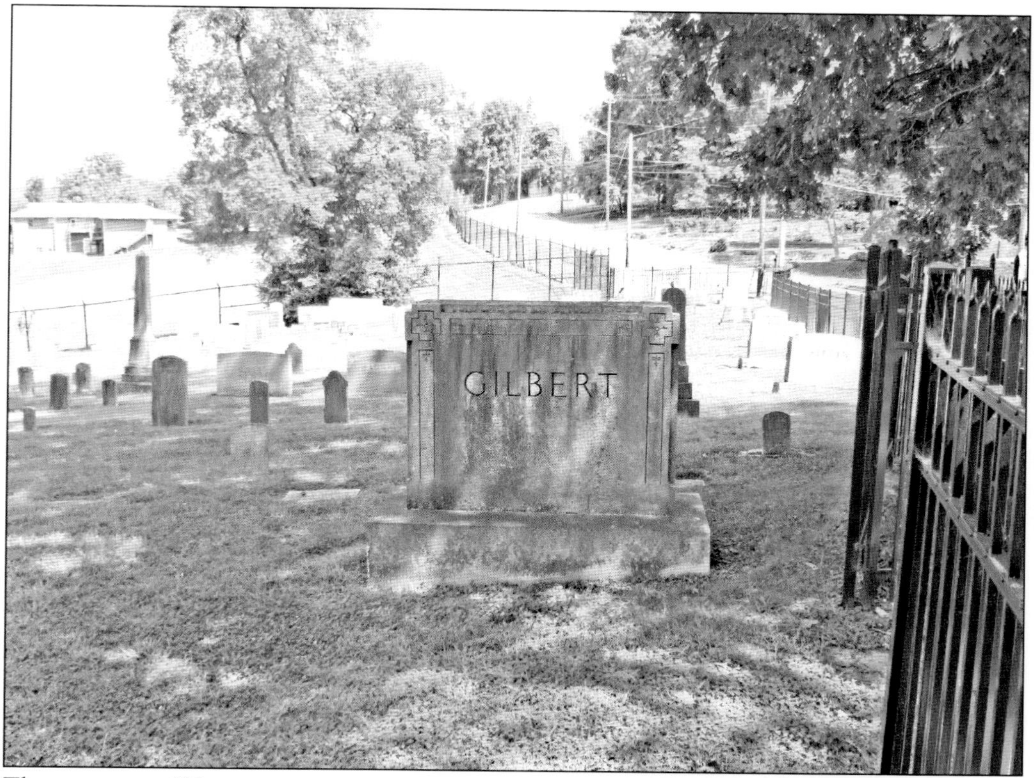

There are over 400 graves at the Island Home Baptist Church Cemetery. Some notable graves include that of Mr. Pally Anderson, who was awarded the Pulitzer Prize for Journalism in 1929, and famed World War II pilot Lt. James D. Gilbert. Lieutenant Gilbert was originally buried on the island of Guam; however, his remains were later found and re-interred at Island Home Baptist Church Cemetery. (Courtesy of Island Home Baptist Church.)

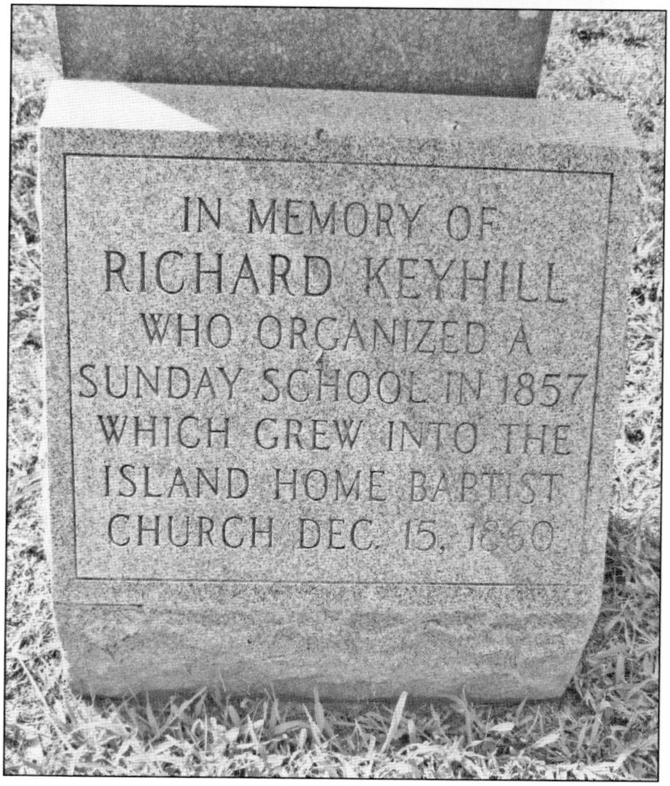

A monument on Island Home Baptist Church property was dedicated to founder Richard Keyhill. (Courtesy of Island Home Baptist Church.)

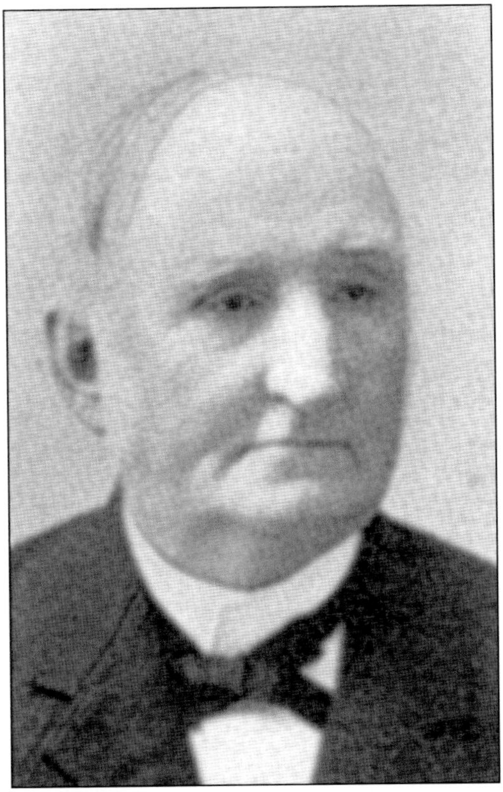

Col. Perez Dickinson was an integral part of the history of South Knoxville, having an estate called Island Home. In 1878, the church that would become Island Home Baptist Church (then called Holston Baptist Church) needed additional space to build. Colonel Dickinson agreed to donate a few acres to the church and the name was changed to Island Home Baptist Church. (Courtesy of Island Home Baptist Church.)

Richard Keyhill and his wife established a Sunday school class in a log structure in 1857 for those living just south of Knoxville in the Cedar Hill community. This Sunday school flourished and grew to become Island Home Baptist Church. (Courtesy of Island Home Baptist Church.)

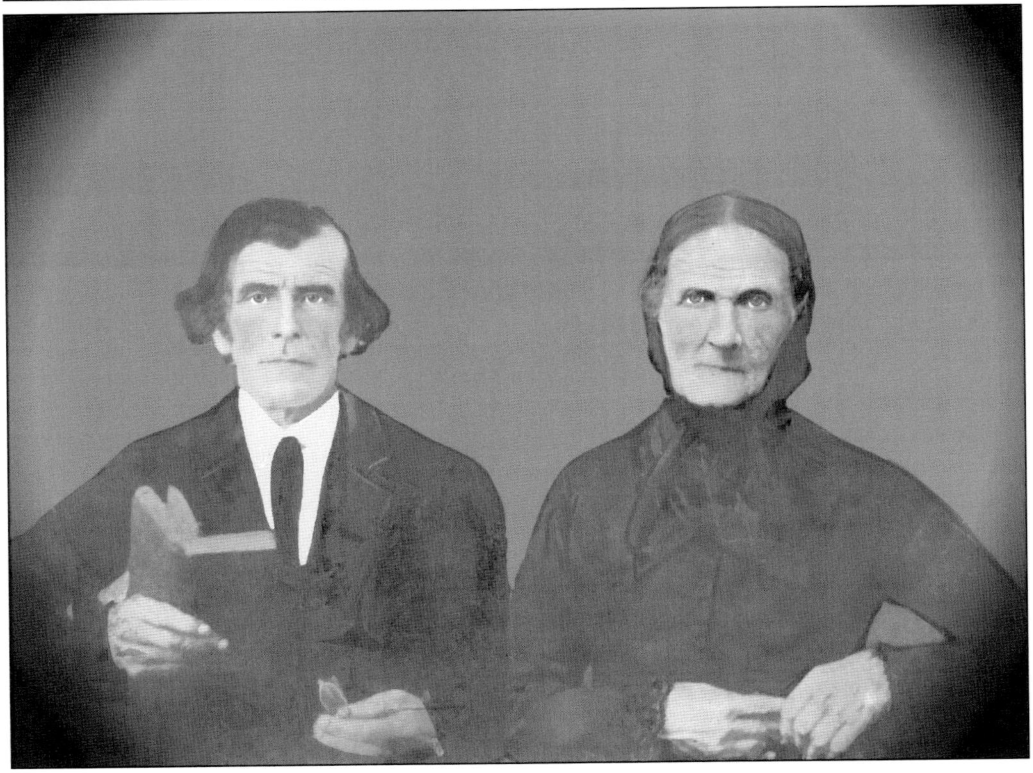

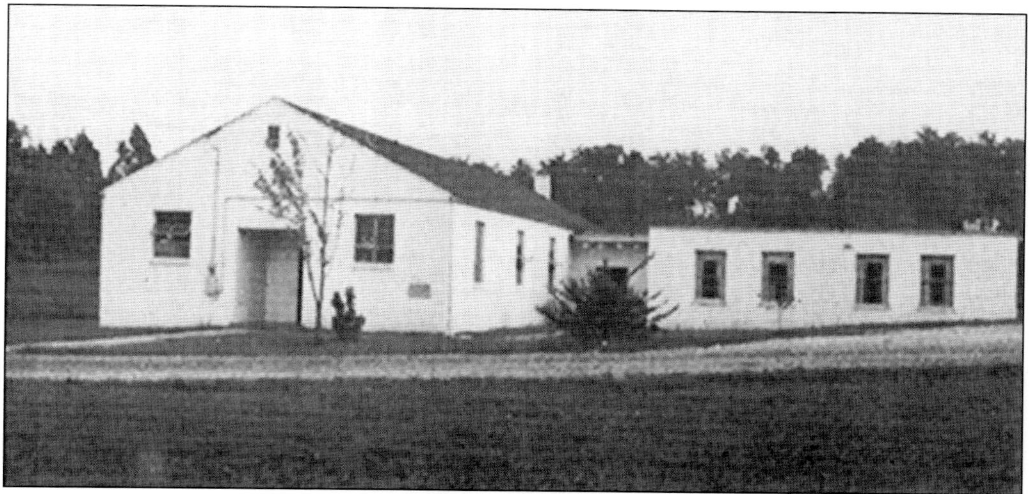

In the 1950s, Island Home Baptist Church purchased land in the Meades Quarry area to establish a mission church. On September 9, 1956, the Meadow View Baptist Church (above) was dedicated with 99 charter members. (Courtesy of Island Home Baptist Church.)

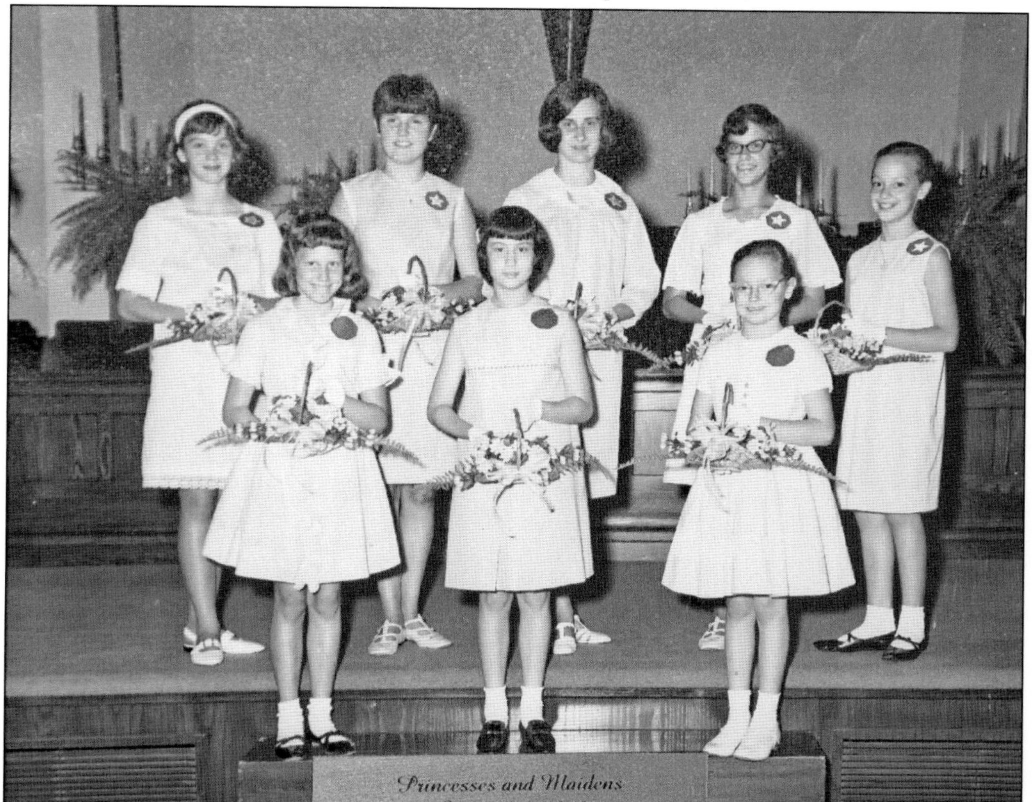

The Girls Auxiliary at Island Home Baptist Church began as the Young Ladies Missionary Society in 1904. After completion of a challenging curriculum of Bible study, personal research, and presentation known as the Forward Steps, a young lady could achieve certain ranks that reflected court titles at a coronation service. This image shows girls receiving the rank of queen at a coronation service in 1963. (Courtesy of Island Home Baptist Church.)

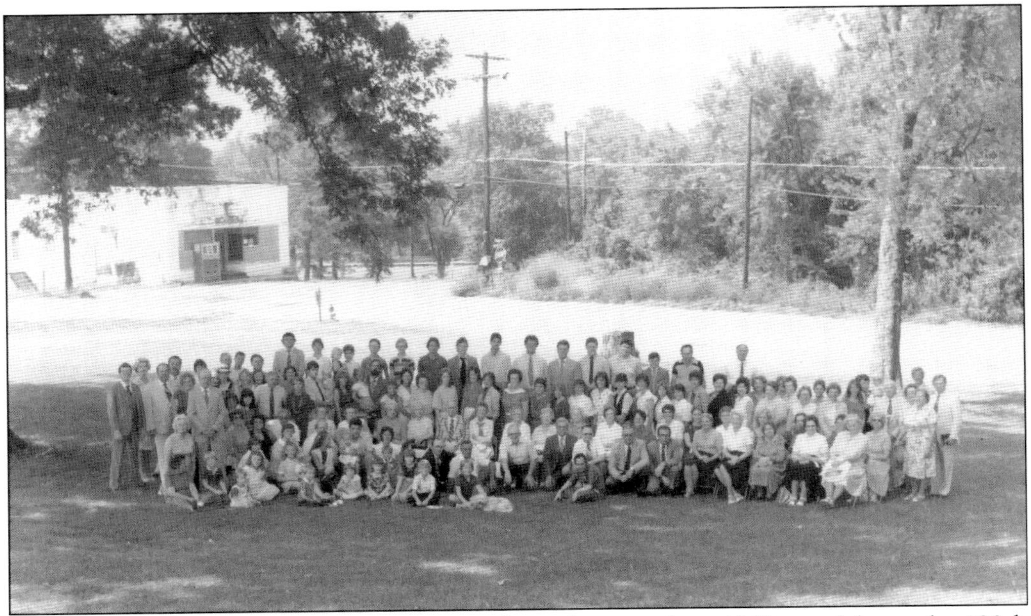

Island Home Baptist Church members pose for a photograph in 1960 to celebrate the 100th anniversary of the founding of the church. (Courtesy of Island Home Baptist Church.)

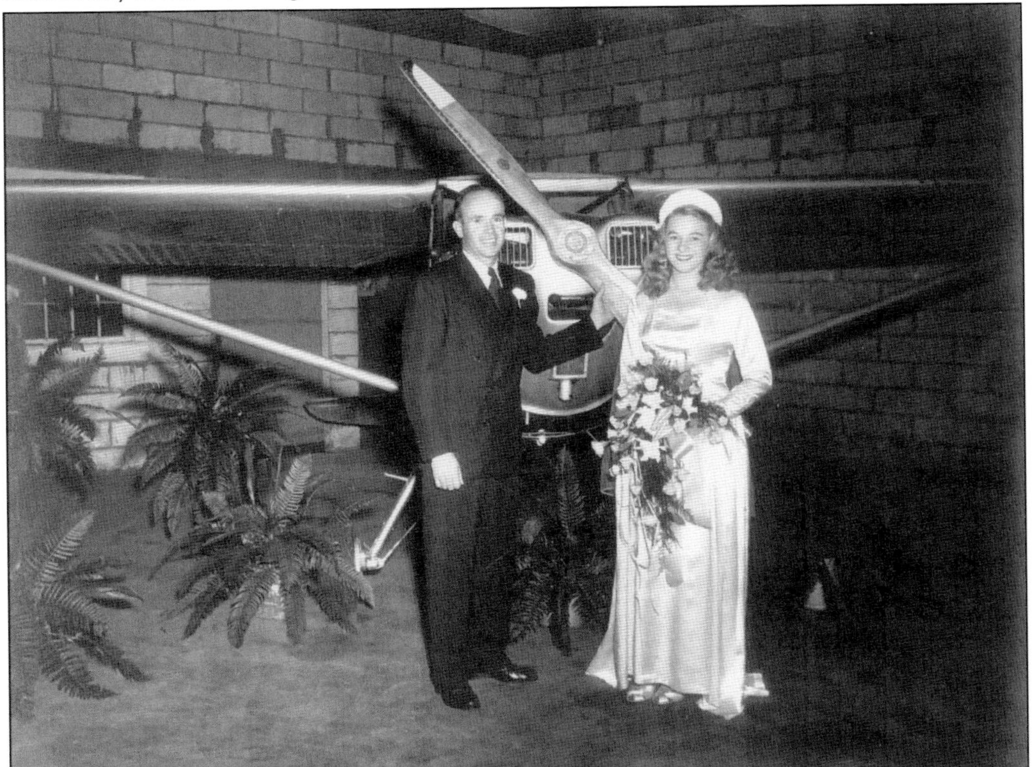

Church members Ora Wattenbarger and Fred Kautz married in the hangar at Island Home Airport in 1947. The Downtown Island Airport is still in operation, serving the South Knoxville community. (Courtesy of Island Home Baptist Church.)

In 1860, 13 members of a Sunday school led by Richard Keyhill met four miles south of Knoxville and decided to form a church. Four of these 13 charter members who formed the Cedar Ridge Baptist Church (later Island Home Baptist Church) are shown here. (Courtesy of Island Home Baptist Church.)

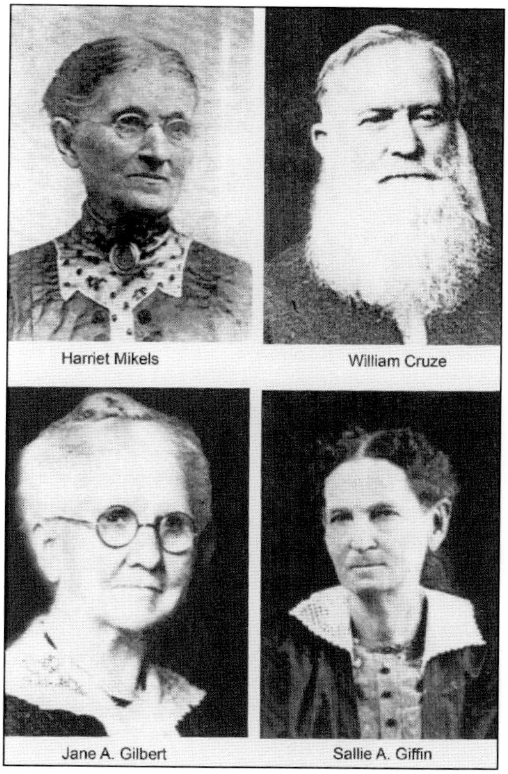

This is one of the many beautiful stained glass windows located throughout the sanctuary and church—stunning treasures that have always provided light and warmth to the people. (Courtesy of Island Home Baptist Church.)

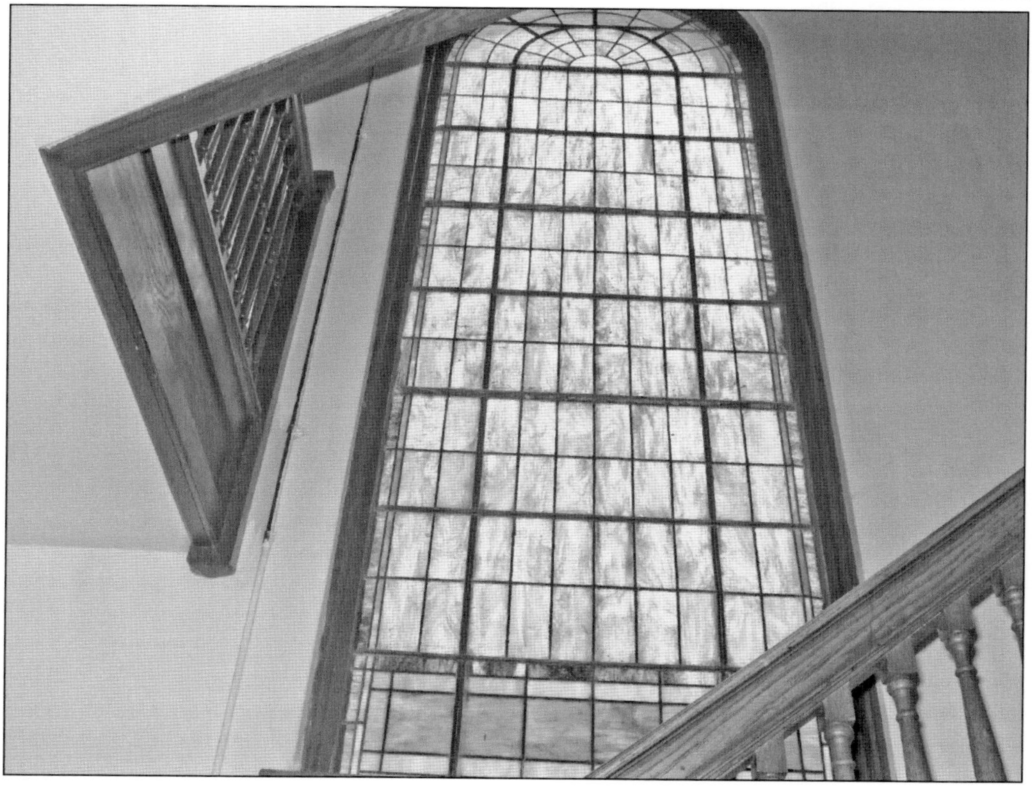

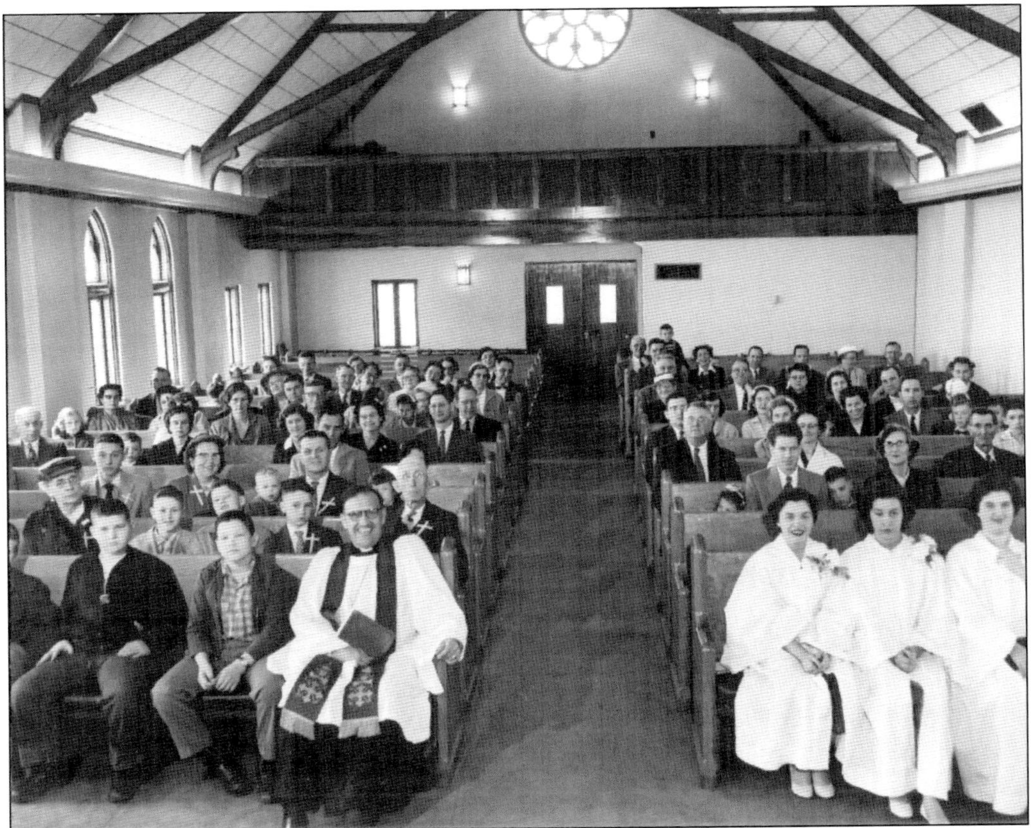

This is a photograph of Gloria Dei Lutheran Church from March 25, 1956. The pastor in the front row is Rev. Gerald North, who organized Gloria Dei. This image celebrated a few early milestones for the congregation: Palm Sunday, Confirmation Sunday (the three young ladies in the front row dressed in white robes would be affirming their faith), and the congregation's date of charter. (Courtesy of the archive collection of Gloria Dei Lutheran Church.)

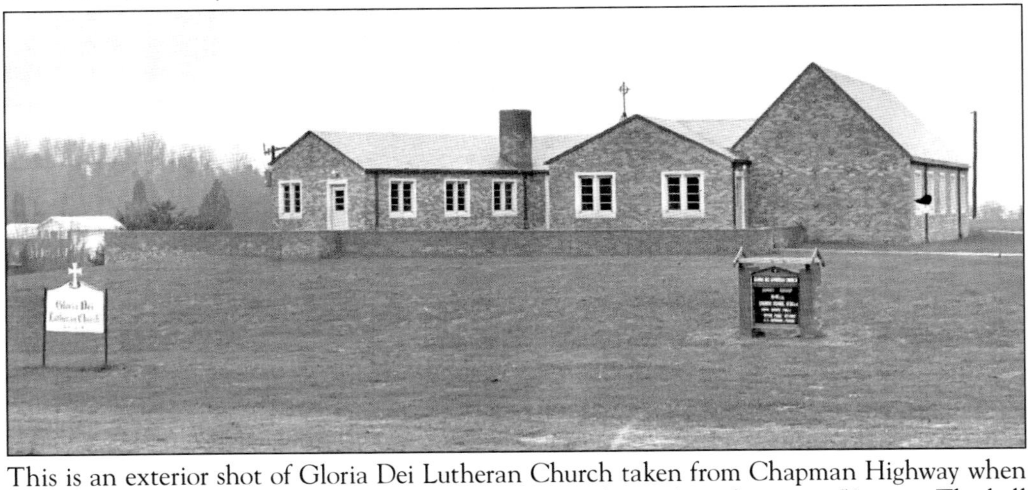

This is an exterior shot of Gloria Dei Lutheran Church taken from Chapman Highway when the church was first built in 1961. The building hasn't changed much in over 50 years. The bell tower, a new roof, and several trees were added; otherwise, it's much the same today. (Courtesy of the archive collection of Gloria Dei Lutheran Church.)

Six

Recreation

Recreation has been an important part of the City of Knoxville from its founding. Recreation in South Knoxville began to truly develop when Col. Perez Dickinson established his Island Home in the late 1800s.

This tradition was further expounded upon when visionaries Harry and Alice Ijams purchased 20 acres of land in South Knoxville in 1910. The land later became a center of nature-related activities, as well as the local Girl Scouts, and eventually a public nature park called Ijams Nature Center.

Upon the establishment of the Great Smoky Mountains National Park in 1941, South Knoxville played an instrumental role as the gateway to the park, with Chapman Highway running directly through South Knoxville.

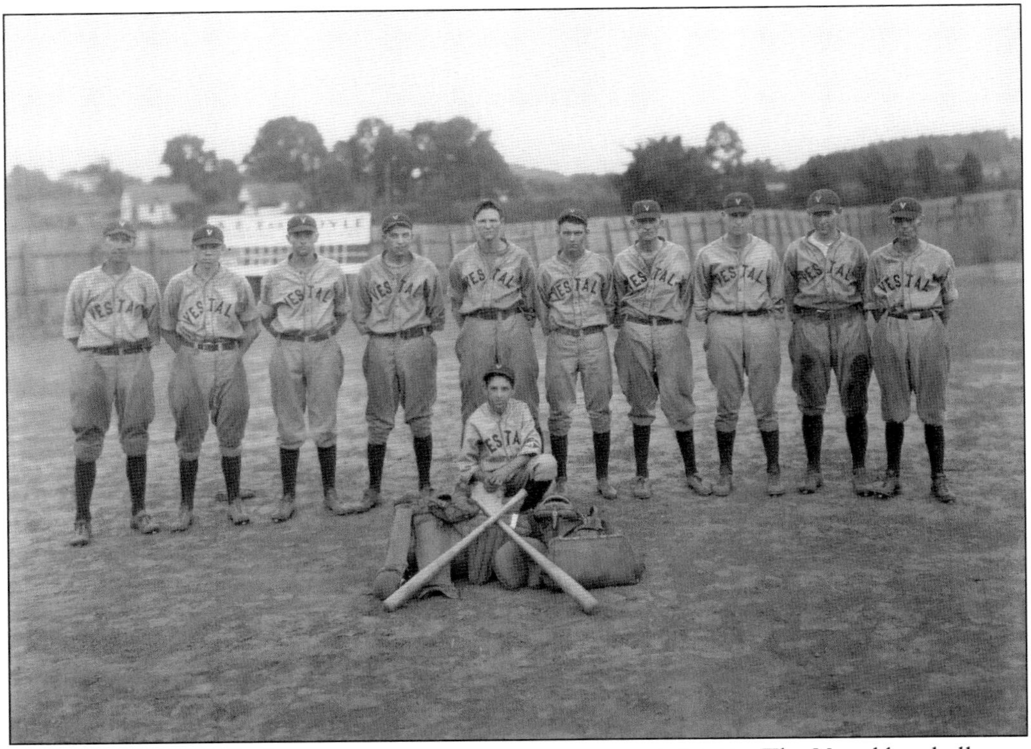

The Vestal baseball team is shown in the 1910s. (Courtesy of Thompson Photograph Collection, McClung Historical Collection.)

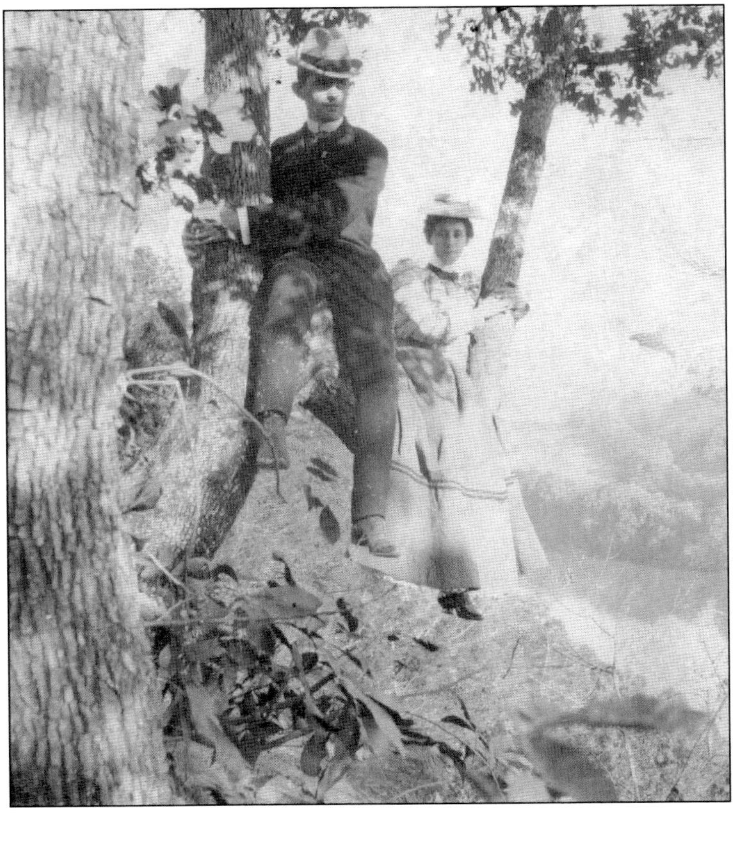

In 1910, Harry and Alice Ijams purchased 20 acres of land overlooking the Tennessee River. The property, formerly part of Perez Dickinson's Island Home estate, soon became a natural haven for a growing family and later Girl Scouts, bird watchers, and ultimately nature lovers. This c. 1905 photograph was taken overlooking Dickinson Island around the time that the couple were married. (Courtesy of Ijams family collection.)

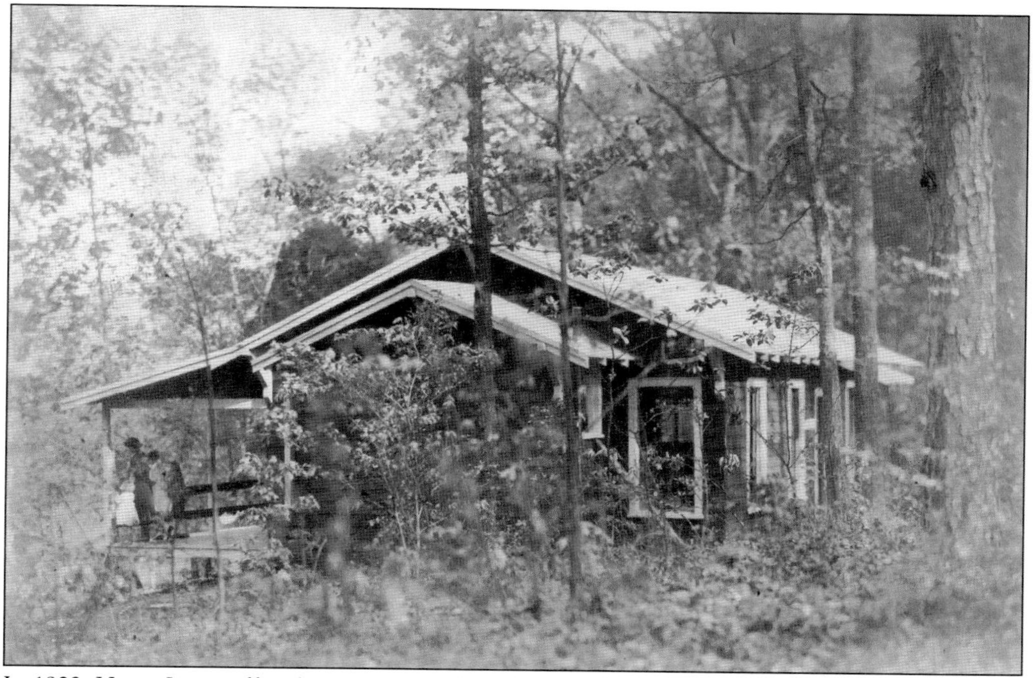

In 1922, Harry Ijams offered space on the Ijams farm to the East Tennessee Audubon Society to build a member's clubhouse in return for protecting a bird habitat, resulting in a loss of a 1,000-acre preserve dubbed by the *Knoxville Sunday Journal* as the "city of birds." The building itself was named the Magnolia Woodward Lodge in honor of the lady who is credited with making the state of Tennessee's first Christmas bird count in 1902. (Courtesy of Jane Crouch Williams.)

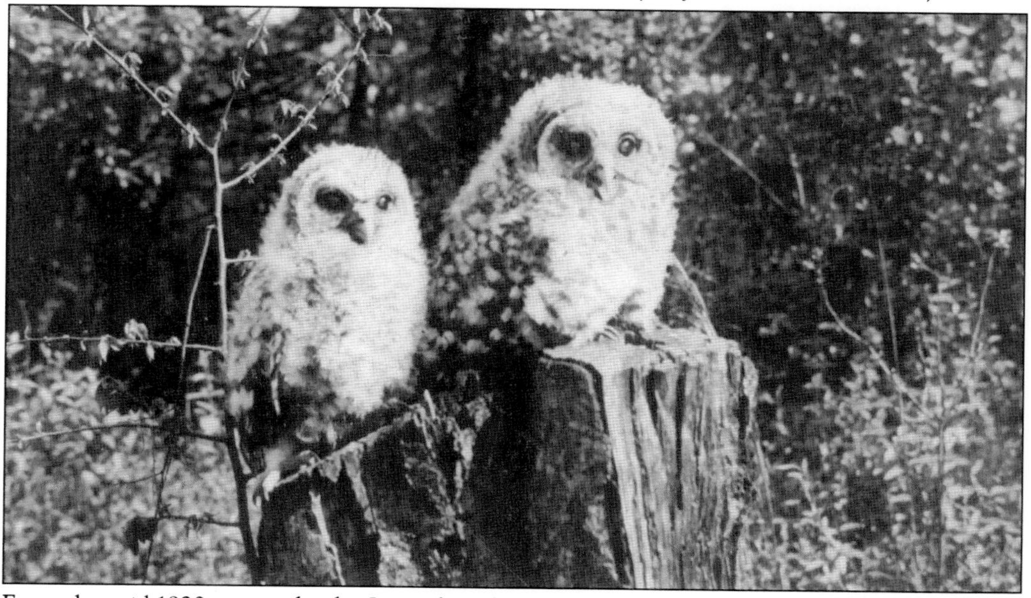

From the mid-1920s onwards, the Ijams farm became known as the bird sanctuary. In addition to East Tennessee Audubon Society activities, a new splinter group, led by Harry Ijams, formed the East Tennessee Ornithological Society to focus more on nature study. Injured birds were regularly brought to Ijams for rehabilitation, including this pair of barred owlets. (Courtesy of Ijams family collection.)

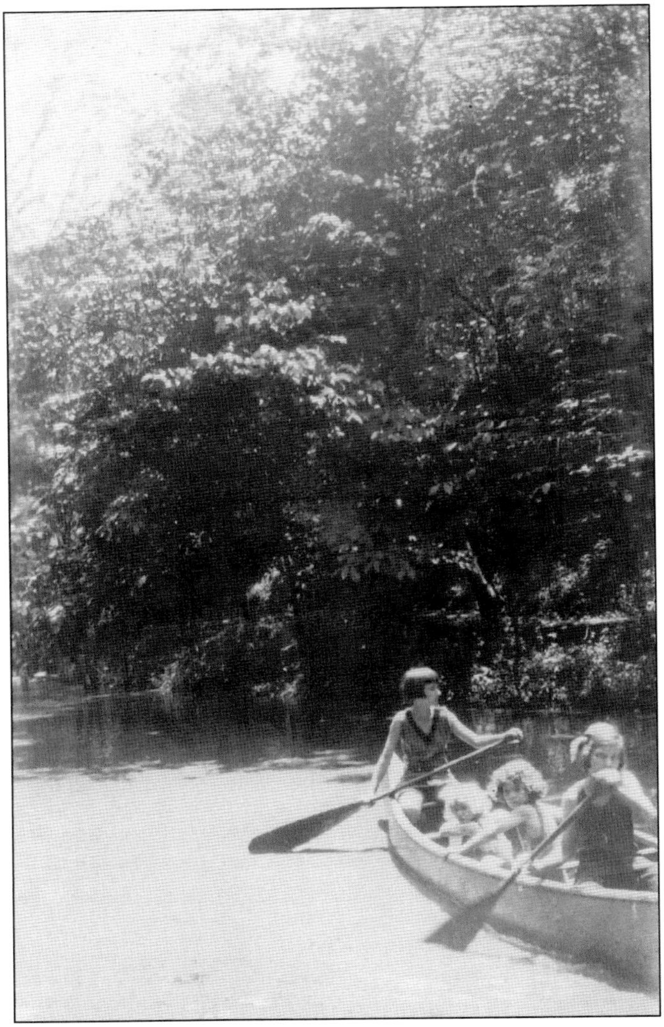

Harry and Alice Ijams raised four daughters to enjoy the outdoors as much as they did. In time, all of the girls became accomplished naturalists and Girl Scouts. Elizabeth, the eldest, became director of the Knoxville Girl Scout Council in 1929 and went on to spend her entire career with the national Girl Scout organization. (Courtesy of Ijams family collection.)

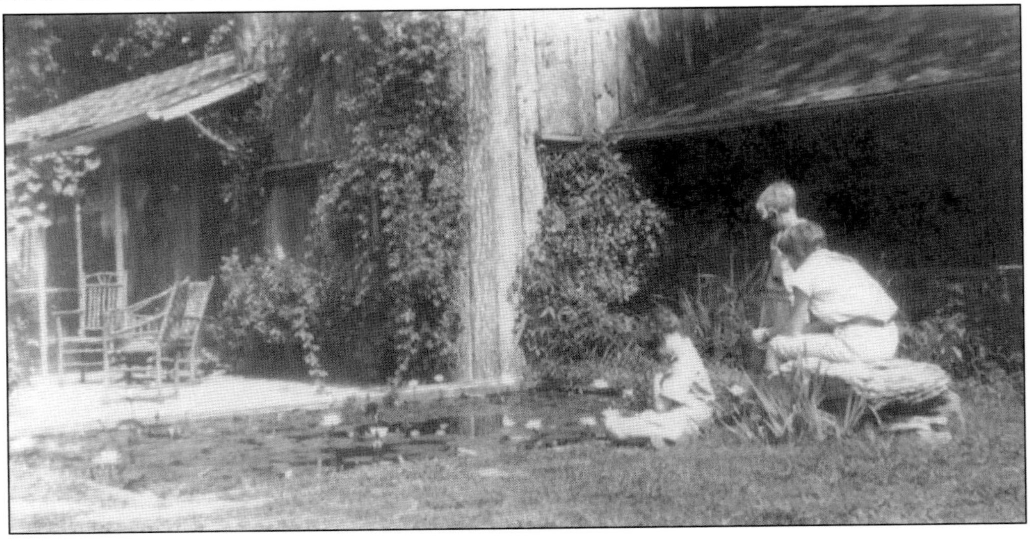

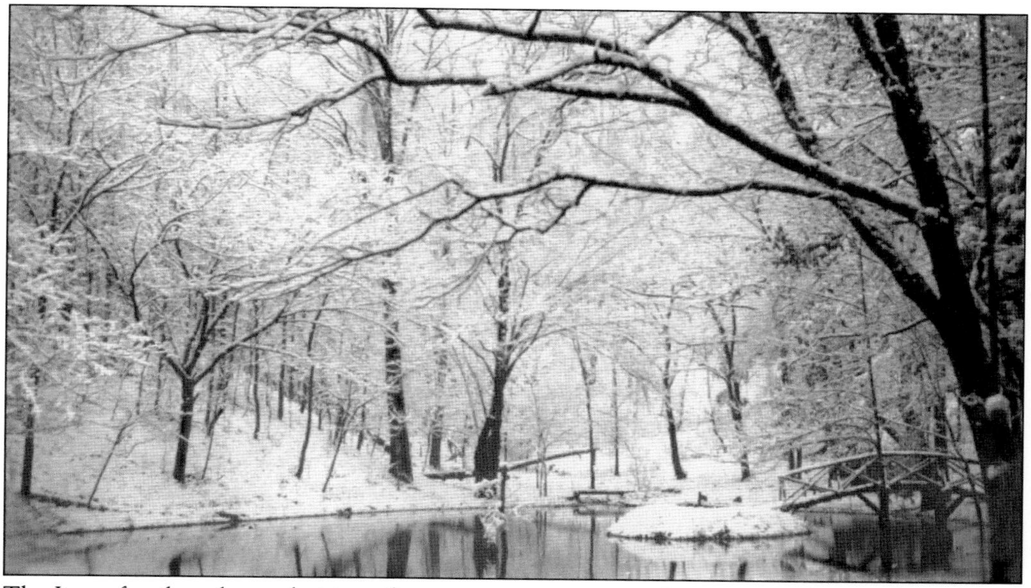

The Ijams family welcomed visitors from across town to visit their property long before the idea was born to make it a public nature park. During the 1930s, Egyptian Lotuses were planted extensively in the large pond and were regarded as one of Knoxville's natural sensations. The pond, still found along the Discovery Trail today at Ijams Nature Center, was originally created by Harry Ijams in 1922 for his daughters to swim in as opposed to the nearby river. (Courtesy of University of Tennessee Special Collections.)

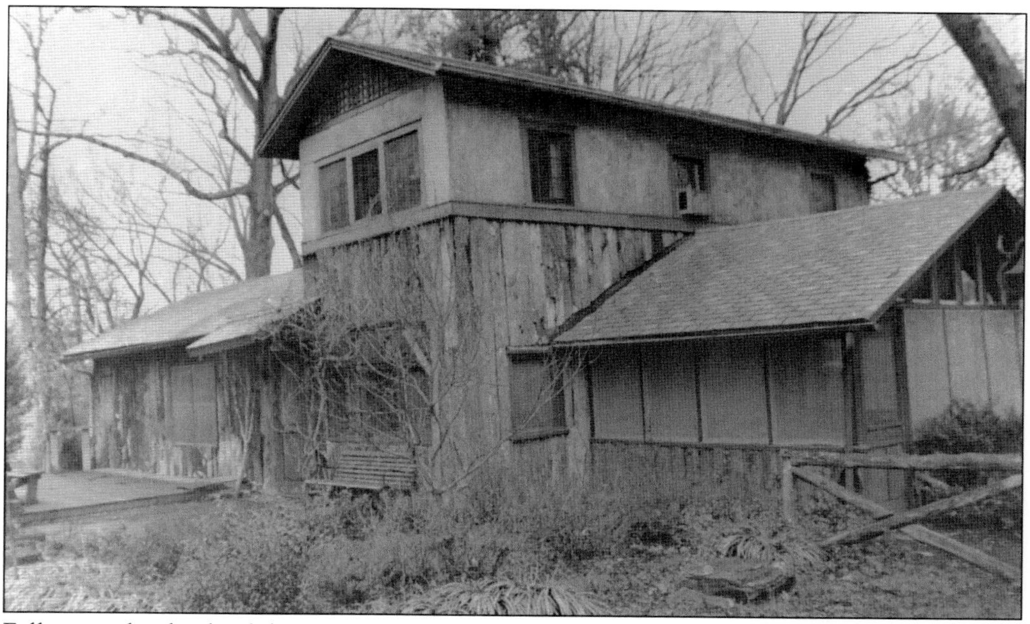

Following the death of their parents, the Ijams daughters decided to sell their family home to the City of Knoxville to become a public nature park. To help make the dream a reality, the Knoxville Garden Club and Knox County Council of Garden Clubs jointly engaged in raising funds to refresh the grounds and refurbish the Ijams house as a clubhouse. Following four years of hard work, Knoxville's new nature park was dedicated on the eve of the Dogwood Arts Festival in April 1968. (Courtesy of Ijams family collection.)

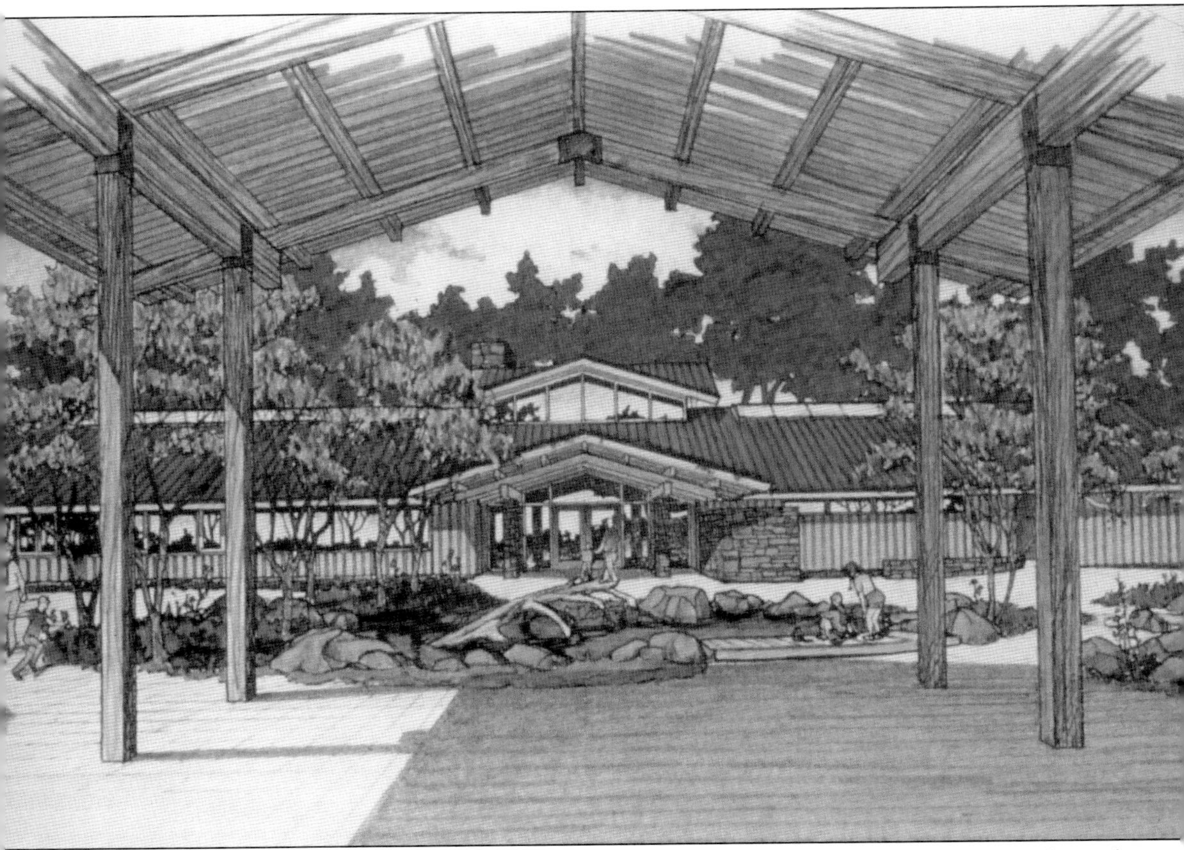

In 1976, Ijams Nature Center became formally established as a nonprofit organization charged with the mission of protecting the park. Along with maintaining the park as a wildlife sanctuary, the new organization began to steadily increase the number of environmental education offerings to school groups, Boy Scouts, and Girl Scouts, as well as the general public. A major capital campaign in the early 1990s allowed the park to swell to 80 acres, and a new environmentally conscious visitor center was designed by local architects McCarty, Holsaple, McCarty. It was opened in May 1997. (Courtesy of Ijams family collection.)

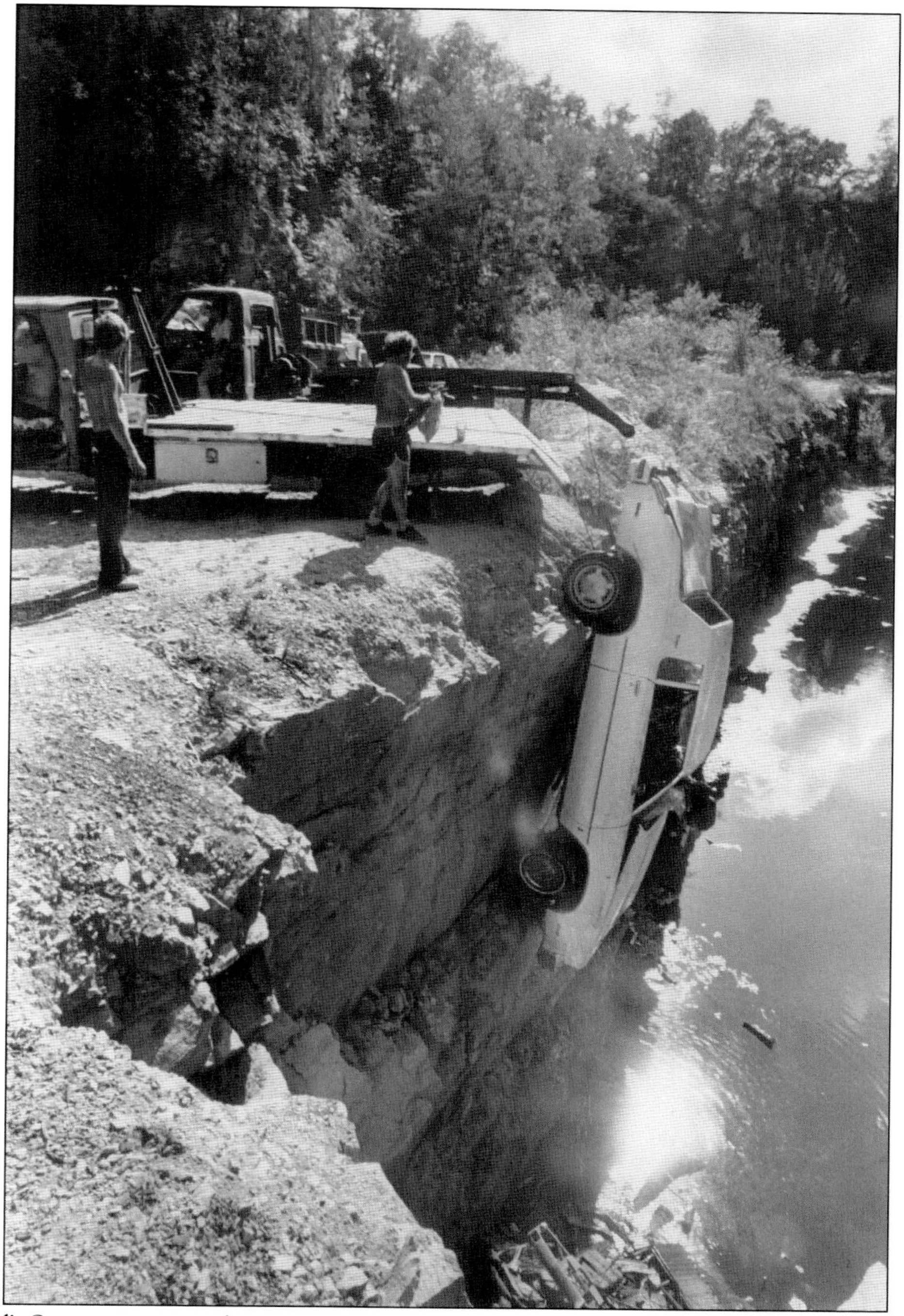

Mead's Quarry was once a burgeoning center extracting Tennessee marble for local and national buildings and monuments. Following the Great Depression, agricultural lime was produced there. Despite numerous efforts by South Knoxvilians to beautify the site for community benefit, it had become an illegal dump and eyesore since operations ceased in 1978. However, in 2001, Knox County purchased the property including the 25-acre lake, which was a common place to illegally dump trash and industrial waste. Here, a 1986 Buick Regal is hauled out during a community cleanup. (Courtesy of Ijams Nature Center.)

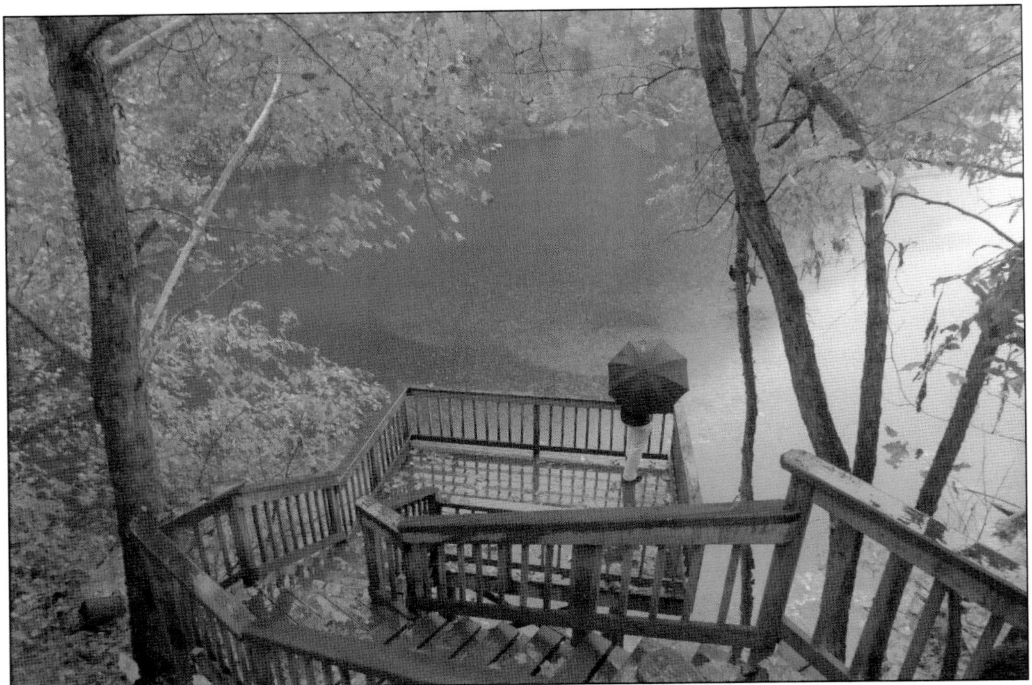

Hundreds of community volunteers contributed to the restoration of Mead's Quarry, which opened to the public in May 2005. Following the demolition of the derelict lime kilns and extensive trash removal, nature trails and an observation deck showcase the imposing cliffs and calming views across the lake. Despite decades of industrial activity and dumping, many visitors are surprised to discover how clean the water is, as evidenced by the occasional sighting of freshwater jellyfish. (Courtesy of Paul James.)

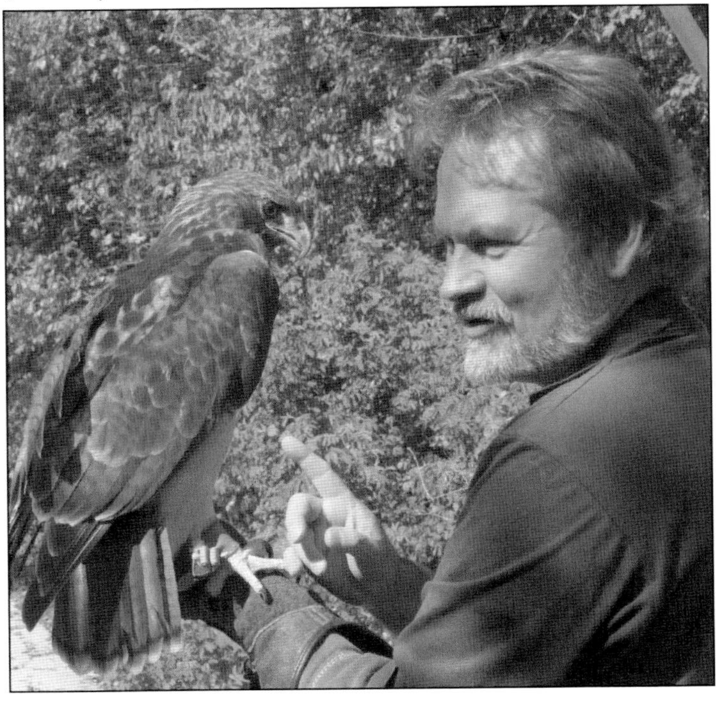

Using birds as educational ambassadors to teach the value of conservation has been a constant theme since the days of the Ijams family. Here, senior naturalist Stephen Lyn Bales shows an injured, non-releasable red-tailed hawk as part of a nature program at Ijams Nature Center. Such presentations are a popular component of school field trips and Scout workshops. Over the years, the Ijams cared for animals including owls, vultures, snakes, opossums, turtles, and other wildlife. (Courtesy of Vicki Henderson.)

Ijams Nature Center is now a 275-acre wildlife sanctuary. In addition to traditional school field trips, a particular focus is providing a nurturing environment to introduce children to the wonders of the natural world through the First Child in the Woods program, day camps, and birthday party adventures. (Courtesy of Bruce Cole.)

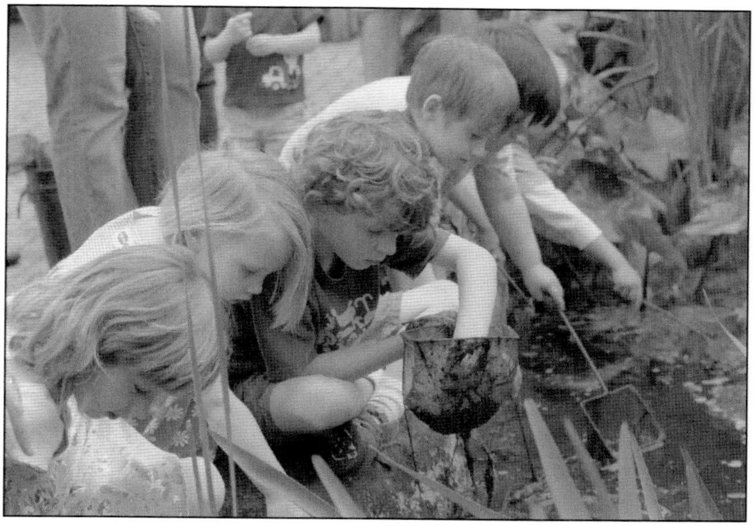

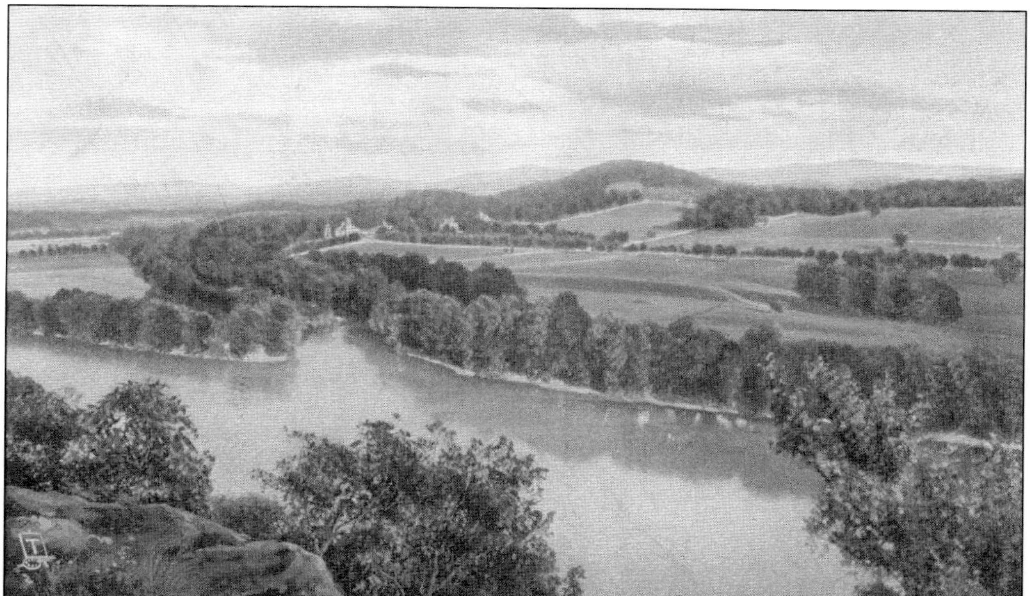

This c. 1903 postcard shows large tracts of undeveloped land in South Knoxville. The land on the south side of the Tennessee River was owned by Massachusetts-born businessman Perez Dickinson. Dickinson Island became an airport in 1930. The inlet in the center of the image leads to Ijams Nature Center and the waterfront to the right of the island is now Island Home Park. (Courtesy of Paul James.)